Liquid Ecclesiology

Liquid Ecclesiology

The Gospel and the Church

By

Pete Ward

BRILL

LEIDEN | BOSTON

Library of Congress Cataloging-in-Publication Data

Names: Ward, Pete, 1959- author.
Title: Liquid ecclesiology : the gospel and the church / By Pete Ward.
Description: Leiden ; Boston : Brill, 2017. | Includes bibliographical references and index.
Identifiers: LCCN 2017013434 (print) | LCCN 2017024261 (ebook) | ISBN 9789004347359 (E-book) | ISBN 9789004345591 (hardback : alk. paper)
Subjects: LCSH: Church. | Ethnology–Religious aspects–Christianity. | Church and minorities. | Evangelicalism.
Classification: LCC BV600.3 (ebook) | LCC BV600.3 .W373 2017 (print) | DDC 262–dc23
LC record available at https://lccn.loc.gov/2017013434

Typeface for the Latin, Greek, and Cyrillic scripts: "Brill". See and download: brill.com/brill-typeface.

ISBN 978-90-04-34559-1 (paperback)
ISBN 978-90-04-34735-9 (e-book)

This book is printed on acid-free paper and produced in a sustainable manner.

Printed by Printforce, the Netherlands

Contents

Acknowledgements

Liquid Ecclesiology grew out of ongoing conversations of the Ecclesiology and Ethnography network. Parts of this book were presented at network meetings at Luther Seminary and at St John's College, Durham. I want to thank Christian Scharen, John Swinton and Paul Fiddes for their continued collaboration on Ecclesiology and Ethnography—much of what is written here benefited greatly from their support and conversation. I also want to thank Mirjam Elbers from Brill for her support and enthusiasm for the Ecclesiology and Ethnography project. I am grateful to those who have read the manuscript at various points, including Paul Fiddes, Tanya Riches, Mathew Guest, Jonas Idestrom, Clare Watkins, Mike Higton, Andrew Root and Chris Russell. Thank you for your feedback and comments. I am particularly grateful to Jonny Baker for the photo for the cover illustration. I also want to thank my Research Assistant Avril Baigent for compiling the index for this volume. A part of the Introduction was published in a more detailed form in *Studia Theologica*,[1] while sections of Chapter 2 were first published in the *Journal of Youth and Theology*.[2] The material on the worship service in Thurso in Chapter 4 was written with Heidi Campbell and first published in *The International Journal of Practical Theology*.[3] I am grateful to the *Studia Theologica, Journal of Youth and Theology* and the *International Journal of Practical Theology* for permission to reproduce sections from these articles.

1 Pete Ward, "Ecclesiology and Ethnography with Humility: Going Through Barth," *Studia Theologica* (July 2016).

2 Pete Ward, "Union with Christ: The Subplot of Evangelical Soteriology," *Journal of Youth and Theology* 2/1 (2003).

3 Pete Ward and Heidi Campbell, "Ordinary Theology as Narratives: An Empirical Study of Young People's Charismatic Worship in Scotland," *International Journal of Practical Theology* 15/2 (2011).

Introduction

"Ecclesiology is the new rock and roll." This casual remark, made to me by the head of a major mission organisation,[1] neatly encapsulates the growing interest in the study of the Christian Church. Ecclesiology is the "new rock and roll" because the Church has moved to centre stage in a wide variety of conversations. Whether it is in missiology or systematic theology, biblical hermeneutics or Christian ethics, the nature and function of the Church has become a pressing theological topic.[2] In the study of doctrine in particular, the Church is at the heart of recent debates about the Trinity.[3] As part of this renewed interest in the Church, academic[4] and popular works[5] on ecclesiology have proliferated. Neither is interest in the Church confined to theologians. In the social sciences, the study of the Church has become a major concern, leading to a rise in congregational studies and a focus on Christian communities in religious and cultural studies, and the

1 Philip Mountstephen, Chief Executive of the Church Mission Society.

2 For example, see Stephen Bevans and Roger Schroeder, *Constants in Context: A Theology of Mission for Today* (Maryknoll, NY: Orbis, 2004); Darrell L. Guder, ed., *Missional Church* (Grand Rapids, MI: Eerdmans, 1998); James W. McClendon, *Ethics: Systematic Theology Volume 1* (Nashville, TN: Abingdon Press, 2002); Stephen Fowl, *Theological Interpretation of Scripture* (Eugene, OR: Wipf and Stock, 2009); and Christian Scharen and Aana Marie Vigen, eds., *Ethnography as Christian Theology and Ethics* (London: Continuum, 2011).

3 See for example, Miroslav Volf, *After Our Likeness: Church as the Image of the Trinity* (Grand Rapids, MI: Eerdmans, 1998); and John Zizioulas, *Being as Communion: Studies in Personhood and the Church* (Crestwood, NY: St Vladimir's Seminary Press, 1985).

4 See for example the activities of the Ecclesiological Investigations Group and their various publications, http://www.ei-research.net.

5 There are too many to list, but examples might include Cheryl M. Peterson, *Who is the Church? An Ecclesiology for the Twenty First Century* (Minneapolis, MN: Fortress Press, 2013); Craig Van Gelder, and Dwight J. Zscheile, *The Missional Church in Perspective: Mapping Trends and Shaping the Conversation* (Grand Rapids, MI: Baker, 2011); Graham Fancourt, *Brand New Church? The Church and the Postmodern Condition* (London: SPCK, 2013); and Michael Moynagh, *Church in Every Context: An Introduction to Theology and Practice* (London: SCM, 2012). Probably the most popular text on contemporary ecclesiology is Rick Warren, *The Purpose Driven Church: Growth Without Compromising your Message and Mission* (Grand Rapids, MI: Zondervan, 1995).

 | DOI 10.1163/9789004347359_002

sociology of religion.[6] Most notably, an anthropology of Christianity has emerged.[7]

While academics have discovered a renewed interest in the Church, there has also been something of an explosion of discussion, debate, and ecclesial experimentation within the churches themselves. This "big conversation" about the Church takes a variety of forms. Whether it is writing about Church growth, or programmes for congregational development, discussion about a missional Church or fresh expressions of Church, Church planting or new missional communities, ecclesiology has become an immediate and deeply felt arena for reflection and dialogue in the Christian community.[8] The burgeoning of academic and popular writing on the Church is matched by the extraordinary creativity that is being expressed in communities, in churches, and in denominations themselves. Ecclesial innovation and experimentation is not just a matter of thought, but is also one of action. Quite simply, the Church is being reshaped and reimagined as a myriad of new ecclesial forms burst onto the scene. These forms include mega-churches, multi-site Churches, virtual churches, café churches, youth churches, and cell churches. There are too many to list here, but such developments add substance to the remark that ecclesiology has become "the new rock and roll."

Ecclesiology, Ethnography and the Liquid Church

At the same time that ecclesiology has become central to theology and to some areas of the social sciences, a debate has begun to develop. The debate

---

6 For example, see Nancy T. Ammerman, *Congregation and Community* (New Brunswick, NJ: Rutgers University Press, 1997); Robert A. Orsi, *The Madonna of 115th Street: Faith and Community in Italian Harlem 1880-1950* (New Haven, CT: Yale University Press, 1985); James B. Twitchell, *Branded Nation: The Marketing of Megachurch, College Inc and Museum World* (New York: Simon and Schuster, 2004); Gerado Marti and Gladys Ganiel, *The Deconstructed Church: Understanding Emerging Christianity* (Oxford: Oxford University Press, 2014); and Mathew Guest, *Evangelical Identity and Contemporary Culture: A Congregational Study in Innovation* (Milton Keynes, UK: Paternoster, 2007).

7 Fennella Cannell, ed., *The Anthropology of Christianity* (Durham, NC: Duke University Press, 2007); and Tanya M. Luhrmann, *When God Talks Back: Understanding the American Evangelical Relationship with God* (New York: Vintage Books, 2012).

8 For an account of some of these developments, see John Walker, *Testing Fresh Expressions: Identity and Transformation* (Farnham, UK: Ashgate, 2014); also Robert Doornebal, *Crossroads: An Exploration of the Emerging-Missional Conversation with a Special Focus on Missional Leadership and its Challenges for Theological Education* (Delft: Eburon, 2012); and Doug Gay, *Remixing the Church: Towards an Emerging Ecclesiology* (London: SCM, 2011).

is centred, although not exclusively so, in the Ecclesiology and Ethnography network.[9] It was the writing of theologians, working independently of one another, and all advocating a turn towards ethnography, that initially sparked the network into life. While it is important to note that such an approach to ecclesiology is common in mission studies and also in the study of liturgy, what is new is that theologians from a range of perspectives have started to see the importance of applying ethnographic insights to doctrine.[10] In 2000, Nicholas Healey made an impassioned plea for what he called a practical-prophetic ecclesiology. At the heart of this kind of ecclesiology he envisioned a turn towards ethnography.[11] Healey argued that ecclesiology should consider the "concrete response" of the Church to its Lord by utilising notions of culture. He acknowledged that sociological and anthropological studies of the Church had been undertaken for many years, but argued that these did not ask theologically-orientated questions, or at least, did not ask the kind of questions that were of pressing interest to theologians. Healey concluded that "the church needs to introduce its own, theological form of cultural analysis, which we can call ecclesiological ethnography."[12] In the same year, in an article published in the *Scottish Journal of Theology*, entitled "Ethnography is Dogmatics," Nicholas Adams and Charles Elliott discussed the importance of what they call "descriptions of the world" for theological work.[13] In 2005, Christian Scharen wrote "Judicious Narratives: Ethnography as Ecclesiology." This article, which was also published in the *Scottish Journal of Theology*, picked up on the significance of ethnography in theology and made an explicit connection to ecclesiology.[14] In 2007, Mary McClintock Fulkerson published her study *Places of*

9 For more on Ecclesiology and Ethnography see http://www.ecclesiologyandethnography.com.

10 Louis J. Luzbetak, *The Church and Cultures: New Perspectives in Missiological Anthropology* (Maryknoll, NY: Orbis, 1963), is a classic text and also offers a good account of the interaction between anthropology and mission studies. In the United States, the Liturgical Press has published a whole series of ethnographic studies of worship. Excellent examples are Mary McGann, *A Precious Fountain: Music in the Worship of an African American Catholic Community* (Collegeville, MN: Liturgical Press, 2004); and David Mellott, *I Was and I Am Dust: Penitent Practices as a Way of Knowing* (Collegeville, MN: Liturgical Press, 2009). See also Christian Scharen, *Public Worship and Public Work: Character and Commitment in Local Congregational Life* (Collegeville, MN: Liturgical Press, 2004).

11 Nicholas M. Healy, *Church, World and the Christian Life: Practical-Prophetic* Ecclesiology (Cambridge, UK: Cambridge University Press, 2000).

12 Healy, *Church, World*, 168-169.

13 Nick Adams, and Charles Elliott "Ethnography is Dogmatics: Making Description Central to Systematic Theology," *The Scottish Journal of Theology* 53/3 (2000): 339.

14 Christian Scharen, "Judicious Narratives: Ethnography as Ecclesiology," *The Scottish Journal of Theology* 58/2 (2005).

Redemption, in which she sought to unite perspectives gained from her own ethnographic work in a congregation with broader theological themes.[15] Mary Clark Moschella's work, *Ethnography as Pastoral Practice*, was also significant in that it addressed practitioners directly and encouraged empirical work as part of ministry.[16] In 2008, the Action Research in Church and Society group (ARCS) produced a report entitled *Living Church in a Global City*.[17] The report offered a series of case studies using action research to develop an understanding of theology in the practice of churches and other Christian organizations in London. The ARCS group developed through this work their understanding of "theology in four voices" (operant, espoused, formal and normative), that they saw as being entwined with practice in each of the contexts.[18] This rise in interest in an ecclesiology that is theologically orientated and yet also able to make use of empirical, and in particular, qualitative methods of enquiry, led directly to a series of conferences organised by the Ecclesiology and Ethnography Network.

Two volumes emerged from the conferences: *Perspectives in Ecclesiology and Ethnography* and *Explorations in Ecclesiology and Ethnography*. These conferences were largely focused on the methodological possibilities of and limits to an ecclesiology that is both empirical and theological. The term "ethnography" has a particular history in anthropology, but because it has already gained some traction in the theological world, those involved in the network understand the phrase as referring in a more informal way to any kind of qualitative enquiry. The first two conference volumes therefore explore methodological concerns about the relationship between qualitative empirical research and theological discussion on the Church.[19] Writers from quite different theological positions explore the relationships between the kind of knowledge that

---

15 Mary McClintock Fulkerson, *Places of Redemption: Theology for a Worldly Church* (Oxford: Oxford University Press, 2007).

16 Mary Clark Moschella, *Ethnography as a Pastoral Practice: An Introduction* (Cleveland, OH: Pilgrim Press, 2008).

17 Deborah Bhatti et al., *Living Church in the Global City: Theology in Practice* (ARCS Project, 2008).

18 Helen Cameron et al., *Talking about God in Practice: Theological Action Research and Practical Theology* (London: SCM Press, 2010). This paradigm of "the four voices" is discussed in more detail in the case study in Part II.

19 For material from the Ecclesiology and Ethnography conversation, see the journal linked to the network, *Ecclesial Practices* (Leiden, Brill); and also Scharen and Vigen, eds., *Ethnography as Christian Theology;* Pete Ward, ed., *Perspectives in Ecclesiology and Ethnography* (Grand Rapids, MI: Eerdmans, 2012); Christian Scharen, ed., *Explorations in Ecclesiology and Ethnography* (Grand Rapids, MI: Eerdmans, 2012). There have been a

is produced through qualitative empirical research, and the ways of knowing and seeing that are appropriate within theology.[20] In this work, I develop these arguments further, but with a specific focus. I want to show how qualitative empirical research can contribute to the theological discussion that is taking place in the Church. Qualitative research does this, I believe, by disciplining the theologian to pay particular attention to the complex and often contradictory nature of lived faith. This attention leads to a theology of the Church that attempts to take account of these complexities and contradictions. This task is not so different from the kinds of negotiation with, and indeed inspiration, that theologians have found in continental philosophy for instance. Yet with qualitative empirical work, the complexity and difficult nature of the material arises from what is observed and its subsequent analysis, rather than from philosophical reasoning. My intention in this volume is to demonstrate how theological approaches that can emerge as a result of paying attention to lived expression have a degree of theological sophistication, and at the same time an inevitable connection to life and actual communities. I reach for the notion of a "Liquid Ecclesiology," because it expresses the dynamic and fluid understanding of the Church that comes from the complexity, ambiguity, and nuance that characterizes the lived expression of the Church. While the terms Liquid Ecclesiology and Liquid Church are my own, the concerns and interests they encompass have been anticipated in previous theological discussion of the Church. As an example of this I discuss the ecclesiology of Daniel Hardy.

Finding the Liquid Church

On the face of it, Daniel Hardy might seem a curious dialogue partner for a Liquid Ecclesiology. Hardy after all represents a significant, and in many ways mainstream catholic, eucharistic focus in Anglican ecclesiology.[21] Yet Hardy's

---

number of other publications seeking to bring together empirical and theological perspectives on the Church and these include Harald Hegstad, *The Real Church: An Ecclesiology of the Visible* (Eugene, OR: Pickwick, 2013); and Neil Ormerod, *Re-Visioning the Church: An Experiment in Systematic Historical Ecclesiology* (Minneapolis, MN: Fortress Press, 2014).

20 This debate has now led to monographs exploring these issues, e.g., Christian Scharen, *Fieldwork in Theology: Exploring the Social Context of God's Work in the World* (Grand Rapids, MI: Baker, 2015). See also Hegstad, *The Real Church*.

21 Hardy stands in the line of Anglican theology that stretches back to Richard Hooker, passes through S.T. Coleridge, F.D. Maurice and on to Gabriel Hebert and A.M. Ramsey.

ideas, I want to argue, anticipate and to some extent map out the territory that I call Liquid Ecclesiology.

The action of God in the world, Hardy argues, is characterized by what he calls sociality. Sociality (or social life) gives form to the way that humans are fulfilled in the purposes of God. So for Hardy, "the forms of social life are closely connected with the free self determination of God in Christ; and their dynamic—how they move—is closely connected with the vitality and direction of God in the Holy Spirit."[22] The Trinity, therefore, originates social forms, both in the Church and in society as whole. Thus it is possible to speak of particular forms of social life—whether they are political or legal institutions—as sites where the Trinity is involved in the freedom of people to be social.[23] Hardy's focus is on both divine action and social forms, which suggests some notion of divine visibility. The work of God can be seen in society and also in the life of the Church. Yet alongside sociality, Hardy introduces the more dynamic and fluid notion of holiness as the moving and affective action of God in the world. Holiness, he says, is intrinsically relational and Trinitarian.

Holiness refers to the way that God is active in the world. God's holiness, says Hardy, is "self maintaining and performative.... For God is a crucible of holiness, a refining fire in the enacting and extending of it, rightly evoking religious affections such as fear, hope, love, hatred, desire, joy, sorrow, gratitude compassion and zeal."[24] God sends forth light that generates relationality. This light can meet with resistance and lesser forms of relationality, i.e., fragmentation. This fragmentation of humanity is burnt away by the death of Christ on the cross. Thus God's holiness is a fire "by which all holiness is generated and sustained in its relation to all else—eventually refines even that which opposes it, thereby healing the fragmentations introduced by those who resist it."[25] Holiness is the direction (or movement) of God. It is relational, but it is also performative, in the sense that it needs to be performed by humans

---

In contemporary ecclesiology, his work is significant for a range of writers. See, for instance, Julie Gittoes et al., *Generous Ecclesiology: Church, World and the Kingdom of God* (London: SCM, 2012); and Stephen Pickard, *Seeking the Church: An Introduction to Ecclesiology* (London: SCM, 2012). See also Martyn Percy, *Shaping the Church: The Promise of Implicit Theology* (Farnham, UK: Ashgate, 2010), 6. Percy's work is interesting because he cites Hardy in support of his own project, which brings sociological and theological perspectives into conversation with contemporary ecclesiology.

22 Daniel Hardy, *Finding the Church* (London: SCM Press, 2001), 24.

23 Hardy, *Finding the Church*, 24.

24 Hardy, *Finding the Church*, 16.

25 Hardy, *Finding the Church*, 17.

in history.[26] This performance takes place in society and also in the church. "The ways by which the holiness of God may be enacted in the world reach far beyond what is conventionally associated with religion."[27] Hardy asks if it possible to talk of the holiness of God being "mediated" other than through "all the dimensions of life in the world, natural, ecological, societal, political, economic and cultural symbolic."[28] The extended live action of God beyond and within the Church lies at the heart of the idea of a Liquid Church, where the strong division between Church and society is made fluid by the work of the Spirit that passes through, moves within, and is active beyond the more solid boundaries of the Church.

Sociality is likened by Hardy to "skin." Skin, he says, represents the thin layer of relations that connect all human beings. The connections between individuals give life to this social skin. The world and society, he suggests, are "universally" natural, social, and highly complex. This is a picture of how the world and society "actually are."[29] The historical location of sociality, or, as Hardy calls it elsewhere, the social transcendent, introduce a dynamic that is particular to human agency.[30] Human society, he suggests, is inevitably situational in nature. Hence social institutions, laws and political organisations are contingent. The same is true of economic relations of production and consumption, of family relations as well as language symbols and culture.[31] Talk of the social as a universal or a transcendent does not therefore preclude movement; rather it encompasses a dynamic shifting and complex reality. This complexity finds its origins in the Trinitarian life of God. Hardy illustrates the dynamic presence of God in society by speaking of the mission of St Paul. Paul was called on his missionary journeys and what he discovered was the presence of Christ in the world. "He found that the world itself was not empty but filled with the presence of Christ—a Christ-like place, so much so that travelling the world was for him a constant finding of Christ."[32] The result was that St Paul found the peoples of the world to be themselves Christ-like, and his travels were a constant rediscovery of Christ.[33]

---

26 Hardy, *Finding the Church*, 15.

27 Hardy, *Finding the Church*, 17.

28 Hardy, *Finding the Church*, 18.

29 Hardy, *Finding the Church*, 85.

30 Colin Gunton and Daniel Hardy, eds., *On Being the Church: Essays on the Christian Community* (Edinburgh: T and T Clark, 1989), 44.

31 Gunton and Hardy, *On Being the Church*, 44.

32 Gunton and Hardy, *On Being the Church*, 46.

33 Gunton and Hardy, *On Being the Church*, 46.

The foundation and the texture of this universal social aspect of life have their origins in God. Here Hardy draws a connection between universal sociality and the Church through the idea of catholicity. Catholicity is not the preserve of the Church alone; it relates to universal sociality. Universality is for Hardy the work of God in the world. "That is the full meaning of catholicity in its Christian sense, the universality in which we live by the grace of God."[34] God's work in the world therefore is to be seen in the "skin" of social relations, nourishing "interrelatedness."[35] All of this should not be taken to mean that social life is in itself always or inevitably "benevolent." The social skin, says Hardy, is often diseased. It is often a leprous skin covered in lesions, "a tissue of lost people who have lost the meaning of the world, of lost security, of lost freedom, of love and friendship lost through separation and abandonment, of lost peace, lost innocence, lost homes, lost well-being, lost countries, lost lives—agonizing losses which befall people who yearn for better."[36]

The human forms of civil society do not in themselves fully present holiness in society. Holiness and sociality for Hardy are linked to the twin notions of *extensity* and *intensity*. The life of God, Hardy says, is nothing less than an engagement with "the extensity and manifoldness of the world."[37] Extensity refers to the movement of God's truth and holiness in the world. This movement involves an individual as well as a societal dynamic. Here Hardy seeks to read the Christian faith against the grain. Alongside the concentrations of the bible, Church and belief (intensity), there is a call to a "spread-out-ness." As Hardy puts it: "We need to think of Christian faith as by nature *spread out*, as something *extended* by its 'spread-out-ness'."[38] The extended, or as I might want to phrase it, fluid life of God, is paralleled with the invitation to intensity. Intensity is performed within the Church as it gathers around the sacrament, but it is also a call to a deeper and more centred spiritual life of prayer.[39] This intensity is an "earnest desire, that is a rational, passionate intensity of heart, soul, mind and strength."[40]

As has been said, Hardy sees culture as complex and dynamic. Rather than offer faith a fixed form, his ecclesiology acknowledges that the work of God takes place within and through this cultural fluidity. Social forms move and

34 Hardy, *Finding the Church*, 84.
35 Hardy, *Finding the Church*, 84.
36 Hardy, *Finding the Church*, 85.
37 Hardy, *Finding the Church*, 159.
38 Hardy, *Finding the Church*, 110.
39 Hardy, *Finding the Church*, 159.
40 Hardy, *Finding the Church*, 111.

change and the dynamic movement of God shifts across time. This fluidity extends to the Church as well as to the wider society. Hardy accepts that churches take different social forms. This is not simply or entirely the result of historical or cultural distinctiveness. He argues that churches have a "logic" and this logic can itself become a source for renewal and change. The very idea of what it is to be the Church can give rise to different ecclesial forms over time and within culture. The social forms of the Church therefore become a vehicle for this idea.[41] Here again Hardy suggests that cultural dynamics bring in fluidity in ecclesial forms. This fluidity is not simply in the collective expression of journey, however. The journey towards extensity and spiritual intensity that Hardy envisages for individual believers also implies a movement and dynamic that is in some respects liquid. I thus want to suggest Hardy anticipates some of the central notions of a Liquid Ecclesiology. Before moving on, it is thus worth summarising the central ideas in my previous work, entitled *Liquid Church*.

Liquid Church[42]

The ideas that eventually formed *Liquid Church* arose from a reading of Zygmunt Baumann's *Liquid Modernity*.[43] Baumann describes the shift from solid forms of social and economic life to less fixed and more fluid relations. This insight into changes in cultural life and community relationships led me to reflect on the ways the Church might also become liquid. Baumann, I should point out, is deeply sceptical of the growing fluidity in society, and so my use of his ideas was reading him against the grain. Nevertheless, I argued that the idea of a Liquid Church enables a way of thinking about the Christian community that takes the fluid nature of culture seriously. As a result, it enables a Liquid Ecclesiology, i.e., a way of seeing existing Church life as a fluid form, and it suggests a way of seeing the Church as a place of divine action in the wider society. To adopt Hardy's terms, Liquid Church develops notions of extensity by paying close attention to the communicative practices that shape both the Church in particular and society in general.

Liquid Ecclesiology, I want to argue, is a shift in the theological imagination from solidity or from "Solid Church" to fluidity and "Liquid Church." Solid Church arises from the understanding that Church is a meeting. In other

41 Hardy, *Finding the Church*, 110.

42 Pete Ward, *Liquid Church* (Peabody, MA: Hendrickson, 2002).

43 Zygmunt Bauman, *Liquid Modernity* (Cambridge: Polity Press, 2000).

words, Church is a gathering in one place, at one time, with the purpose of performing a shared ritual. The idea of Solid Church, I will argue at the outset, is a reductive ecclesiology, but this broad categorization carries a theological coherence. If the essence of Church for the Catholic can be said to be the Eucharist, for the Protestant the preaching of the Word, and for the Pentecostal the singing of worship songs, then what these three have in common is a social logic.[44] They all assume a meeting. In other words, Solid Church is built upon the deep theological assumptions that make up what Catholics, Protestants and Pentecostals understand as the Church. The point about Solid Church then is that it has a deep hold on the imagination of the Christian community, such that it is almost impossible to think of Church as being anything other than a meeting. This hold is what I call "the affective gravitational pull of the Church."[45]

Solid Church, it must be stressed, is the product of a popular ecclesial imagination rather than considered academic ecclesiology. Hardy's ecclesiology, for instance, qualifies the intensity of the Church gathered round the Eucharist with the call to extensity. Both are places of divine encounter for Hardy and this in a sense is what Liquid Ecclesiology is seeking to foreground. Hardy also suggests that while sociality is universal, the social forms in which sociality is expressed shift over time and in relation to culture. Liquid Ecclesiology takes this notion and focuses on the way that culture operates. Thus it is important to say right at the outset that a more fluid understanding of Church does not do away with gathering. Neither does it downplay the importance of key practices such as preaching, celebrating the Eucharist, gathering and fellowship, or singing praise and worship songs, or what Hardy describes as intensity. What Liquid Church does argue, however, is that fluidity is a characteristic of both divine being and of human culture. Fluidity therefore takes place both in meetings and outside of them, and this picks up again on some of Hardy's ideas of the dynamic relationship between holiness, intensity and extensity. Liquid Ecclesiology focuses on the way the divine life passes through the walls and links Church with the wider society. Hence it embraces the sensibility that sees living water as not contained within the Church. By the power of the Spirit, this living water flows within, between, and around the Church and the wider society. Samuel Trevor Francis expresses in his nineteenth century hymn as follows:

44 This is a typology that I first suggested in *Selling Worship* (Milton Keynes, UK: Paternoster, 2005).

45 Pete Ward, "Blueprint Ecclesiology and the Lived: Normativity as a Perilous Faithfulnes," *Ecclesial Practices* 2/1 (2015), 74-90.

Oh the deep, deep love of Jesus, vast unmeasured boundless free.
Rolling like a mighty ocean in its fullness over me.
Underneath me all around me flow the currents of thy Love.
Leading onward leading homeward to thy glorious rest above.

The love of Jesus is not contained within Church meetings. It flows underneath within, and around. This love is there in the world and in the Church. It is the love of Jesus that makes the Church more than a meeting. Liquid Church embraces and is embraced by this love. At the same time, the liquid love of God, the living water that rises in the believer through the work of the Spirit, is paralleled by the fluid nature of cultural expression. I accept these observations are not remarkable in and of themselves. Most ecclesiology will develop patterns of theology that reflect this crucial dimension. Liquid Ecclesiology is not seeking to simply generate a theory or theology in isolation from the habituated sensibility of Solid Church, however; it wants to take seriously the social and cultural power of ecclesial culture. Liquid Ecclesiology is a cultural theology in the sense that it seeks to interact with patterns of practice and thinking that are operant in the lived expression of the Church. Liquid Ecclesiology is theological and theoretical then, but it develops theology through a deep interaction with cultural expression and the lived. Liquid Ecclesiology is a theology that takes cultural expression seriously as one part of the paradox of the Church.

Church Dogmatics: a Fork in the Road

Daniel Hardy's ecclesiology serves as a helpful dialogue partner for Liquid Ecclesiology. I have shown the substantial, and perhaps unexpected overlap in concerns, while also setting out how a Liquid Ecclesiology might take these ideas in new directions. Hardy is not the chief dialogue partner for this project, however. As I have been developing these ideas I have also been wrestling tacitly with Karl Barth's ecclesiology.[46] I accept that Barth is also an unlikely dialogue partner for this project, in that he is openly sceptical of any kind of theology that deals with the social or the historical. Barth's objections are extremely important, and they raise a theological caution that anyone engaged

46 Parts of this section have previously been published in a more detailed form in Pete Ward, "Ecclesiology and Ethnography with Humility: Going Through Barth," *Studia Theologica* (July, 2016).

in ethnographic work in ecclesiology must take seriously. At the same time I want to argue that, read with respect, but also with a certain transgressive sensibility, Barth might be extremely helpful, not just in what he appears to rule out in ecclesiology, but also because of his clear focus on ecclesiology.

I want to start my interaction with Barth with the opening section of *Church Dogmatics* (I.1), which starts with the assertion that dogmatics is "the scientific self examination of the Christian Church with respect to the content of its distinctive talk about God."[47] This understanding of the task of the theologian represents something of a fork in road. It is a fork in the road because it appears to offer the possibility for a kind of theology that interacts with the lived expression of the Christian Church. Of course Barth does not take this route.[48] In fact, his ecclesiology, as Kimlyn Bender has demonstrated, developed as a rejection of any kind of social or historical analysis as part of the theological task. Liquid Ecclesiology takes the other direction, however, and goes down the road that Barth rejected. This move is not meant as a rejection or a repudiation of Barth's ecclesiology. Bender suggests that future ecclesiologies would be wise to go through Barth, rather than to attempt to go around him.[49] Going through Barth requires consideration of why he is so cautious about an ecclesiology that draws on sociological forms of research. Barth's caution leads to a series of theological checks and balances in ecclesiology. In taking the other fork in the road, Liquid Ecclesiology does not reject these theological parameters. It seeks instead to explore the possibility of a theology that has Barth's theological considerations as a framework, and which then sets out to complete what Barth appears to say the task of dogmatics is. In other words, while broadly accepting the Christological framework that Barth sets out, Liquid Ecclesiology seeks to pay attention to the distinctive talk of the Church. This is what I call the other path, the fork in the road, and it starts by wondering what if the theologian takes this starting point in *Church Dogmatics* at face

47 Karl Barth, *Church Dogmatics* I.1 (Edinburgh: T and T Clark, 1975), 3.

48 Bender defends Barth from Healy's critique, i.e., that Barth is not sufficiently "concrete" in his ecclesiology, by pointing out that Barth does discuss ecclesial practices in *CD* IV.3.2. These practices do not define the Church, however. Bender makes the point that for Barth the investigation of practices is the preserve of practical rather than dogmatic theology. (Bender, *Karl Barth's Christological Ecclesiology*, 275.) Sociological descriptions of the Church should not form part of dogmatics, but they have a place in Christian ethics and practical theology (Bender, *Karl Barth's Christological Ecclesiology*, 276; Barth *CD* IV.3.2, 859-860.) Barth's sociological descriptions of the Church come from the prevalence of such work in the nineteenth century and his desire to maintain the theological character of the Church. (Bender, *Karl Barth's Christological Ecclesiology*, 276.)

49 Bender, *Karl Barth's Christological Ecclesiology*, 285.

value? What might happen if the task of dogmatics actually involves paying close and disciplined attention to the continual and ongoing expression of the Church? How might this change ecclesiology? So while accepting that this is not exactly Barthian in approach, Liquid Ecclesiology has developed through a dialogue with Barth. Before moving forward down this alternative road, it is important to spend a while considering why, given his starting point in *Church Dogmatics*, Barth takes the route that he does.

Barth's ecclesiology is a rejection of any approach to ecclesiology that is based on social or historical analysis. Behind this move it should be noted there is a specific historical and cultural location to Barth's theology. (There is an irony here that is worth enjoying for a moment.) As Bender has shown, Barth is concerned throughout his career to define the Church against "Neo-protestantism" and Roman Catholicism. The first reduces Christ to human experience, and the second incorporates Christ in institutional practice. As Barth puts it in *Church Dogmatics:*

> The only possibility of a conception of dogmatic knowledge remaining to us on the basis of Evangelical faith is to be marked off on the one hand by the rejection of an existential ontological possibility of the being of the Church (i.e. Neo-protestantism) and on the other hand by the rejection of the presupposition of a constantly available absorption of the being of the church into a creaturely form, into a "There is" (i.e. Roman Catholicism).[50]

The being of the Church is Jesus Christ and it is freedom of the Spirit that brings about Christ's presence, rather than institutional forms or inward piety. Barth's ecclesiology, says Bender, is based first and foremost in his understanding of election. The Church is the Church in the election of Jesus Christ. This election "precedes" human action. This is not a collaborative partnership. God and man do not have "dealings" with each other. Rather, it is God who is active. The activity of humanity has no place in this election; it is the action of God that instead elicits a response.[51] Humanity is "elected" in the humanity of Christ. So for Barth, the divine freedom is that Jesus Christ is both the electing God and the elected human being.[52] The Church exists because Christ exists;

---

50 Barth, *CD* I.1, 41, quoted in Bender, *Karl Barth's Christological Ecclesiology*, 96.

51 Barth, *Church Dogmatics* II.2 (Edinburgh: T and T Clark), 176, quoted in Bender, *Karl Barth's Christological Ecclesiology*, 116.

52 Bender, *Karl Barth's Christological Ecclesiology*, 117.

it lives because Christ lives. The "Christian community can be what the human nature of its Lord and Head is."[53] This Christological orientation limits the possibility of seeing the Church through history or through visible social forms. This problematic is illustrated by Barth with a geometrical analogy. Christology, he says, is like a vertical line meeting a horizontal line. The horizontal represents human sin.[54] Justification, the work of God, is the point where the vertical and the horizontal intersect.[55] So for Barth, the Church is an event, a moment when these lines intersect. The language of event does not preclude talk of the Church as institution. Indeed, the Church as event can only exist in concert with the "flesh and blood" of communities. But, says Bender, for Barth the relationship between event and the historical social form of the Church cannot be reversed.[56]

The relationship between the divine and human in ecclesiology is Christologically "ordered" for Barth. This is what George Hunsinger has identified as the Chalcedonian pattern of relations between the divine and the human in Barth's theology. The pattern consists of a unity, a differentiation, and an asymmetry of relations.[57] This pattern is derived by Barth from a Chalcedonian Christological definition whereby in the relation of human and divine in the person of Jesus Christ there is a unity, but this unity leaves the distinction between divinity and humanity in place and there is an irreducible hierarchy of relations. By analogy, this pattern extends to the Church. Here the asymmetry in relations is understood through the patristic ideas of *anhypostasia* and *enhypostasia*.[58] These are again firstly Christological, and only by analogy extended to the Church. *Anhypostasia* is a negative assertion that the human in Jesus Christ does not have any existence apart from the Word. *Enhypostasia* expresses the related view that the human has a real and complete existence in the Word. The *anhypostatic/enhypostatic* pattern means that the intersection of divine activity cannot be read off the life of the Church. "The pattern whereby the church can be understood as the indivisible unity of a divine event and

53 Karl Barth, *Church Dogmatics* IV.2 (Edinburgh: T and T Clark, 1958), 59-60 quoted in Bender, *Karl Barth's Christological Ecclesiology*, 150.

54 Bender points out that the analogy of intersecting lines is a significant development from Barth's earlier work in Romans. Here the work of God in the world is likened to a tangent that just touches the edge of a circle. The tangent being the work of God and the circle the sinful world. Bender, *Karl Barth's Christological Ecclesiology*, 168.

55 Barth, *Church Dogmatics* IV.1, 643, quoted in Bender.

56 Bender, *Karl Barth's Christological Ecclesiology*, 168.

57 Bender, *Karl Barth's Christological Ecclesiology*, 4.

58 Bender, *Karl Barth's Christological Ecclesiology*, 4, see also Karl Barth, *Church Dogmatics* I.2 (Edinburgh: T and T Clark, 1956), 163.

a historical and human institution in irreducible and unconfused distinction is the Christological pattern of Chalcedon and the anhypostatic-enhypostatic logic, whereby the church is a single reality composed of a divine call and a human society in asymmetrical relation, the second entirely dependent upon the first."[59]

What follows from this is that the Church, rather than being accessible to sociological observation, can only be understood as an object of faith: *Credo ecclesiam*. As such it is impossible to grasp its reality through historical or indeed empirical means. The Church is essentially a mystery. This does not mean that the lived community can be ignored, because for Barth the opposite is the case. The Church is a community of believers present in history, but it is only the Church because of God. "The Church is, of course, a human earthly-historical construct, whose history involves from the very first and always will involve human action. But it is this human construct, the Christian Church, because and as God is at work in it by his Spirit."[60] There is a human "action" that builds the Church, but what makes this truly the Church is the work of God. In commenting on the Apostles' Creed, Barth rejects notions of the invisibility of the Church. The Church is visible; we believe in its existence. This means that each congregation is a congregation of Christ. "Take good note, that a parson who does not believe that in this congregation of his, including those men and women, old wives and children, Christ's congregation exists, does not believe at all in the existence of the Church. *Credo ecclesiam* means that I believe that here at this place, in this visible assembly, the work of the Holy Spirit takes place."[61] It is in this concrete and particular congregation that the Holy Spirit becomes "event." Yet there is always a struggle between the empirical Church and the "true" Church. The "true" Church emerges as a quickening of the Spirit as human work to build up the community into the true Church.[62] The Church exists as it responds to the Holy Spirit. The "true" Church is made by the free working of the Holy Spirit. This work is predicated on the historical and social, but it is not reduced to this. The historical form of the Church makes the invisible visible, but only as the Holy Spirit is at work.[63] "The Christian community, the true Church, arises and is only as the Holy Spirit works—the quickening power of the living Lord Jesus Christ."[64] So the Church as an article of faith

59 Bender, *Karl Barth's Christological Ecclesiology*, 168.

60 Barth, *CD* IV/2, 616.

61 Bender, *Karl Barth's Christological Ecclesiology*, 143.

62 Barth *CD* IV/2, 617.

63 Bender, *Karl Barth's Christological Ecclesiology*, 171.

64 Barth *CD* IV.2, 617 see in Bender, *Karl Barth's Christological Ecclesiology*, 171.

(*Credo ecclesiam*) does not preclude the "concrete" nature of the Church. Indeed, the opposite is the case, because the Holy Spirit calls the community into existence. So, says Bender, the real Church should not be sought apart from the historical manifestation of the community, but within its historical forms. Yet the true Church is only perceived in the historical by means of faith.[65] To see the Church only on the historical plane is to fail to understand the true nature of the Church.[66] The Church there has a reality and a mystery that coincides with the incarnation. "The glory of Jesus Christ was hidden when he humbled himself, when he took flesh He was obedient to God, when He destroyed our wrong, when he established our right. So, too, the glory of humanity justified in him is concealed. And this means that the glory of the community gathered together by him within humanity is only a glory which is hidden from the eyes of the world until His final revelation so that it can be only an object of faith."[67] Barth's theology therefore sets the question of visibility at the heart of ecclesial reflection.

Reduced Visibility

The project that I propose is not without its problems. Indeed, some might argue that the whole enterprise is mistaken. Before returning to Barth and what it might mean to "go through his theology," the issue of visibility and invisibility needs to be investigated. Writing from within the Ecclesiology and Ethnography conversation, John Webster adopts a Barthian rejection of the theological possibilities of ethnography. He warns of the limits of empirical research in our ability to "see" the real nature of the Church. Ecclesiology, he argues, must be viewed in hierarchical terms. For Webster, "a theology of the Church cannot simply be a phenomenology of ecclesial social history, but an inquiry into that history's ontological ground in the being and works of the church's God."[68] For Webster, it is not so much that the empirical study of the Church is impossible, but rather that there should be a hierarchy of understanding between the origin of the Church and the phenomena of the Church. Webster's contention is that the empirical study of "phenomena" will always be limited. It will see something, but it will inevitably be frustrated because

65 Bender, *Karl Barth's Christological Ecclesiology*, 171.

66 Bender, *Karl Barth's Christological Ecclesiology*, 177.

67 Karl Barth *CD* IV.1, 656-657, quoted in Bender, *Karl Barth's Christological Ecclesiology*, 174.

68 John Webster, "'In the Society of God': Some Principles of Ecclesiology," in *Perspectives on Ecclesiology and Ethnography*, ed. Pete Ward (Grand Rapids, MI: Eerdmans, 2012), 200.

of its limitations.[69] There are two kinds of theological investigations into the Church. The first is enquiries into the origin of the Church which is the task of dogmatics. The second deals with the phenomena of the Church. But there is a problem here, says Webster, because these phenomena are "elusive." The phenomena are "signs whose matter does not inhere in themselves; they have a special visibility; they do not exhaust themselves in their natural manifestation."[70] For Webster it is this hierarchy of knowing that is important, rather than a specific methodology. As he puts it: "In the order of knowing, which comes first is probably a matter of indifference."[71]

On the face of it, Nicholas Healy is more optimistic about the prospects for an ecclesial ethnography. Modern theology, he argues, suffers from over abstraction. What he calls the "blueprint" approach to doctrine, "can lead to reductively abstract and theoretical views of the church."[72] For Healy, there is one crucial drawback to this form of ecclesiology: it provides very few tools that enable theologians to critically examine the "concrete identity of the Church." "Ecclesiology is not about the business of finding the single right way to think about the church, of developing a blueprint suitable for all times and places. Rather, I propose that its function is to aid the concrete church in performing its tasks of witness and pastoral care within its ecclesial context."[73] By context, Healy is not talking about a setting that is separate from the Church, and neither is he advocating some kind of correlation between theology and this context. He is talking instead about the ways in which the Church is part of, and intertwined with, cultural and historical developments. "The concrete church, living in and for the world, performs its tasks of witness and discipleship within particular, ever shifting contexts, and its performance is shaped by them."[74] Ecclesiology has developed in response to events. So Healy criticizes doctrinal theology as being abstract, and yet his consideration of the possibilities for ethnographic work is also a little sceptical. Writing in *Perspectives on Ecclesiology and Ethnography*, Healy presses on the limits of ethnography for theological construction. The action of God cannot be read directly from the practice and communal life of the Church, because the lived is complex and so often contradictory in nature.

69 Webster is taken to task on the issue of the limits and possibilities of empirical work in ecclesiology by his colleague, Chris Brittain, see Brittain, (2014) 5-30.

70 Webster, "In the Society of God," 221.

71 Webster, "In the Society of God," 221.

72 Healy, *Church, World*, 38.

73 Healy, *Church, World*, 38.

74 Healy, *Church, World*, 39.

Visibility and invisibility are categories that run deep in ecclesiology. Claims to be able to "see" the action of God in the world are obviously problematic, but I want to argue that this caution should not simply be applied to empirical work. It applies in equal measure to the theologian. The theologian is constructing a theology and it is worth asking why this construction is privileged over the work of someone who pays close attention to the expression and life of a community, and where the writing that ensues is also a construction. This question gains some force when theological understandings of the Church are so clear that the action of God takes place in and among this communal life. This is not to say that such attention to lived communities in order to discern the action of the divine is straightforward. Discerning the work of God is determined by the being of God. Empirical work in ecclesiology and ethnography should therefore be fundamentally "theological" in nature, and not only theological, but spiritual i.e., a relational knowledge. Thus in ecclesiology Christ is known only as the knower is also known. This, I would argue, is true in all theological work, be it work with texts or work that focuses on the lived expression of communities. This relational dynamic is set within the contingent nature of theological expression, however. Theology is construction and this sensibility must introduce limitations and reflexivity into ecclesiology.

Visibility and the Affective Gravitational Pull of the Church

In contemporary thinking it has become commonplace to root theologies of the Church in the doctrine of God. In particular, a number of theologians have generated social theologies of the Trinity as the basis of the Church, although more recently, some others have questioned the wisdom of this approach in ecclesiology. Stephen Holmes is one among many theologians who are finding problems with the social doctrine of the Trinity as a "blueprint" for ecclesiology.[75] Holmes develops his critique by addressing some of the assumptions about Trinitarian theology and arguing how those who advocate a social doctrine of the Trinity have, in his view, misread the tradition. Along the way he makes an interesting observation about the relationship between theology and reasoning about the Church. Holmes points out that John Zizioulas and Miroslav Volf have very similar Trinitarian theologies, yet these theologies appear to fund contrasting and contradictory ecclesiologies. Holmes observes

75 Parts of the next section were published in *Ecclesial Practices* as "Blueprint Ecclesiology." and the Lived: Normativity as a Perilous Faithfulness."

that while for Zizioulas Trinitarian theology leads to a hierarchical and structured pattern for the Church, for Volf, by contrast, it leads to a more democratic and participatory ecclesiology. Although they have very similar "blueprints" in terms of their readings of the Trinity, each appears to conclude that these plans support very different—in fact diametrically opposite—ecclesiologies. Zizioulas is, of course, an Orthodox theologian and Volf (at the time of writing) is Free Church.[76] Holmes appears to have uncovered what I have elsewhere called the "affective gravitational pull of the Church."[77] The affective gravitational pull of the Church refers to the way ecclesial patterns become deeply habituated in believers. This habituation is evident among theologians, where, despite the claim to be reasoning theologically, habituated norms of ecclesial affiliation appear to hold sway. So, having done the complex reasoning that Trinitarian theology seems to require, the resulting ecclesiologies appear to divide along rather predictable lines. The Orthodox Zizioulas settles for hierarchy, and the Free Church Volf for shared leadership. This calls into question the whole project of ecclesiology as a means of generating a framework for the Church. It is rather like a situation where two builders are given the same plans and one builds a bungalow and the other a five-storey block of flats. The point here is that there appears to be something more than theological reasoning at play. What can be observed is the affective gravitational pull of the Church.

Gravitational pull describes the way that ecclesial traditions shape and condition reasoning. Traditions are affective because they are inhabited, lived in, and simultaneously habituated and internalized. Theologians are, in this sense, no different from any other Christians, in that their tradition in the Church shapes how they reason. It is worth introducing Karen Kilby's critique of social Trinitarianism as projection here.[78] Kilby argues that the God in God's self is "hidden" from us, such that it is not possible to directly reason from the economic to the immanent Trinity. Those who advocate social doctrines of the Trinity appear to have seized this "hiddenness" as an opportunity, however. What by rights is not known and shouldn't be known—the apophatic—has been filled by the social and political concerns of the theologian. Kilby judges this to be "projection." These observations on social Trinitarianism in effect echo Albert Schweitzer's critique of the liberal lives of Jesus, i.e., that liberal

76 Stephen R. Holmes, "Three Versus One? Some Problems of Social Trinitarianism," *Journal of Reformed Theology* 3 (2009): 77-89.

77 Ward, "Blueprint Ecclesiology and the Lived: Normativity as a Perilous Faithfulness."

78 Karen Kilby, "Perichoresis and Projection: Problems with Social Doctrines of the Trinity," *New Blackfriars* (October, 2000); and Karen Kilby, "Is an Apophatic Trinitarianism Possible?" *International Journal of Systematic Theology* 12/1 (January, 2010).

theology recreates Christ in its own image.[79] There is a deep irony here, and one that is not lost on Kilby, because those who want to utilize Trinitarian theology in ecclesiology are doing so because they want to insulate themselves against "liberal" theology based in experience. The assertion that the Church is rooted in the being of God is intended to provide a theological assurance against the prioritization of the lived as seen in the prevailing move towards culture and contextualisation. Kilby's suggestion that these theologies are some kind of projection undermines this assurance somewhat. Traditional ecclesiology might not be the kind of idealised, or normative "plans" that the designers claim. The work of Holmes and Kilby is deeply significant, but there is a further move that neither of them quite makes, and this relates to the appropriation of Social Trinitarianism in the Church.

Trinitarian theology has been enthusiastically taken up in ecclesial discourse. This taking up is deeply significant because it indicates a symbiotic relationship between theology and the lived. To illustrate this, it is worth quoting Catholic theologian, Catherine LaCugna:

> The heart of the Christian life is to be united with the God of Jesus Christ by means of communion with one another. The doctrine of the Trinity is ultimately therefore a teaching not about the abstract nature of God, nor about God in isolation from everything other than God, but a teaching about God's life with us and our life with each other. Trinitarian theology could be described par excellence as a theology of relationship, which explores the mysteries of love, relationship, personhood and communion within the framework of God's self revelation in the person of Christ and the activity of the Spirit.[80]

Here the Trinity is swimming in a cocktail of ideas: community, relationship, and communion with one another. These concepts are precisely what Kilby identifies as projections, and as such they represent the aspirations of the contemporary Church. We want these things. We are drawn towards this vision of ourselves. These ideas lay bare the affective gravitational pull of the Church. They reassure us in the face of the disintegration of community, the rise of consumerism, and the hegemony of the self, that the Church embraces another way. The irony here is that this "other way," read as projection, is not the

79 Albert Schweitzer, *The Quest of the Historical Jesus* (London: A.C. Black, 1911).

80 Catherine Mowry LaCugna, *God For Us: The Trinity and Christian Life* (San Francisco: Harper Collins, 1991), 1.

robust theological understanding of the Church that it purports to be. It is, in effect, another version of what Heelas and Woodhead call the subjectivization of religion.[81] The only difference is that it is the collective or communal self that is centre stage.

What this brief discussion of Social Trinitarianism demonstrates is the fluidity of theological discourse itself. Theology is liquid because it utilizes culturally-conditioned forms of expression: it is construction. The idea of affective gravitational pull is an attempt to factor in the extent to which culture, here manifested as tradition and embodiment, plays a decisive role in theological reasoning. The point of this observation is that it relativizes the normative claims of theology to shape a vision of the Church through privileged forms of reasoning. This does not mean that theology plays no role in Liquid Ecclesiology: the opposite is the case. It simply means that the theological voice that draws on the tradition should be positioned for what it is, i.e., "construction." It is faith seeking understanding. The theologian builds a world, but the status of this world is not guaranteed, nor does it have any particular claim to apprehend the divine. At the same time, this does not mean that the divine is closed off from theological discourse. Theology is part of the expression of the Church and as such conditioned and contingent. Theology does not have any special claim to visibility, but neither is it occluded from the vision of God. The point is that what theologians say about God is a contested and contesting field, and to claim anything beyond that is problematic. Ecclesiology is liquid, in other words.

Exactly the same needs to be said of theologically-informed qualitative work on the Church. In fact, qualitative enquiry is characterized by a continual focus on the way the researcher brings theoretical and personal perspectives into their research. These perspectives are often foregrounded, not to claim any kind of "objective" knowledge—since it is accepted that such knowledge is problematic—but rather to develop a dialogue between the researcher and the research context. Liquid Ecclesiology identifies how this reasoning itself is part of "expression" and therefore contingent. While this does not preclude any attempt to seek a theology of the Church, it accepts that such a project does not stand on any kind of self-evidently sacred or supra-cultural ground. Rather, the reasoning needs to take place with a weather eye on how culture, tradition, and embodiment play a powerful role in reasoning. All of this is to argue that reasoning about divine action through theology or through theologically-

81 Paul Heelas and Linda Woodhead, *The Spiritual Revolution: Why Religion is Giving Way to Spirituality* (Oxford: Blackwell, 2005), 2-5.

informed empirical work is fluid and contested. This is what critical realism calls epistemic relativity.

Critical Realism and Perilous Normativity

The limits of theological expression are suggestive of the epistemological framework offered by critical realism.[82] Critical realism, says Andrew Wright, is characterized by ontological realism, epistemic relativism, and judgmental rationality.[83] *Ontological realism* is the assertion that there is a distinction between the realm of knowledge and the realm of the real. “Objects exist and events occur in reality whether we are aware of them or not.... So there is a crucial distinction to be made between ontology and epistemology. Once the distinction between ontology and epistemology is established it becomes possible to develop a rich account of the contours of reality.”[84] *Epistemic relativism* resists both enlightenment certainty and postmodern scepticism. Ontology has a primacy over epistemology because reality precedes the knowledge of that reality. Our knowledge is limited, however, and therefore it is epistemologically relative.[85] Knowledge lies between the extremes of absolute certainty and radical scepticism and it consists in reasoned attachment to positions. Knowledge is “faith seeking understanding.”[86] “The affirmation of epistemic relativism acknowledges the limits of our knowledge, but does not deny either the actuality of genuine knowledge or the possibility of establishing better knowledge in the future.”[87] *Judgemental rationality* recognizes that not all accounts of reality are equal. It is possible to make judgements between differing expressions of knowledge. There are neither secure foundations for knowledge nor fixed criteria for deciding between truth claims in knowledge, but nevertheless, rational discussion is possible, in fact it is necessary. As Wright puts it, “The priority of ontology means that we must adapt our epistemic tools in response to the objective demands of reality, rather than adjust reality to bring it into conformity with our epistemic tools.”[88] Knowledge is contextual rather

82 See Alister McGrath, *A Scientific Theology: Volume 2, Reality* (London: T and T Clark, 2001), 234-244.

83 Andrew Wright, *Christianity and Critical Realism: Ambiguity, Truth and Theological Literacy* (London: Routledge, 2012), 10-13.

84 Wright, *Christianity and Critical Realism*, 10.

85 Wright, *Christianity and Critical Realism*, 11.

86 Anselm, quoted in Wright, *Christianity and Critical Realism*, 13.

87 Wright, *Christianity and Critical Realism*, 13.

88 Wright, *Christianity and Critical Realism*, 13.

than foundational. Knowledge is built through a creative process and once it is expressed it is subject to revision and correction. Yet both constructs and the means by which we may decide between competing explanatory forms of knowledge are subject to revision. They are provisional. Judgemental rationality, says Wright, is rather like a court of law where different forms of knowledge and information are at play in the pursuit of the truth.[89]

A critical realist perspective introduces a significant analytical framework into ecclesiology. Blueprint ecclesiologies rest on the assertion that the being of the Church is derived from the being of God. Normativity therefore arises from a kind of privileged access to ontology. Theological method, reason illuminated by the Spirit, gives access to the "isness" of God and the "isness" of the Church, but what is meant here by ontology is quite distinct from the understanding of ontology within critical realism. For critical realism, ontology refers to the "real," but the description of this "real" is epistemological and therefore relative. In other words, while knowledge is formed in relation to the real, any account of "what is" does not operate in the field of ontology. Blueprint ecclesiologies tend to conflate epistemology and ontology. In fact, this merger lies at the heart of their claim to authority. This is what Wright calls enlightenment certainty. The certainty in blueprint ecclesiology comes from complex associations of ideas. The first part of the chained set of ideas is the assumption that truth can be attained at the level of abstraction. Abstract descriptions of the Church are then articulated with a claim to expressing ontological truth, i.e., being able to speak about what really "is." What really is, it is claimed, has its roots in a deeper knowledge, the knowledge of God. This heady mix is the habituated mode of operation for theological discussion.

Critical realism suggests a move beyond the attempt to find a fixed theological reference point for ecclesiology. First, it identifies doctrinal discussion as epistemologically relative. Despite the claim to operate at the level of what is, critical realism reads blueprint ecclesiologies as accounts of the real and not as ontology itself. As such, these accounts are relative, open to challenge and revision. At the same time, a critical realist perspective allows the possibility that there is an ontological reality beyond our accounts of that reality. Thus ontology in a critical realist perspective is present, but it is closed off as a privileged field of discourse. Critical realism short circuits the link that theologians have been inclined to make between abstraction, ontology, and revelation, but it opens the door for a kind of ecclesiology that can interact with the doctrinal as situated knowledge, i.e., as part of the lived. It does this

89 Wright, *Christianity and Critical Realism*, 14.

while resisting the tendency to entirely collapse the doctrinal into the cultural, however. The critical realist perspective also frames a theologically informed, qualitative method. Here also the real is accepted as the lived expression of the community (and within and through this the work of the Spirit), with accounts of the real accepted as contested and "epistemologically relative." These accounts are constructed in relation to the real, but are never taken to be identical with it.

Critical realism re-orientates the discussion around visibility and invisibility. Instead of the position where the action of God is invisible and human social patterns are by contrast visible, critical realism suggests that the real is visible and accounts of the real are always provisional. The real here relates not simply to divine presence, but also to the lived expression of the Church. Empirical work is therefore also problematic in relation to the real. This means that there are two kinds of "real" at play in ecclesiology that is drawing on empirical work. The first relates to the lived as the real. The second is theological, and relates to the possibility for either a theologically-oriented empirical work or a theology that works with texts to have access to the "real," i.e., to the divine presence. The point is that this second "real" is not inaccessible to theological work either in the empirical form or in the more traditional forms, but what is produced, i.e., the accounts of the real—or what I would call "the construction"—is epistemically relative. The epistemic relativity needs to be combined with a theologically-oriented epistemology, however, which would insist that "seeing" the divine either in texts or in empirical data requires a positioning in relationship, i.e., faith. The real in ecclesiology is only accessible as the basis for belief through the relational dynamic of the Holy Spirit. I explore this idea in Chapter 9 as the call to "abide," although abiding is both attention and relational wonder. Abiding is the condition for ecclesiological ethnography in that both theology and empirical work seek to express the work of Jesus Christ in the human.

Going through Barth

When returning to Barth and the task of "going though" his theology, it is worth starting with the contextual location of his work. As I stated earlier, Barth's theology is constructed in opposition to two ecclesial polarities, what Bender calls neo-protestantism and Roman Catholicism. Liquid Church has a similar starting point. It shares a reaction against the first of these, neo-protestantism, i.e. theologies of the Church based on experience alone, but rather than embrace Roman Catholicism instead, seeks the alternative of a "blue print ecclesiology, as Healy calls it, or the construction of ecclesiology purely as an ideal. In advocating the need for attention to the lived expression of the Church, my intention is not to advocate experience or the "ultimate concern" of individuals or communities as an adequate basis for ecclesiology. At the same time, it is important to resist the assumption that the theologian writing a theoretical ecclesiology has some kind of ability to "see" that has priority over the experience of lived communities. The dichotomy between empirical or culturally-generated theological perspectives and those developed by scholars working from texts is in my view a false one. The central issue is the distinction between the presence of Jesus Christ in the Church and the ability of the theologian working either with text or with empirical data, or preferably both, to speak of the presence of Christ in, with, and through human expression. Taken in this way, I think it is possible to heed the warning that Barth lays down concerning the task of ecclesiology without necessarily accepting the limitations he sets out for empirical and historical methods.[90]

I agree with Barth that the basis for ecclesiology is Jesus Christ. What I do not accept is that the construction of the theologian affords unproblematic access to ontology.[91] At the same time I would argue that the theological task is essential. It is the calling of the Church to express the gospel and as part of that expression there needs to be reflection and critique. The theologian therefore has a crucial role. This role requires both a searching after the presence of Christ in the lived expression of the Church and also the continual reinterpretation of the tradition of the Church in relation to changing culture and contexts. This task is necessary because culture is fluid. It is also necessary because

90 The Chalcedonian pattern of relations that Hunsinger has identified in Barth is suggestive, but inherently problematic. Deborah van Deusen Hunsinger, *Theology and Pastoral Counselling: A New Interdisciplinary Approach* (Grand Rapids, MI: Eerdmans, 2010). It is suggestive because this pattern reinforces the priority of the "theological" in ecclesiology. By theological I do not mean the ways of speaking and constructing that are associated with theologians. I mean divine presence and action. The critical realist perspective acknowledges this ontological priority, while accepting the epistemic relativity of any attempt to express this ontology. The point here is that this caution needs to be extended to the Chalcedonian pattern itself. There needs to be a certain theological modesty here. The notion of *anhypostatic*/*enhypostatic* relations is itself a construction. The reality of the incarnation is closed off from the theologian and this construct is an attempt to make sense of the humanity and divinity in Jesus Christ. Chalcedon, I would argue, maps out the possibilities and the limits of speech about Christ, but as it does so it traces our unknowing rather than our knowing.

91 It is worth noting that Barth is clear also that there are significant limits to the theologians' ability to see Jesus Christ (Barth, *CD* I.1, 3-24).

through the power of the Holy Spirit Jesus Christ is present in the Church as wind that cannot be predicted, as light that illuminates cultural practice, and as living water that flows in, around and through the expression of the Christian community. Cultural fluidity shapes ecclesiology, because meaning, practice and communication are always in movement. Raymond Williams speaks of culture as a way of life. Culture, he says, is a "structure of feeling."[92] This way of life is "as firm and definite as 'structure' suggests, yet it operates in the most delicate and least tangible parts of our activity."[93] Culture is organic in nature and yet it manifests itself in organization. Like an organism it shifts and changes over time.[94] There is a sense in which it can only be made visible to those who are within its organism, but at the same time "visibility" may be restricted by the sense that this is simply the way things are. Hence Williams can talk about the mystery of cultural transmission. "One generation may train its successor, with reasonable success, in the social character or the general cultural pattern, but the new generation will have its own 'structure of feeling', which will not appear to have come 'from' anywhere."[95]

It is the fluidity of culture and the nature of divine presence that determines the orientation of a Liquid Ecclesiology. For Barth, the Church is apprehended by faith. It is therefore a mystery to be received rather than an object for study. The task of ecclesiology rests on the conviction that the Church is the object of faith. Faith because it has its being in Jesus Christ, but faith also, I would add, because Christ is present in and through the fluid and often imperfect expression of the community. Faith then precedes and shapes the rational task of ecclesiology. This is Anselm's classic description of theology as "faith seeking understanding." For Barth, faith does not indicate the agency of the believer so much as the way in which the being of God structures what it means to believe. The being of God, he argues, precedes the questions of the Christian.[96] Liquid Ecclesiology rests on a similar conviction, but faith, i.e., belief in the Church, lies at the heart of ecclesiology also as a practice of abiding.

With Barth, I accept that neither of these offers an unproblematic account of divine action. Where I part company is in the caution that Barth expresses concerning the significance of the historical and the social in ecclesiology.

92 Raymond Williams, *The Long Revolution* (Harmondsworth, UK: Penguin Books, 1961), 64.

93 Williams, *The Long Revolution*, 64.

94 Williams, *The Long Revolution*, 65.

95 Williams, *The Long Revolution*, 65.

96 Karl Barth, *Anselm: Fides Quaerens Intellectum: Anselm's Proof of the Existence of God in the Context of His Theological Scheme* (London: SCM Press, 1960).

For Barth, the true Church is "event." This episodic affirmation of the presence of Christ makes sense in relation to Barth's chief concerns about neo-protestantism and Roman Catholicism. Liquid Ecclesiology seeks to embrace some of the Christological grounding of ecclesiology that Barth advocates, but it sees the presence of Christ in the cultural as fundamental. Chapter 2 sets out the case for this orientation towards the Christ within the lived expression of the community. Rather than attempt to create a boundary around the "true" Church, I advocate a theology of paradox and kenosis as the basis for relationship: Christ present in the imperfect expression of the Church. It is the fact that expression is always imperfect that necessitates the task of theological ethnography. The point here is that expression in the lived community of the Church is not simply imperfect, it is multi-layered, characterized by a plurality of voices. I seek to illustrate this dynamic through an extended case study examining the expression of the Gospel in contemporary evangelical/charismatic churches. This case study is there to illustrate how taking account of the actual proclamation of the Church, i.e., what Barth appears to say is the task of dogmatics, is far from straightforward. Communities and individuals appear to live comfortably and often without awareness of the mutually contradictory or incompatible theological implications of shared cultural expression. These layers of ambiguity might be taken as a prompt to retreat to the safer ground of doctrinal theology. This is a mistake. Doctrinal theology is just as compromised even where doctrines have been agreed by Church councils. Instead, the call is to believe in the Church as the body of Christ that is divided and yet somehow one; in conflict and yet called to unity; sinful and yet also a place of blessing. This is what it means to believe in the Church.

Scripture and Theology

Abiding in Christ is the call to worship and adoration as the starting point for discerning Christ in the scriptures and in the community of the Church, the body of Christ. The approach to scripture developed in this book sits within a wider turn towards a theological understanding of scriptural interpretation. The scriptures, argues Stephen Fowl, are the work of human writers. They reflect the diverse languages, histories and cultures of their authors. The scriptures and those who were responsible for preserving, editing and organising these texts were subject to "social, material and institutional forces," although the relative significance of these may be an area for discussion. Despite these contextual and contingent factors behind the text and canon, Christians understand scripture as the word of God. As Fowl puts it, "Christians are committed to the notion that Scripture is the word of God. In, through, or in spite of its clearly human, historical characteristics, Christians confess that Scripture repeats, conveys, or reflects the words of the living God."[97] Scripture therefore remains the standard against which any expression of the faith is to be assessed. Theological interpretation of scripture, says John Webster, should be understood from a theological perspective that locates the bible and its reception in the Church within the "scope of the progress of the divine word."[98] This approach to scripture rests on an understanding of what it "is," i.e., "Holy Scripture, God ministering his Word to human beings through human servants, and so sharing with them the goods of knowledge of himself."[99] Scripture therefore forms part of the self-communication of the Trinitarian God. It is situated within the relational movements of glorification, sending and breathing. Coming to scripture as a place of abiding and transformation is therefore to be drawn into and to participate in the life of God; to be indwelt and to indwell. This participatory understanding of the work of the Spirit through the scriptures embraces rational thought and a range of hermeneutical strategies, but it finds its being in the being of God.[100] Scripture is to be understood as part of the activity of the Trinitarian God that "is graciously directed to drawing humanity into ever deeper communion with God and each other."[101] It is for this reason that scripture needs to be at the heart of communities as the means for continual encouragement and reflection. As Fowl puts it, "Scripture is primarily addressed to communities and it is within Christian communities that believers are to be formed and transformed to enhance their movement into ever deeper communion with God and each other."[102]

The particular theology of abiding drawn from John's Gospel that I advocate in this book rests on the move towards the theological interpretation of scripture. Scripture is here understood as a place of divine encounter and transformation, but I have put a priority on the gospel narratives and in particular the Gospel of John as providing a framework for a constructive engagement in analysis and critique of the Church. The focus on John is not an argument for the priority of one gospel over the other writings in the New Testament. It

97 Fowl, *Theological Interpretation*, 2.

98 John Webster, "Editorial," *International Journal of Systematic Theology* 12/2 (April 2010): 116.

99 Webster, "Editorial," 116.

100 Francis Watson, "Hermeneutics and the Doctrine of Scripture: Why They Need Each Other," *International Journal of Systematic Theology* 12/2 (April 2010).

101 Fowl, *Theological Interpretation*, 9.

102 Fowl, *Theological Interpretation*, 51.

is simply a lens that allows for a corrective reordering of the way that theology has operated in relation to practice in the Church. The argument is that contemplation of Jesus Christ in the actual words of scripture is the place where God is revealed. This revealing calls for worship and only thereafter reflection, and then construction. Worship involves a reordering in the presence of Jesus Christ—Jesus Christ seen in the scriptures but made present through the work of the Holy Spirit who leads the Church into truth. This "truth" is not doctrine or proposition, but a person, Jesus Christ, which does not mean that doctrinal formulation has no place in the Church, because the Church is called to express and communicate Christ in cultural forms. The point is that theological construction, because it is provisional, needs always to be reformed and reframed through the practice of contemplation of Jesus Christ. This worship has deep and significant parallels with the lived spirituality of the contemporary Church. The practice of singing worship songs is a coming into the presence of Jesus Christ through the work of the Holy Spirit. Times of worship are moments of abiding and contemplation that transform and revivify the Church. This basic sensibility is deeply significant. It is not a sellout to consumerism; it is the fragment of life in the Church that I believe needs to be grasped and renewed through a more scriptural orientation. The "you" of the worship songs needs to become the Jesus of the gospels, not the other way round. So a critical analysis of the cultural forms of the Church is a way of paying attention to the way that practice generates particular forms of theological expression. This is what it means to reflect, i.e., to seek the presence of Jesus Christ in the life of the Church and to do this through disciplines of paying attention. The fluidity of the Church is part of its life in the Spirit, but this life needs attention precisely because it is life. Attention comes through a critical and sustained curiosity about how Church is lived out in social forms, but these forms are only "seen" as they are brought into worship through the contemplation of Jesus Christ in the scriptures. This in a sense is complexity coming into the presence of complexity. The complexity of the lived finds its orientation and re-orientation in the life that is Jesus Christ. This is what it means to worship in Spirit and in Truth and to be reformed in the image of Christ.

The Gospel and the Church

Barth's starting point for *Church Dogmatics* i.e., "the scientific self examination of the Christian Church with respect to the content of its distinctive talk about God" locates the gospel at the centre of the theological task and hence in ecclesiology. Liquid Ecclesiology finds its orientation in the fluidity of culture, but it derives its origins from the presence of Christ in the Church and in the world. This inevitably raises the question of the gospel in relation to the Church, because it is the gospel that is the good news of Jesus Christ and hence the origins of the Church. It is tempting to see the gospel as a fixed point in a fluid culture. The Church has its message, and this is the rock that can stand amidst the ebb and flow of culture. Appeal to the gospel as the firm basis for the Church is not unusual. Liquid Ecclesiology challenges this simplified approach to theological expression, however, by arguing that if there is a "fixed" point in the gospel, then this needs to take account of the cultural nature of all ecclesial expression. The problem with the gospel as a fixed point can be illustrated from two quite different theologians: the Anabaptist, James McClendon, and the Anglican, Michael Ramsey.

The Gospel, McClendon argues, is the starting point for a vision of the Church as a moral and ethical community.[103] The ethical life of the Church finds its orientation in the "great story" of the Old Testament and the New Testament and Jesus Christ is the heart of this story.[104] McClendon has a vision of the Church as people who inhabit and are inhabited by this story. The gospel presents a "strange world" of the Kingdom of God. But this strange world is an open story that can be entered by believers in the present.[105] The Gospel story gives rise to three motifs that shape the life of the Church as an ethical community. Firstly, the Church is located within the story as a band of travellers who are on *the way*. Thus the gospel presents the Christian life as a road or a journey.[106] For those who are on the way—the journeying people of God—there is the experience of a growing awareness of a particular responsibility for fellow travellers. McClendon calls this responsibility *watchful care*. Christians are not individual travellers, but a community in relationship. Linked together as brothers and sisters the "congregation" pledges to watch over each other on the road.[107] The third motif is that of *witness*. The Church is not a closed group of believers, but an open circle of care.[108] The Church expresses care by sharing the Gospel with the wider society and offering care in the world. McClendon therefore develops his ecclesiology around a people shaped by this narrative journeying together on the way and called to a particular ethic expressed as a

103 McClendon, *Ethics* 47.
104 McClendon, *Ethics* 48.
105 McClendon, *Ethics* 338.
106 McClendon, *Ethics* 48.
107 McClendon, *Ethics* 51.
108 McClendon, *Ethics* 53.

way of life in their congregation and in the wider society. For McClendon, this ecclesiology arises from an overtly Anabaptist vision of the Church.

In *The Gospel and the Catholic Church*, Michael Ramsey also takes as his starting point the relationship between the gospel and the Church.[109] The Church, he argues, does not find its relevance in social engagement or in generating what he calls international policies that attempt to remedy the ills of the world.[110] Rather, the Church finds its point of reference in "the death of Jesus the Messiah, and…the deeper issues of sin and judgment."[111] The Church is shaped by the gospel of Jesus Christ who has died and who has risen again.[112] This is the work of Christ on the cross, bringing about a new humanity. "Christ is here defined not as the isolated figure of Galilee and Judaea but as one whose people, dead and risen with him are his own humanity. Membership of the Church is to die to self i.e. to be utterly dependent on the body.[113] The fact of Christ includes the fact of the Church."[114] The Church, he argues, is the people of God. "The individual Christian exists only because the body exists already."[115] Through baptism individuals are incorporated into the body of Christ and it is as part of this corporate body that they experience grace. The link between baptism and the gospel mirrors Ramsey's overall conviction that the shape of the Church should be derived from the gospel. "The Church's outward order expresses its inward meaning by representing the dependence of the members upon the one Body wherein they die to self."[116] The Church's outward order, he argues, is not a matter of indifference, but is supremely important because the visible Church tells the gospel.[117] Order, he suggests, exists in three main elements: baptism, the Eucharist and Episcopacy. Baptism is the act where a person is brought into a new relationship with Christ,[118] and in a continual response to this baptism the believer lives out their Christian life. It is in the Eucharist that the Church's life is gathered together. In fact, for Ramsey, all of life is brought to the Eucharist.[119] The bishops in the Church

109 Michael Ramsey, *The Gospel and the Catholic Church* (London: Cowley, 1936).

110 Ramsey, *The Gospel*, 3-4.

111 Ramsey, *The Gospel*, 4.

112 Ramsey, *The Gospel*, 5.

113 Ramsey, *The Gospel*, 44.

114 Ramsey, *The Gospel*, 33.

115 Ramsey, *The Gospel*, 38.

116 Ramsey, *The Gospel*, 2.

117 Ramsey, *The Gospel*, 50.

118 Ramsey, *The Gospel*, 58.

119 Ramsey, *The Gospel*, 118-119.

are central because they are the ones who show that the community is gospel oriented, not just in the present, but throughout Christian history in the succession of bishops from New Testament times.

Both McClendon and Ramsey seek to build their ecclesiologies from the gospel. What is remarkable is that, given what appears to be a shared starting point, they have generated two very different visions for the Church. The one is clearly Anabaptist and the other is High Church Anglican. And what is clear is that not only have they argued for quite different kinds of Churches, the one hierarchical, sacramental and static, and the other more oriented towards ethics, congregation and movement, they also express the gospel in quite different ways. Both are participatory at heart. For McClendon, the story incorporates the believer; for Ramsey the believer is incorporated into the body of Christ, the Church, but these forms of participation signal quite different gospel sensibilities. In other words, the "gospel" is problematic as a fixed starting point for developing ecclesiology. The gospel appears to be itself part of expression and theological construction. Having said this, there is the paradoxical position that both McClendon and Ramsey press, that "the gospel" must be at the heart of ecclesiology. It is a mistake to conclude from this that the task is simply to clarify what the gospel is and that these theologians have somehow made a wrong turn. The point is that the evaluation of any ecclesiology needs to take account of the expression of the gospel, and the ways in which that gospel is embodied. In other words, there is a theological task that requires an engagement with expression and the lived, but also a revisiting of the scriptures and the Christian tradition. This is the task of Liquid Ecclesiology.

Part I: Currents in the Liquid Church, deals with the theological and cultural theories that shape Liquid Ecclesiology. A theology that is empirically orientated needs to be theological. Theology can of course be manifest through empirical research, but there are ways of speaking and writing that are distinctively theological in both tone and method. In the following chapters, I develop a theology of Gospel and Church as the basis for a Liquid Ecclesiology. I make this move in order to situate Liquid Ecclesiology within a wider theological conversation and also to develop a theological frame for the empirical. This frame is itself a "construct," and I have constructed it in order to shape what is then illustrated further in the Case Study in Part II.

The theological voice is necessary to the argument, but it is also presented with self-knowing, i.e., the consciousness that it is provisional. In adopting a theological voice in these chapters, I am aware that this is a voice that seeks to be rooted in the tradition and has the confidence to speak of the work of God in the world. To speak in this way of the work of God reveals a confidence that is perhaps less evident in empirical research, or perhaps the empirical researcher needs to be more hesitant with a theological voice. Speaking and discerning in a theological voice is an essential aspect of ecclesiology and ethnography. Yet adopting a theological voice and using this as a starting point is a deliberate move. It is a construction, but it is a construction that is made with a measure of self-awareness. I am acknowledging that what I say, even as it may claim "normativity," is epistemologically relative. This point should not lead to hesitancy, however. The Church needs theological speech and would die without it, in fact. Theological speech offers ways of living, a perspective and a vision of transcendence. There is thus something of a Catch 22 situation here. It is necessary to speak theologically in order to confidently express the life of God in the world and in the Church. It is right and necessary that this way of speaking makes claims and seeks to change the way that we live as the Church and as humanity. At the same time, we must acknowledge and accept that such a way of speaking is not definitive. This is what it means to be faith seeking understanding.

Chapter 1 argues that the Church and the Gospel have their being in Jesus Christ. The presence of Christ in the world and in the Church shapes the Church and the gospel. This presence has its origins in the "crazy love" of God. The fluid being of the Church is dynamic, relational and made ever youthful by the work of the Holy Spirit. The Church and the gospel are expressions in culture, and therefore a limitation of the divine presence. They are the humiliation of the Word in the Church. Chapter 2 sets out the case for the paradox at the centre of ecclesiology. The paradox is that the Light of the World transforms and yet is also communicated within the expression of the Church. The Light shapes individuals and a way of life in the community, but as it does so it is paradoxically limited to the partiality of cultural forms. Chapter 3 explores how, through the work of the Spirit, the presence of Christ in the Church is fluid, a fluidity that is matched by the way culture works. Cultural forms shift their meaning across time and within communities. The gospel cannot be preserved as if it were somehow outside or above culture. Instead, the Church has accepted that the Gospel finds its authenticity in Jesus Christ, as he is revealed in scripture and also in the embodied and expressed tradition of the Church. While it is evident that both the scriptures and the Church are culturally bound, this does not mean that all and any kind of expression is acceptable or above criticism. Chapter 4 explores the content of the gospel message in relation to the idea of a "grand narrative" of the Church.

Part II: Discerning the Liquid Church, A Case Study, shows how these theological and cultural frameworks operate in the expression of the Church. The case study focuses on the gospel as it is understood and has operated in contemporary evangelical and charismatic churches. The case study illustrates how close attention to the fluidity of expression and the dynamics of culture, making use of a variety of methods of empirical research, can generate a multilayered understanding of an issue in ecclesiology. In this case, the issue is how the gospel relates to the Church. The case study takes the form of discourse analysis and it centres on the lived expression and communicative practices of the Church. This analysis serves to illustrate how qualitative empirical work can both enrich and also challenge theological discussion about the Church. Discourse analysis brings together a range of different empirical data to generate an analysis of the expressive and cultural communication of elements within the contemporary Church. The case study deals with the contemporary evangelical/charismatic Church in the United States and the United Kingdom. The case study takes as its starting point the widely-held view that the gospel is unchanging, while the Church has a responsibility to continually adjust its life and expression to the changes in culture. The notion of espoused and operant theology is used to explain how in practice the evangelical expression of the Gospel has become disconnected from the everyday lived practice of the contemporary Church. Chapter 5 looks at the idea of an unchanging gospel and how expression itself has made this idea possible. Chapter 6 traces how the desire to communicate the faith, particularly among young people, has led to the adoption of more subjective forms of expression. It is argued that the concentration on the self and a personal relationship with God has led to the more objective Gospel becoming less and less significant. Chapter 7 traces this split between the espoused Gospel and the operant faith of the Church through a detailed discussion of contemporary worship.

Part III: Remaining the Liquid Church, develops the notion of judgment and normativity in Liquid Ecclesiology. Chapter 8 examines the case study and explores the specific issues and problems that arise from a separation of Gospel and the lived practice of the Church. In Chapter 9 these perspectives are then used as the starting point for a discussion of normativity in ecclesiology as the practice of abiding. Finally, Chapter 10 sets out how abiding might become part of the lived expression of the Church through theological education.

Liquid Ecclesiology and Normativity

Liquid Ecclesiology: Gospel and Church is thus an attempt to explore an ecclesiology that takes full account of culture and the divine being of the Church. The gospel is central to this project as it is the gospel that forms the heart of the community. Once it is accepted that this gospel is itself cultural and therefore fluid, questions arise concerning the continual faithfulness, authenticity, and legitimacy of the Church. In other words, the whole issue of normativity in theology arises. Liquid Ecclesiology accepts that theological arbitration as it has traditionally been conducted is not an entirely acceptable solution. This is because theological expression is itself cultural and therefore fluid. Fluidity need not be seen as inherently problematic, however. Liquid Ecclesiology takes as a main tenet that there is a symbiotic relationship between the divine being and the cultural expression of the Church. Both are moving and alive, i.e., more liquid than solid. Thus while theologians are able to generate distinctions and make deliberations when they limit themselves to "ideas," the lived, living, indwelling, and indwelt Christian community requires a more compromised and muddied form of analysis, i.e., an analysis that accepts its own limitations and its own contingency. Such an observation does not preclude the practice of ecclesiology or the necessity for judgement. Normativity remains a key function of ecclesiology. I simply argue that this practice needs to be reoriented.

The re-orientation of ecclesiology rests on the notion of "abiding," which has two aspects. The first is a turn towards worship and wonder. Worship and wonder are focused on Jesus Christ revealed in the scriptures. Secondly, abiding refers to the practice of discernment. This is the discipline of paying close attention to the cultural expression of the Church. This attention is also a practice of worship and wonder since its primary orientation is towards the presence of Jesus Christ in the Church and also in the world. Abiding is the call to return continually to Jesus Christ to be transformed as a community. Abiding operates as normativity in the Liquid Church. This normative function is not only necessary, it is essential. Because of the gravitational pull of the Church, normativity appears to be a perilous activity without guarantees. This ambiguous and muddied aspect of ecclesiology is part of its situation in the lived. Abiding is thus inherently perilous.

Normativity, reconstituted as abiding, describes an ecclesial practice. Fundamentally this means that normativity, as abiding, comes with none of the guarantees that traditional ecclesiology might expect. Normativity is not simply delivered through the genre of theological rationality and the ability to make distinctions in the ideal. Neither can it be achieved by privileging the voice of the trained theologian. Being part of the expression of the Church locates the theologian in the flow of tradition and as part of the prayer of the community. Abiding is not simply the prerequisite for knowing (and being known), it is its primary location. What this means is that the "product" of theological creativity, presented as knowledge, is not in and of itself normative.

Normativity is always located in the lived. The theological product is thus the approximation to normativity. It is always contingent. If judgment is simply deciding between competing idealized accounts, then normativity can operate by an exchange between theological products. This kind of normativity is not at all what is required in ecclesiology, however, because judgment has implications for the social and the cultural. Churches have to take material form. They are "things." The connection to the material and historical requires ecclesiology to forge some kind of connection with the particular. Normativity in ecclesiology calls for something more than this, i.e., a way to develop judgment in relation to the contingent. Liquid Ecclesiology draws attention to the gravitational pull of the embodied. What this means is that normativity operates in relation to the lived and as part of the lived and this is precisely what this book sets out to explore.

PART I

Currents in the Liquid Church

CHAPTER 1

The Gospel and the Church

The starting point for constructing a Liquid Ecclesiology is theological. In other words, a Liquid Ecclesiology sets out a way of seeing the relationship between the expression of the Church and the being of the Church. The key to this theological way of seeing is the gospel. What I mean by the gospel and how it is nuanced in theological and cultural terms is explored in depth in the following chapters, but I want to suggest the theological starting point for understanding the Church lies in the gospel. The gospel is at the heart of two crucial conversations concerning the Church. The first relates to how the Church takes a social form in society. The second relates to how the Church is studied. It is the gospel that brings these two conversations together and generates a theological orientation both for the remaking and making of Church, and also for the critical and creative conversation around how Church is to be studied. Taking the fluid cultural and theological dimensions of the Church seriously requires a consideration of the gospel. However, the gospel and the Church have a prior connection in Jesus Christ. They find their being in Jesus Christ. This ontology is itself "fluid." Liquid Church is therefore fluid because of the being of God. It is this being that finds its echo in the fluidity of culture, and the paradox of ecclesiology lies in developing theological understanding that takes account of the presence of Jesus Christ in and through the culturally contingent and imperfect expression of the Church. The gospel, then, relates crucially to the moving and dynamic presence of Jesus Christ in the world. This chapter explores the nature of divine presence, drawing on the notion of *manikos eros*, the "crazy love of God," to describe the character of Christ's interaction with the world. This leads to a discussion of connection between the expression of the Church and Jesus Christ. The theme of humiliation is developed to explore the self-emptying that characterizes both the incarnation and the presence of Christ in the Church.

Jesus and the Church

The relationship between the gospel and the Church is in Jesus Christ. It is Jesus the vine who is also the way the truth and life.[1] So if we ask what the

1 John 15: 1; and John 14:6.

 | DOI 10.1163/9789004347359_003

Church "is," or what the gospel "is," the answer in both cases is Jesus Christ. The being of the Church and the gospel lies in Christ, but this identification is not equal. There is a broken line of connection between the Church, the gospel, and Christ. This unequal identification does not weaken the connection to Christ, since it arises from the freedom and transcendence of God. God is always beyond our knowing, revealed and yet partially veiled. The Church and the gospel act as this veil of social and cultural expression, so it is in the context of this veiling, rather than despite it, that it is possible to say that the gospel is the gospel of Jesus Christ and the Church is the Church of Jesus Christ. "Where-ever Jesus Christ is," says Ignatius, "there is the Catholic Church."[2] This expression does not operate the other way round, however. It is not always possible to say that where the Church is, there is Christ in quite the same way, not least because it is a sad fact that the Church often does not live up to its calling, and there are times when the Christian community does as much to obscure Christ as it does to reveal him. The same unequal dynamic of identification can also be applied to the gospel.

The gospel is where Jesus Christ is present. This is the meaning of the verse in the first chapter of Mark's Gospel: "Jesus came to Galilee, proclaiming the good news of God, and saying, 'The time is fulfilled, and the kingdom of God has come near; repent and believe in the good news'" (Mark 1:14). The gospel of the Kingdom is proclaimed, but he is himself the coming Kingdom. Jesus is the Kingdom and he is the gospel. The gospel, then, like the Church, "is" Jesus Christ. Here again it is possible for Christians to "miss proclaim" and obscure the life of Christ in their message. Yet it is in and through the cultural expression of Church that Christ chooses to be present. So Jesus "is" the answer to what the Church and the gospel "are," but this ontological relationship is complex. The unequal relationship between the Church and the presence of Christ is a fundamental aspect of all ecclesiology. The dynamic of the presence of Christ and the social and historical contingency of the Church lies behind all of the issues that relate to Gospel and culture and contextualization. It also operates in questions of mission and the future shape of the Church. Most importantly, the unequal identification between Jesus Christ, his Church and the Gospel, remains the touchstone for issues of judgment in relation to the life of the Church.

Churches of all kinds are prone to believing their own myths and absolutizing particular cultural expressions as the truth. The only possibility for

---

2 Ignatius, "Epistle to the Ephesians," *The Apostolic Fathers with Justin Martyr and Irenaeus*, trans. Philip Schaff, Vol 1 of *The Ante Nicene Church Fathers* (Grand Rapids, MI: Eerdmans, 2001), 90.

correcting problems and bringing the Church to "judgment" lies in the person of Jesus Christ. Judgment here does not mean an eschatological reckoning, but the possibility of correcting, renewing, and reforming the Church in each new cultural context. Renewal is essential because of the cultural veil of expression. The building blocks that the Church uses to proclaim the gospel afresh in each generation are cultural, and are therefore only approximate to Christ. Approximate expression is a given, not simply because of cultural or social imperfection, but because of the overwhelming being of God. In encounter with this God, the only response is wonder and worship. Expression should always be qualified by humility. It is this encounter with God as overwhelming presence that orientates the true relationship between the Church and the gospel. In worship, the Church is led to see its place in the sweep of God's Trinitarian life and the outpouring of passionate and crazy love for the world.

Church, Gospel and the World

The Church and gospel have their being in Jesus Christ, because all things find their origin in him. Christ is the image of God and "in him" all things in heaven and on earth were created (Col 1:15). Creation and the Church are joined, according to Colossians, by a common relationship with Christ. The Church, like creation, is held together "in Christ," who is its head (Col 1:18). Being joined to the body comes through hearing the gospel and believing, but this relationship had its origins before creation (Eph 1:13). The blessing that is shared by the Church therefore has its beginning in the freedom of God to choose humanity. As the writer to the Ephesians puts it: "He chose us in Christ before the foundation of the world" (Eph 1:4). The choice is for the world and it is this that the Church enjoys. God's love is for the whole world created and sustained in Christ, and on the cross it is all creation that is reconciled and redeemed (Col 1:20). The Church then shares in a gospel that gathers all things into the life of God through Jesus Christ. Sealed with the Spirit, believers are promised an inheritance of "redemption" as the people of God (Eph 1:13). This gathering of love in the Trinitarian life of God incorporates the entirety of creation (Eph 1:10). "He himself is before all things, and in him all things hold together" (Col 1:17), and as the image of God, Christ is "the firstborn of creation"(Col 1:15). So the fullness of Christ is the fullness of God, "and through him God was pleased to reconcile to himself all things, whether on earth or in heaven, by making peace through the blood of his cross" (Col 1:20). This is the fullness that the disciples have seen in the incarnation and in the cross (John 1:14): the word made flesh, full of grace and truth. This is the glory of God, seen at creation, in the incarnation, and on the cross, and it is a foretaste of glory that is to come. The cross of Christ then represents a pivotal point between what came before creation and what comes as the fulfilment of creation. “In him we have redemption through his blood, the forgiveness of our trespasses, according to the grace that he lavished on us” (Eph 1:8). The Church indwells and is indwelt by the lavishing of this love of God: Father Son and Holy Spirit. Church and gospel therefore have their being in this love, because God is love.

Love is animated before creation in the Trinitarian being of God. Love extends to the free choice of humanity and the creation of the world, and love is the gathering of “all things” in Christ. As the writer of Ephesians puts it, “And he has put all things under his feet and has made him the head over all things for the church, which is his body, the fullness of him who fills all in all” (Eph 1:23). The Church is “particular” and marked, because it is part of this wider movement of God towards the world. The gospel similarly can only be understood as having its being in Christ when it is seen in like manner. The expansiveness of the gospel does not come from a more developed theology. It comes from the being of God. God precedes and exceeds our knowing and expression. The Church and the gospel do not contain or ever fully express the being of God that gives them life. They are rather continually conditioned and renewed by the Spirit, making Jesus Christ known in and through cultural expression. The Church and the gospel are therefore “preceded” by the love of God for the world. God so loved the world that he sent his Son (John 3:16). There is therefore an order of relations that situates the gospel and the Church in the life of God and the lavishing of grace on creation. The love God has for the world gives rise to the Church, not the other way round.

The Crazy Love of God

If the Church and the gospel find their being in the presence of Christ then it also needs to be made clear that this presence is not guaranteed by a particular kind of expression or by distinctive cultural forms. In other words, Christ is not made present by saying the right words, or doing the right things, or organizing the right way. At the same time, the paradox is such that it is only in particular ways of speaking, doing, and social organization that Christ is present. This presence comes from the freedom of the Spirit. Through the Spirit, Christ is present because God is love. But love does not simply explain why Christ is present; love also shapes the manner of that presence. It is this manner, rather than particular kinds of expression or social forms, that determines the relationship between the Church and the gospel.

In *The Life in Christ*, the fourteenth century Orthodox theologian, Nicholas Cabasilas, uses the term the *manikos eros*, or "crazy love," to speak of Christ's presence:

> Just as human affection, when it abounds, overpowers those who love and causes them to be beside themselves, so God's love for men emptied God He does not stay in His own place and call the slave, He seeks him in person by coming down to him. He who is rich reaches the pauper's hovel, and He displays His love by approaching in person. He seeks love in return and does not withdraw when he is treated with disdain. He is not angry over ill treatment, but He sits by the door and does everything to show us that He loves, even enduring suffering and death to prove it.[3]

The presence of Christ in the Church and in the gospel arises from, and is characterized by this crazy impassioned love. Jesus Christ, as the being of the Church, is not a principle or a theory.[4] The presence of Christ in the Church is a passionate self-emptying that is seen in the washing of the disciples' feet, the identification with humanity in the sharing our baptism, and ultimately in his death on the cross. This is the love that is experienced by the Church, as Christ through the power of the Spirit is made present. The identification of Christ with the Church and the message that it is called to proclaim is rooted, grounded, and empowered by this crazy love. Love points to what it means to be Church and what it means to share the gospel with the world. The love of God is shown in the image of Christ as one who patiently waits outside to be welcomed in. "Listen! I am standing at the door, Knocking; if you hear my voice and open the door, I will come in to you and eat with you, and you with me" (Rev 3:20). This is the crazy devotion of the lover who waits around on the street just happy to be near the place where their beloved lives. Impassioned for humanity, Christ waits for the encounter with those whom he loves. As Christ sits by the side of the well in the heat of the day waiting to meet a woman who comes to draw water, so too is he present in his Church and in the world. Drawn to those who grieve, and to those who meet to celebrate a

---

3 Nicholas Cabasilas, *The Life in Christ*, trans. Carmino J. Decatanzaro (Crestwood, NY: Saint Vladimir's Seminary Press, 1974), Book 6: 644-645, 162-163.

4 It is worth noting in this flow of theological assertion that saying this is itself a theory. In other words, I am caught here in a paradox that is the consequence of epistemic relativity. In speaking theologically, in adopting the theological voice, it is necessary to construct theory. This theory is not the presence of Christ, yet in order that I might speak of Christ not as theory, I must construct theory. This is the Catch 22 of ecclesiology.

wedding, he is moved to pity for those who have a suffering child, or for those who struggle with political power and responsibility. This is the kenosis of the Son who loves enough to draw alongside humanity. The crazy love of God is made manifest in Christ, who is energized by impassioned love to be "near" in these kinds of places, and in these kinds of ways. This crazy love is shaped by *kenosis*, the self-emptying (Phil 2:7), suffering, and glory. This is grace and truth, the fullness of God in Jesus Christ, and it is this fullness that shapes the Church and the gospel. For the presence of Christ in the Church and the gospel is not based on abstract theology or correct definition, or on the right kind of ritual, practice, and order. The "is" of the Church and the gospel is a response to, and a joyful sharing in, the crazy love of God.

Sharing in the crazy love of God represents a call to follow Christ as presence in the world. The Church experiences the personal and passionate presence of Christ in its ongoing life, but this presence is also there *in the same way* outside the Church. The love of God means that Christ is drawn to wait and be present alongside everyone and anyone, as they pass through the joy and the troubles of life. When families and communities gather together, Christ is present. Whenever people mourn and lament the death of a loved one, Christ is there, and when people are moved by art and music, or by the beauty of creation, Christ is there. This presence is not a generalized principle of divine life. Christ is present because of the crazy love of God. The presence is personal and intentional. Church and gospel therefore find their origin and their point of reference in this crazy love seen in the Church and outside the Church. It is this love that continually calls the Church to a renewed and restored life empowered by the Spirit.

The Liquid Renewal of the Spirit

Christ is present in the Church and in the world, through the work of the Holy Spirit. Irenaeus speaks of the Spirit as also constituting the being of the Church. "For where the Church is there is the Spirit of God; and where the Spirit of God is there is the Church; and every kind of grace; but the Spirit is truth." The Spirit works to vivify and to keep the Church youthful. Faith has been received and preserved in the Church and "by the Spirit of God, renewing its excellent vessel, causes the vessel itself containing it to renew its youth also."[5] The youthful renewal of the life of the Church comes from the Spirit of

5 Irenaeus, "Against Heresy," III, xxiv, 1, in *The Apostolic Fathers*, 458.

God. This is the Spirit promised by Jesus to the disciples, who will lead them into "truth." This truth is not primarily a set of ideas, or a theology, and neither is it a form of organization, or religious ritual. The truth is the person of Jesus Christ who is made present to the Church through the work of the Spirit. As the gospel of John expresses it, '"When the Spirit of truth comes, he will guide you into all truth; for he will not speak on his own, but will speak whatever he hears and he will declare to you the things that are come. He will glorify me, because he will take what is mine and declare it to you."[6] The truth that John's gospel points to is a person.

Through the work of the Spirit the Church is to be continually renewed and made youthful in each generation. This animation of the people of God gives rise to the sense that the Church is not static, but is always moving, and developing. So what the Church "is," i.e., the "being" of the Church, is perhaps best seen as something that is characterized by movement and this movement comes from the presence of Christ through the work of the Spirit. This movement then is not simply what happens in the Church, it is also the call of crazy love to follow the divine passion in the world. The crazy love of God means that the Church has a vocation to be animated by the Spirit, and a calling to be fluid in its form as it responds to the challenge of crazy love of God, both inside the community, and outside. The Church is therefore a living organism, always changing, moving, and growing. This organic notion of being runs throughout the biblical imagery of the Church. The presence of Christ, and being joined to Christ, are fundamental to these metaphors of the Church, and each carries within it the changing dynamic of growth. The Church as a body grows toward Christ. As it is written in Ephesians, the Church must not be blown about by every kind of doctrine, "[b]ut speaking the truth in love, we must grow up in every way into him who is the head, into Christ from whom the whole body, joined and knitted together by every ligament with which it is equipped, as each part is working properly, promotes the body's growth in building itself up in love" (Eph 4:15-16). This is a picture of the Church that individually and corporately grows up into maturity in Christ. It is Christ as the head who binds individuals together into the body.[7] The body imagery in Ephesians therefore has this organic quality.

The Church is an organism moving towards completion, through being bound together as ligaments and joints in the body. This growth motif is found

6 John 16: 13-14; see also 14:25 and 16:6-10.

7 C. Leslie Mitton, *The Epistle to the Ephesians: Its Authorship, Origin and Purpose* (Grand Rapids, MI: Eerdmans, 1951), 157.

elsewhere in Ephesians also. The new people of God have been formed into one body through the cross of Jesus Christ, bringing together Jews and Gentiles. The people are shaped into the temple of the Lord, built on the foundation of the apostles and the prophets. Christ himself is the cornerstone of this building. "In him the whole structure is joined together and grows into a holy temple in the Lord; in whom you also are built together spiritually into a dwelling place for God" (Eph 2:21-22). This is a vision of the Church as the gathering together of peoples through Christ, both Jews and Gentiles, who together have access, "in one Spirit to the Father" (Eph 2:18). There is fluid movement of people here, journeying towards encounter with God in the temple. The journey is vivified and animated in the Spirit. The Church journeys towards the temple, and is at once formed into the temple, and in that temple divine encounter takes place. "The temple is 'in the Lord', even as it is a dwelling place 'in or by the Spirit'."[8]

The image of the temple is also found in 1 Peter 2: 4-5 where Christ is spoken of as the "living stone." Once rejected, there is now an invitation to come to him, "like living stones let your self be built into a spiritual house, to be a holy priesthood, to offer spiritual sacrifices acceptable to God through Jesus Christ" (1 Pet 2:4). The cornerstone for the temple is the living resurrected Christ. Just as he is living, so those who journey towards him are also made alive. This is a creative mixing of metaphor that expresses the complexity of the Church that is both material and spiritual. Living stones are somehow both structure and organism, and hence the image of the building is transformed from solidity to organic fluidity. Brought to life, the stones are collectively made by God into his temple. Believers are in the process of "being built" together into the house of God. The temple that is made of people replaces the physical temple in Jerusalem in the New Testament (for example, Mark 14:58; 15:29, John 2:19. 4:21, 23-24; Acts 7:48; 17:24). "The House of God is no longer to be thought of as a physical building, but as a living house in which God lives."[9] It is the place where God dwells and yet this dwelling is now seen as being within individuals and the community. Christ is the cornerstone, the basis for the life, and yet there is an animation of the presence of God that brings the stones together. The construction of the living temple does not cease.

The Church is not "set in stone" once it has been built. The animation of the Spirit is continual. Christ does not cease to be alive once located as the

8 Everett Ferguson, *The Church of Christ: A Biblical Ecclesiology for Today* (Grand Rapids, MI: Eerdmans, 1996), 129.

9 Peter H. Davids, *The First Epistle of Peter: New International Commentary on the New Testament* (Grand Rapids, MI: Eerdmans, 1990), 87.

cornerstone and neither do the believers. The presence of God is therefore a continual revivifying, as the church is being made alive and formed into the temple of God. It is this life energy that makes the Church a fluid community. The Church is Liquid because made so by the work of the Holy Spirit: living water wells up in believers and overflows as the crazy love of God.

The Humiliation of the Word

Liquid Ecclesiology starts with the conviction that the Church has its being in the life of God. So the answer to the question about what the Church "is," is Jesus Christ, and similarly, the answer to the question of what the gospel "is," is also Jesus Christ. The Church and the gospel are related through a shared "ontology" in the being of God. This being is characterized by the crazy love of God. Love introduces a dynamic that is shared both inside and outside the Church, by the self emptying of Christ, patiently waiting for the various ways that people respond and turn in fitful and partial ways towards the light. It is the Spirit that makes Christ present to people. The Spirit is at work, both inside and outside the Church, seeking to make Christ present and known. The Spirit therefore is the animating force that makes the Church ever youthful. The life of the Spirit shapes communal life and it draws believers into the wider society. "God is Love, and those who abide in Love abide in God and God abides in them" (1 John 4:16). Crazy love is the energising movement that passes in a fluid way through the walls of the Church and back again. So the being of the Church is shaped by the fluid life of God, but there is a paradox here because the Church is also, and always, a cultural expression. The expression of the Church is a sharing in the crazy love of God, but it is also and always "cultural," i.e., it is made by people and by communities.

Christ through the Spirit chooses to be present in and through the cultural expression of the Church. This is an aspect of crazy love because it too is self-limiting. Hence Christ is both revealed and veiled in the cultural forms that the Church must use to express faith. This cultural expression includes the liturgy of the Church, the gathering and social life of community, and the gospel that the Church proclaims.[10] These expressions are animated, or made youthful and alive by the Spirit, and they become indwelt by the presence of Christ. Expression does not encompass or deliver the presence of Christ, however. Dietrich Bonhoeffer speaks of the incarnation as a self-limiting of God

10 Cultural expression includes this particular attempt at generating a theology of the Church and any kind of empirical analysis of the Church.

in and through revelation. In human form Christ becomes a stumbling block (*scandalon*), apparently confining the divine in human form. The incarnation, says Bonhoeffer, is therefore the humiliation of the Word.[11] This humiliation is repeated in the life of the Church, where in the sacraments, preaching, and gathering, Christ is present. The presence of the resurrected and ascended Lord, is also a *scandalon*, it is a "second humiliation."[12] The presence of Christ in the Church, Bonhoeffer argues, is not as a set of ideas, but as a relationship. "He is not a universally accessible idea but the word perceived only where he allows himself to be perceived."[13]

The sacraments, Bonhoeffer says, actually teach the limitations of doctrine. In the sacraments, the Church is taught that God is not contained solely in ideas.[14] Christ is not conveyed in general truths, but through a personal address. Christ is present "for me" in personal relational ways in the life of the Church.[15] Quoting Luther, he says, "So it is one thing if God is there, and it is another if he is there for you."[16] This relational dynamic is played out most decisively in the gathering of the community. The community, Bonhoeffer argues, is itself a revelation. "The Word is in the community in so far as the community is a recipient of revelation. But the Word is also itself community, in so far as the community is itself revelation, and the Word wills to have the form of a created body."[17] So the Christian community does not simply "represent" Christ; it is the body of Christ. Christ is not only the head of the Church. He is also the community itself.[18]

The self-limitation of Christ in the life and expression of the Church is a humiliation, because that life and expression are always partial. Cultural expression is not partial, because culture is somehow tainted or inherently problematic or always inclined to error. These perspectives generally mask the belief in the Church and its expression as somehow beyond or above culture. Cultural forms are a humiliation because of the transcendent nature of the being of God. In the incarnation, humanity is transformed, and through the resurrection it is taken into the life of God. Christ continues in human form transformed by glory. Humanity, and by extension human culture, are recapitulated

11 Dietrich Bonhoeffer, *Christology* (London: Collins, 1966), 46.

12 Bonhoeffer, *Christology*, 47.

13 Bonhoeffer, *Christology*, 51.

14 Bonhoeffer, *Christology*, 54.

15 Bonhoeffer, *Christology*, 47.

16 Bonhoeffer, *Christology*, 48.

17 Bonhoeffer, *Christology*, 60.

18 Bonhoeffer, *Christology*, 60-61.

in death and resurrection. This reworking and reincorporation into God mean that while human society and cultural expression continue to be sinful and imperfect, they are also capable of being taken up in revelation. This gathering of all things into God has its origins in creation and it has its pivotal point in the cross of Christ, but it has its fulfilment in the final gathering of all things at the end of time. It is in this fluid sweep of the movement of crazy love that Church and Gospel are to find their orientation. They are a humiliation not because they are "cultural," but because they struggle to express fully the being of God. At the same time the flaws in expression and social life continue to show through. The Church is the body of Christ, but it is always prone to error.

Expression and Problems

Liquid Ecclesiology is not alone in focusing the discussion of the Church on the dynamic play between culture and divine presence. Ecclesiology in general has grown out of the understanding that the social and theological are in tension in the life of the Church. Gerard Mannion and Lewis Mudge argue, for instance, that attention to the lived is a particular distinctive in the theology of the Church. They point out that most of the key doctrinal formulations concerning the Church have developed in relation to the cultural and the lived. As a result, the doctrine of the Church has not generally been worked out in the abstract, but has emerged from the persistent and repeated failings of the Christian community in history. They indicate the way that Christian theology has always sought to interact with what they call the "historical-sociological-institutional footprint" of the Christian community.[19] In other words, the understanding of the gospel is itself located in the historical and the communal. The social reality of the Church forms a part of the theology of the community, such that versions of the faith are "constructed" that correspond to particular circumstances and historical contingencies.[20] Authentic ecclesiology, they argue, always seeks to explore what the advent of Jesus Christ means in the form of a community. Ecclesiology is speech about God, but this speech is never entirely abstract. Instead it is speech that takes account of a "certain kind of witnessing, serving, community."[21] Hence it is central to the task of ecclesiology that "bearing in mind the changing nature of society and culture and

19 Gerard Mannion and Lewis Mudge, eds., *The Routledge Companion to the Christian Church* (London: Routledge, 2008), 3.

20 Mannion and Mudge, *The Routledge Companion*, 3.

21 Mannion and Mudge, *The Routledge Companion*, 3.

our relative inability to access this 'reality' can we conceive of a community in which and through which Jesus Christ might become present 'within histories' contingencies'."[22] This dynamic is present in two of the archetypal biblical images for the Church: the body of Christ and the vine.

The Body

This dynamic between a theological understanding of the Church and the gospel, is seen quite explicitly in Paul's letters to the Church in Corinth. The body of Christ metaphor in 1 Corinthians arises directly from Paul's detailed knowledge of the particular problems and failings of the Corinthian church. Thus while there may not be particular people in mind who are seen as the eye, or the hand, of the body, the problems associated with division and elitism in this local church are laid bare throughout the epistle.[23] In teaching about worship and the body of Christ, Paul is forthright: "I do not commend you, because when you come together it is not for the better but for the worse. For to begin with, when you come together as a church, I hear that there are divisions among you and to some extent I believe it" (1 Cor 11:17-18). He goes on to detail how the gathering for the Lord's Supper has been characterised by feasting and drunkenness among some, while others go without food because they are poor. It is in this context that the Church is spoken of as a body that includes difference and distinction.[24] Joined to Christ, in his body the life of the Church is based on unity. Here the practice of spiritual gifts is set in the context of unity. Unity among believers is derived from the oneness of the Spirit and the oneness of Christ.[25] This unity transcends not only ethnic and social differences, but it also forms the basis for a community where there may be "varieties of service" and "varieties of activities" (1 Cor 12:5-6). Ministries of every kind spring from the work of the Holy Spirit. It is the baptism in the Spirit that joins the community together into the body of Christ.[26] Unity is derived from Christ, who is one, but so also is diversity. The force of Paul's argument, says Gordon Fee, is that "even though the body is one, it does not consist of one member but of many." So the body image rests on unity, by being joined to Christ, but it also supports difference.[27]

---

22 Mannion and Mudge, *The Routledge Companion*, 3.

23 1 Corinthians 1: 10-17; 5: 1-13; 6:1-11.

24 1 Cor 12:1-31.

25 1 Cor 12: 4-6.

26 1 Cor 12:13 and 12:27-28.

27 Gordon Fee, *The First Epistle to the Corinthians: New International Commentary on the New Testament* (Grand Rapids, MI: Eerdmans, 1987), 601.

The image of the body arises from particular historical circumstances and it is generated in order to address these. As a theological construct, it is passed down through the scriptures, and it gathers an authority by being repeated as a part of the tradition. The meaning of the term "the body of Christ" should not be dislocated from the historical context that generated the doctrine. The point here is that the normativity of the image of the body arises from the way that it brings the central conundrum of ecclesiology into its own construction. The image is inherently located in the lived, and it has direct implications for the lived, but it simultaneously carries the idea of the presence of Christ and the movement of the Spirit. The image in this sense is an icon of its intent and power for the community of the Church in the present. It is a "living word," a way as well as a truth. As such it brings life through being animated in the Spirit. At the same time it points to the being of the Church, as life and movement, and truth. The actions of individuals and the responses of communities are in no way incidental to the power of the image. The image assumes agency. But as it does so it also assumes fallibility. Churches go wrong and divide themselves in wearingly predictable ways, but the body image is there to generate a turning towards the life in the midst of life. The parts of the body are to be knitted together. This is not simply the idea of a community. The metaphor corresponds to actual communities. It finds its origins in Corinth, but it has purchase in the lived experience of the Church across time and cultures. The body image speaks of the way that growth, movement, and life, are of the "being" of the Church. When talking of ontology and of the gospel, we therefore need to pay particular attention to the actuality of communal living and practice alongside the construction of metaphor and image, because it is only through this kind of attention that what the Church and what the gospel are can be found. This is the basis for Liquid Ecclesiology, i.e., understanding the Church and the gospel as fluid movement.

The Vine

Just as with the metaphor of the body, the being of the Church and its growth are also linked in the image of the vine in John 15. The vine imagery, like the body, carries within it the sense that the Church, even as it is joined to Christ in an organic unity, is still prone to error. In fact, the exhortation to abide seems to imply the requirement for the Church and for individual believers to actively seek to be in continual union with Christ. To cease to do this is to risk being unfruitful and cast aside into the fire. Jesus is the true vine and his Father is the vine grower. The followers of Jesus are the branches. If they do not bear fruit then they will be pruned. But the word that Jesus has spoken to his disciples makes them clean. "Abide in me as I abide in you. Just as the branch cannot bear fruit by itself unless it abides in the vine, neither can you unless you abide in me. I am the vine, you are the branches. Those who abide in me and I in them bear much fruit, because apart from me you can do nothing.... My Father is glorified by this, that you bear much fruit and become my disciples. As the Father has loved me, so I have loved you; abide in my love. If you keep my commandments, you will abide in my love, just as I have kept my Father's commandments and abide in his love."[28] Christian practice springs as a fruit from being made one with Christ, the vine. Apart from the vine there is no fruit. In fact, the unfruitful branches are cut off and they are burned.[29]

The biblical images of the body and the vine address the central paradox of ecclesiology. They both assume human agency, even as they speak of a close, even organic, union with Christ. So the fact that the Church is limited by culture and prone to error is essential to the image in both cases. As a result, the inherent tensions and conflicts between the seen as a participation in divine being and yet also inclined towards sin, division and unfaithfulness are held together. This tension is not ideal, but it is suggestive of the way things are.

Theology and the Lived

So far in this chapter I have argued that answers to what the Church and gospel are, are to be found in Jesus Christ. Both have their being in Christ and therefore the question of the relationship between Church and gospel finds an answer in the "I am" of the gospels. There has been some slippage in what I have been saying so far, however, for while I have strongly asserted that the Church is Jesus Christ, I have spent most of the chapter talking about the "presence" of Christ in the Church. There is a tension around how the Church can be the body of Christ and how Christ can also be present in the Church. This paradox is deeply significant, because it signals how theological reasoning and language are conditioned by the being of God, i.e., that they are epistemically relative and therefore contested, and as a result the ways of speaking and reasoning that we resort to need themselves to be made fluid and movable because of the "difference" of the divine being.

The opening lines of John's Gospel give an indication of the problem of human expression and divine being. "In the beginning was the Word and the Word was with God, and the Word was God. He was in the beginning with God. All things came into being through him, and without him not one thing

28 John 15: 4-5 and 8-10.

29 The image of the vine and abiding therein are explored in more detail in Chapter 9.

came into being. What has come into being in him was life, and the life was the light of all people. The light shines in the darkness and the darkness did not overcome it" (John1: 1-4). The verses speak of the divine in a complex and paradoxical way. The Word is "with God" and the Word "is" God. The fact that these verses and others like them led to the development of the doctrine of the Trinity should not distract us from the way that reason is stretched and turned on its head by these images. The Word is both with and also is God. Explaining how this might, or might not be the case is to miss the point. What these verses are saying is that all talk about God pushes categories and logic and makes them fluid in such a way that what is said and what it is possible to say are determined by who God is rather than any theoretical system. Hence the idea of what it is to "be" something and also to be "with something" is transformed.

This logic of the making fluid of categories is extended from the being of God to the being of the Church. Christ is present in the Church, but Christ is also the head of the body. The body is also the body of Christ. This mixture of imagery is necessary to carry the complexity of divine presence in the Church, but it also makes space for the human and cultural by interrupting the line of reasoning from the lived experience of the Church to the being of God. Hence this theological perspective has a direct relevance to the empirical study of the Church. The Church is joined to Christ and dwells in him and he dwells in the Church, just as the Son dwells in the Father, although the force of this "like" is not to be mistaken for an equivalent. This distinction is emphasized in the notion of "indwelling" or abiding, where the call is for the Church to reach towards the crazy love that is shown in Christ, and also in the relationship between the Father and Son. Love here requires the exercising of persistence and faithfulness. The Church abides in Jesus Christ and Christ abides in the Church. It is the crazy love of God that shapes the indwelling of Jesus Christ in the Church. "Those who love me will keep my words; and my Father will love them, and we will come and make our home in them" (John 14:23). The love that is called out from those who are followers of Christ is an extension of the love of God. "As the Father has loved me, so I have loved you; abide in my love. If you keep my commandments, you will abide in my love, just as I have kept my Father's commandments and abide in his love" (John 15:9-10). The Church therefore is joined to Christ as the vine, and believers are made part of the body of Christ, although "remaining" requires faithfulness to the words of Jesus Christ. Love results in keeping the commandments that he has given.

All of this is really a prelude to saying that the presence of Jesus Christ in the Church is complex. Christ is the vine and the Church is his body. So the

Church has its being in Jesus Christ, but this identification is an incorporation of human culture and sociality into the being of God. This incorporation is inevitable, and unavoidable, and it is important to note that it also sets parameters, or limits, around how the Church and the gospel should be understood. So while the Church is the Church of Christ and the gospel is the gospel of Jesus Christ, it is also true that at any one time or in any one place, both Church and gospel may be less than what they are meant to be. It should be stressed that this observation is not simply about the idea of the Church, but an observation about actual congregations and communities. In other words, it is empirical in nature. This observation does not negate the being of the Church or the gospel, however. Rather, it is simply an introduction to the way that divine being must stretch categories to make them more fluid. So the Church finds its being in Jesus Christ, but it is also and always a human construct, with the consequent challenges that come from this relationship. It is not separated from culture, or set apart from culture, since it carries these forms into what it means to abide. This is the humiliation of the Word and it finds its impulse and its energy in the crazy love of God.

The Gospel, Ecclesiology and Ethnography

This chapter has explored how the being of the Church and the gospel is to be found in Jesus Christ. This theological observation also serves to shape how the Church is to be studied. In other words, there is a theological basis to theological and empirical method, and this theological basis is shared with the way that the culture and expression of Church operates in practice. This is because the expression of theology is itself not distinct from, but it is part of the expression of the Church. More importantly, it is because theological knowing is conditioned by the being of God. Theological conditioning limits what can be said by the theologian, both when adopting a theological voice and also, and crucially, when discussing the Church as it can be observed. Here is where the limits of the theological pattern I have set out bear on empirical approaches to ecclesiology. The Church must be understood through the presence of Jesus Christ, but this relationship cannot be simply and unproblematically reversed.

The Church and the gospel have their being in the person of Jesus Christ. This being is an intense presence; a crazy love that involves the double humiliation of the Word. Such a kenotic ecclesiology should be at one and the same time taken as an invitation to discern the presence of Christ in the world and in the Church, while also accepting that any discernment is provisional. In Part II this paradoxical theological method is explored through a case study.

The case study sets out to show how the expression of the gospel takes place in cultural forms. The shifting nature of culture and of the lived experience of the Church mean that what appears to be a "fixed" form for the gospel in the life of the community has gradually, and perhaps imperceptibly, shifted over time. The result is that the expressed gospel message of evangelical churches has come adrift from the ongoing lived theology of the community. The case study therefore plays a central role in the argument developed throughout this book concerning theological method in ecclesiology that takes account of the complexity of the lived expression of the Church. This leads on the question of normativity and judgement in ecclesiology. In essence, this boils down to the problematic of the presence of Christ in and through the imperfect expression of the Church.

The images of the body and the vine carry within them the essential tension of any theology of the Church and of the gospel. They both speak of the union between human society and Jesus Christ. At the same time they also carry the clear understanding that the Church and believers are capable of being less than they are called to be. Branches, though joined to the vine, may become unfruitful. The body is made up of factions that go against the essential nature of the body by seeking to be distinct. Hence, as Paul puts it, if the foot were to say "because I am not a hand, I do not belong to the body, that would not make it any less a part of the body. And if the ear were to say because I am not an eye, I do not belong to the body, that would not make it any less a part of the body" (1 Cor 12:15-16).

The vine and the body are images that call the Church to be what it "is." At the same time they exhibit realism about the way that the Christian community can often fail to live up to what it is called to be in Jesus Christ. This dynamic is the reason that while it is possible to say that the "being" of the Church is derived from Jesus Christ, it is more problematic to make the identification the other way around. This does not mean that it is not possible to "see" Jesus in the lived expression of the Church, for this after all is the experience of Christians throughout the ages and week by week in churches. Yet at the same time this presence is always veiled or slightly obscured. Christ is present in the Church in cultural forms that convey who he is, while always limited. This basic dynamic between the presence of Christ and the cultural forms of communication is true for the Church, but it is also true for the gospel. In the next chapter, the dynamics that arise from cultural expression and the being of God are discussed as paradox.

CHAPTER 2

The Gospel as Paradox and Light

Liquid Ecclesiology takes the paradox of the Church as a starting point. The paradox here refers to the being of Church. In the first instance, the Church is the body of Christ, but it is also and always a human society. So the paradox identifies the central and enduring problematic of the relationship between the divine and the human in the Church. The paradox finds its point of origin, not in any notion of corruption, or dilution, or reduction of God to culture. Instead it is in the freedom of Christ, in the power of the Spirit, to choose to come close and to be present in the cultural expression of the Church that this paradox is sustained. The paradox of culture and the presence of Christ are operative at a number of levels. These include the limited and partial nature of theological expression, the necessity that the Gospel is true, and the complexities of what it is to live the gospel as communal and individual conviction. Each of these dynamics carries paradox through, within, and around the being of the Church. Paradox is therefore an essential ingredient in understanding the relationship between the gospel and the Church and it needs to be at the heart of a theologically-informed ethnography. In theologically-orientated ethnographic work, paradox has some similarities with what John Swinton and Harriet Mowat call "complexifying." To complexify involves a form of theologizing that takes account of the multilayered and often contradictory data that qualitative research generates.[1] Paradox is not an incidental or an unfortunate by-product in ecclesial existence, however. Paradox comes from the being of God in the world. The Word made flesh is the one who both is and is with God before creation. Paradox therefore curtails ontology in all speech about God, and as such is fundamental to the being of the gospel.

Paradox in ecclesiology acknowledges that the gospel the Church is called to proclaim cannot simply be a message or information. The gospel is Jesus Christ, the Light of the World. The message of the Church therefore does not exist separately from the one who is proclaimed. The message is always, and is already, embodied, embodied in the incarnation, but also embodied as Jesus is made present in the life of the Church, through the Holy Spirit. The gospel as message therefore has two reference points: Jesus as he is known through the

1 See John Swinton and Harriet Mowat, *Practical Theology and Qualitative Research* (London: SCM Press, 2006), 13.

 | DOI 10.1163/9789004347359_004

scriptures, and Jesus as he is continually present in the life and expression of the Church. This correspondence to Jesus Christ structures the content of the gospel message, but it is also a continual reminder that ideas alone, whether understood as doctrine or as theology, do not in themselves guarantee "truth," because Jesus is the truth. At the same time the gospel is a message and therefore ideas. This is the paradox of the gospel and it is the point of departure for an empirically-informed ecclesiology, because it acknowledges that it is possible to examine ideas and doctrine as cultural communication. This examination does not sum up or contain the gospel, because the gospel is Jesus Christ present in scripture and in the ongoing life of the Church. Expression, i.e., the communicative form of the gospel, while it should and must be articulated, is always provisional.

Paradox is significant, because it acts as a continual acknowledgement of the fluid nature of ecclesial expression. The cultural and historical contingency of the gospel as expression inevitably introduces elements of fluidity into Church life, because cultural expression is on the move, contested and contesting. This fluid dynamic is not a contradiction, or a negation of the divine nature of the Church. Instead it arises from the moving, changing, and relational responsiveness of God. The being of the Church is fluid, because of the being of God. This is what it means to speak of the paradox of the gospel. At the same time, fluidity is also a characteristic of culture, because this is the way that culture works. The paradox of the Gospel arises from the presence of Christ in the world. This is a theological statement, i.e., one generated with a theological method and a theological voice—a confidence in speaking of the divine—but it also sets out a frame for theologically-informed empirical research. The intention here is to develop parameters for empirical work and also theological reflection. Again, reflexively, this theological frame is offered with the assumption that it is epistemologically relative and contested, but the Catch 22 of expression means that construction of a theological framework is possible, useful, and I would argue, necessary, in ecclesial method. Theologically-orientated ethnography is therefore situated in a flow, methodologically, and this is why I have given it the name Liquid Ecclesiology.

The Light of the World: Presence, Encounter, and Transformation

Christ is present in the Christian community's expression of the gospel as light transforming the world and the Church. This transformation takes place through the gospel, i.e., through the expression of the Church, although it is always and already *divine presence*. The gospel is the "light of the knowledge of the glory of God in the face of Jesus Christ" (2 Cor 4:6). The Gospel is "light": a mystical illumination that comes through a personal encounter with Christ who is the image of God. This encounter may be conveyed by means of a message, i.e., a particular form of expression or construction, but it can never be reduced to ideas or abstraction alone. The light of Christ shines through, between and upon the gospel expression of the Church. The gospel, as an account of Christ's presence and work in the world, does not operate apart from that presence. It is not a thing in itself and yet it is a thing. It is material expression and therefore culture, but it is also indwelt by the presence of Christ. Yet it is not of the character or nature of the Gospel itself that it is both presence and an account of that presence; it arises, rather, from the nature of divine being. In other words, correct expression or formulation does not in itself guarantee presence or truth, since this is only found in the being of God. At the same time the Church is charged to continually express the Good News of Jesus Christ. This expression is cultural and material. At the same time the expression finds its truth in Christ, who as the light of the world is the image of God. The reflection of glory in the gospel is therefore a Trinitarian energy and animation. The gospel is both an account of the presence of God and the means by which believers are taken up in glory and through divine illumination transformed. This means that the embodied culture of the Church, i.e., the expression of what is being transformed, is not incidental to the gospel but always a part of it. The divine presence is evident not simply in the gospel message, but in the way that this message transforms and renews individuals and the community.

The gospel acts in the life of the Church as a *moment of encounter*. This is not an encounter with truths, but an encounter with the truth. As the gospel of John makes clear, Jesus is the *Logos* through whom all things were made. The *Logos* was "life" and the life was the light of all people (John 1:3-4). It is this same *Logos* made flesh, who reveals the glory of God (John 1:14). "He was in the world, and the world came into being through him; yet the world did not know him. He came to what was his own, and his own people did not accept him. But to all who received him, who believed in his name, he gave power to become children of God, who were born, not of blood or of the will of the flesh or of the will of man, but of God" (John 1:10-13). This encounter is repeated in the Church and the world, in and through the gospel. It is not in the nature or condition of the account that this is cherished and sustained, but in the crazy love of God that such cultural accounts become encounter. While the Light of the world is not encompassed or contained by the accounts, the two are not separate. Account and presence co-exist and this is the mystery of God and the glory of the Church and the world. Encounter implies a relational basis to the gospel and this relationship again carries with it the deep and enduring persistence of embodiment. The gospel is only encounter in the lives of believers and of the community. The truth of the gospel is therefore always relational as it is played out in the world.

Encounter brings about relationship. To receive the light is to become "children of God" and to be born again into the life of the Spirit. What is born of the flesh is flesh, and what is born of the Spirit is Spirit (John 3:16). Spirit birth is a renewal of being, but it effects a relational connection to God. The Light of the World is presence and encounter but this encounter is simultaneously a *transformation*. The gospel is the Light that shone at creation that shines into the hearts of those who encounter Christ in and through expression. "For it is the God who said, 'Let light shine out of darkness,' who has shone in our hearts to give the light of the knowledge of the glory of God in the face of Jesus Christ" (2 Cor 4:6). Transformation is effected through the glory of God, which is the Light of the world enlightening the believer. This Light brings about energizing and animation through the work of the Spirit that gradually changes the believers into the image of Christ. "Now the Lord is the Spirit, and where the Spirit of the Lord is, there is freedom. And all of us, with unveiled faces, seeing the glory of the Lord as though reflected in a mirror, are being transformed into the same image from one degree of glory to another; for this comes from the Lord, the Spirit" (2 Cor 3:17-18). Born anew as children of God, those who receive Christ are transformed and this transformation leads to a new way of life. This is life: walking in the Light. The Light of the World illuminates the way for the believer. So the response to the Light of the World leads to a direction or a way. "I am the light of the world. Whoever follows me will never walk in darkness but will have the light of life" (John 8:12). This transformed "way" is also simultaneously culture and expression and the light of life. Christ present in his Church in the lived and the everyday. Presence, encounter, and transformation all indicate the extent to which the embodied and the lived form an on-going part of gospel. This means that the question about what the gospel "is" cannot be reduced to theological or doctrinal expression alone. The gospel is the Light of the World not because it is a superior philosophy, but because it is a message that gives rise to a way of life and it is precisely this insight that makes a theological ethnography possible.

The Light of the World: Shaping a Way of Life

Through presence, encounter, and transformation, the gospel of the light of the knowledge of the Glory of God in the face of Christ shines in the life of the Church and in the world. The gospel therefore takes a human form: the body of Christ. This human form is not incidental to the gospel. It is not simply the result of the proclamation of the gospel. The embodiment of the Church is to the gospel what the incarnation is to the gospel, because both are Jesus Christ. All talk about the content of the gospel therefore must continually have these two dynamics constantly in mind. Jesus Christ in the Scriptures and Jesus Christ made present in the Church through the work of the Holy Spirit.

The affective and social animation of the gospel in individuals and in the Church is not incidental to the gospel. It is the gospel. The gospel is therefore not simply a means of coming to faith or of being converted. The gospel is to be regarded as the continued and ongoing presence of Christ in the Church. This presence operates as a point of reference. The gospel is continually operative in the Church, because the Spirit is always animating and making it youthful. The Light of the World generates life. This life is not a one-off moment, but a continual vivifying and revivifying. The gospel then is not simply about entry into faith and the life of the Church. Of course the gospel brings about encounter. It is the means whereby Christ is present to the world, and through the response of faith it is how individuals are drawn into the glory of God, born again, and receive the life of God. Yet the life, and the glory, and the new birth, are never simply a moment, because they are ongoing. The water of life wells up and becomes a continual flow, so it is reductionist to limit the action of the gospel to a single moment of conversion, because the gospel is Jesus Christ, the fullness of the Church and of the world in whom all things come together. Encounter with Christ and being joined to him may come through expression of the gospel in cultural form, but it is never solely or exclusively this moment. The gospel is the Light of Christ, which draws the world into relationship with God and just as this relationship is continuous, so the gospel has an enduring place in the life of the Church as it shapes a way of life.

The Light of the World guides the Church to generate culture and sociality. As a result the gospel is continually operative in the Church such that it *shapes a way of life*.[2] The gospel is gospel only as it is made alive, so the made aliveness, i.e., the cultural and social, must form the understanding of what the gospel is, hence the way of life that the gospel shapes is fundamentally and always a part of the being of the gospel. This theological insight again has a direct bearing on the shape and possibility of empirical ecclesiology. It means that the study of the Church is incomplete without paying close attention to the social and the lived. The point here is that it is the gospel that makes this kind of method necessary.

2 Reference to culture and sociality here draw on Raymond Williams' notion of "a whole way of life," Williams, *Culture and Society 1780-1950* (Harmondsworth, UK: Penguin, 1961), 16.

The gospel shapes the life of the Church in a distinctive and unique way. This is because the life of the gospel is the life of God. As a result, theologically-orientated empirical work on the Church is never simply the examination of human culture and agency. The work of the gospel is a new birth into a dynamic and fluid relationship. This is precisely what Nicodemus struggles to understand when Jesus explains the new birth in the Spirit. The Pharisee accepts that Jesus is a teacher who has come from God, but Jesus appears to challenge this more comfortable interpretation by speaking of new birth. Thus Jesus as a teacher and the teaching itself seems to be relocated in a dynamic and fundamental change of life. This is a new birth, for "what is born of flesh is flesh and what is born of the Spirit is spirit" (John 3:6). Any attempt to categorize or comprehend this work of God in the life of those who believe is challenged, not because of doctrinal complexity, but because of the very nature of God. "The wind blows where it chooses, and you hear the sound of it, but you do not know where it comes from or where it goes. So it is with everyone who is born of the Spirit" (John 3:8). It is in this context of mystery and Nicodemus' failure to understand that the archetypal gospel verse of John 3:16 is set. Jesus is making clear that understanding "heavenly things" is problematic. Yet he is the one who has ascended into heaven and also descended. For "God so loved the world that he gave his only son, so that everyone who believes in him may not perish but might have eternal life" (John 3:16). Here again the being of God shapes the possibility for developing an ecclesiology from what can be observed. So while the gospel must be understood in relation to the lived, the basic mystery of the fluid life of God in the world will always condition what can be said. This does not mean that nothing can be said through empirical work about the life of God in the world and in the Church, simply that such talk is contingent, contested and epistemically relative.

The new birth in Christ arises from the love of God in Jesus Christ. It is the crazy love of God that leads to the giving of the Son. Belief in the one who is given leads to eternal life. This life is the new birth, the work of the Spirit that blows where it wills. The new life is not deduced from the giving of the Son, however, neither is it simply generated from doctrine (although it can and must be expressed as doctrine). The new birth grows organically and relationally. It is life not philosophy, organism rather than system. The shaping of life that is seen in the gospel is therefore a living and breathing participation in the life of God. It is the life of God lived in the Church and in the world. So this fluid "life" perspective is there in John 3:16, the verse that for many of those discussed in the case study in Part II has become the archetypical biblical passage that expresses the heart of the gospel. The "life" that comes through the giving of the Son is the new birth that Jesus speaks about with Nicodemus.

As a result the "giving" of the Son for the world, and the response of faith, are linked to the life that comes from the Spirit and this life is hard to comprehend. It cannot be easily predicted or tamed. This life, the life that is given to those who believe and are born again as children of God, is a constituent part of the gospel. It is not just the statement that those who believe have life that forms part of the gospel. It is also the life itself.

Convictions

Liquid ecclesiology is an attempt to integrate a theological voice in the theology of the Church with the multi-layered complexity of qualitative empirical research. This form of ecclesial ethnography, I have argued, has a theological root in the gospel. As a consequence, there are fundamental theological limits to what can be observed of the life of God in the social and the cultural. These limits do not arise from a secularised social scientific method, but from the being of God. In other words, the gospel itself suggests that the presence of Christ in the world and in the Church is both a revelation and also a mystery. At the same time, expression and construction are a necessity for the life of the Church. This necessity is operative both for the theologian and for the life of the Church more generally. The gospel is the life of Jesus Christ in his body. This is what James McClendon calls convictions.

Convictions, for McClendon, refer to the embodied and active links between ideas and the community. He argues that a shared way of life in a community arises from the deep convictions of that community. The expectation should then be that theology will give rise to a shared way of life in the Church.[3] For McClendon, this connection to action and sociality is such that ideas cannot be judged by their merits alone. To illustrate this, he reflects on the moral struggle that Paul refers to in Romans 7. "It is one thing to think the truth, another to live it."[4] Hence, to give an account of faith it is necessary to speak about how this faith is lived, because faith must be "lived out and not just thought about."[5] This is a critical idea in Liquid Ecclesiology: that an account of the gospel must include an assessment of what kind of community and life the particular message gives rise to. The turn to qualitative empirical method in ecclesiology is therefore a response to this theological imperative.

3 McClendon, *Ethics*, 30.

4 McClendon, *Ethics*, 43.

5 McClendon, *Ethics*, 119.

The emphasis on living out the faith in McClendon's thought does not mean that he reduces doctrine to action. His account of theology is not simply a moral or ethical discourse, neither is it a retreat into a discussion of practice as a field that is distinct from belief or doctrine. For McClendon, doctrine and action are merged in a deep identity formation where ideas and who the individual and the community are, become locked together. His term for this is "conviction." Convictions, he argues, "are persistent beliefs such that, if X (a person or a community) has a conviction it will not be easily relinquished and cannot be relinquished without making X a significantly different person (or community) than before."[6] Convictions are therefore not merely characterized by professed doctrine, they are more than opinions or beliefs. Convictions are "deeply self involving" and they reveal what we truly are. They are seen in attitudes and actions. "Thus (in this regard like 'faith') convictions have an affective dimension, while (in contrast to mere emotion) they also have cognitive content, and (in contrast to mere habits) they entail our intentions as well as our action."[7]

The richness of human existence and of human communities means that convictions may operate in a hidden manner. McClendon suggests that learning who we are takes time and attention. For communities in particular, because of their complexity, self-awareness involves paying particular attention to theological reflection. Reflection is necessary because of the powerful role that convictions play in communities, and the way that they can remain obscured from sight. This hidden character, McClendon argues, can disguise the extent to which communities may generate convictions that are theologically problematic. Convictions then are not always benign or even positive in nature. The Christian community is quite capable of living its life out of convictions that contradict the faith or that conflict with that faith. In the history of the Church, tensions and problems have continually arisen between community life and the way that the Gospel is understood.

Convictions, Paradox and the Gospel

Convictions are ideas that shape identity and action, and it is this mix of the cognitive, the affective, and the communal that generates paradox. Paradox

6 James McClendon, *Doctrine: Systematic Theology, Volume 2* (Nashville, TN: Abingdon Press, 1994), 29; see also James McClendon and James Smith *Convictions: Diffusing Religious Relativism* (Norcross, GA: Trinity Press International, 1994), 91.

7 McClendon, *Doctrine*, 29.

relates to a complex mix of relations and dynamics. Central to these dynamics are the issues that arise from the recognition that the cultural expression of the Church, in its contingency and fluidity, is simultaneously a place where Christ is made present. This is the humiliation of the word, the self-limitation of Jesus Christ in the power of the Spirit, in the social and the historical. Humiliation is also paralleled by a further humiliation that takes place in the Church itself. This humiliation arises from the paradoxical nature of the gospel in the world. This paradox is evident in three related complexities. The first of these is the realization that the gospel is always partial and yet also true. The second is the acceptance that the Church has to believe that its message is true. Thirdly, there is the dilemma that what the Church believes is true is always contested and open to challenge

The self-limitation of the Word means that the expression of the Church is *always partial and yet also true*. The expression of the Church is partial because human communication using cultural forms and norms is always inadequate to express the truth of God. It is important not to see this in terms of purity or in terms of a categorical distinction between humanity and the divine. Partiality is not a reference to the impossibility of communication about God, or the inherent sinfulness of this expression. It is primarily an acknowledgement that human expression is limited, and limited forms of expression will always struggle to adequately communicate the infinity of God. The paradox of the gospel is that inadequate expression is made "true" through the work of the Spirit. True here does not mean complete or always correct, but indwelt by the presence of Jesus Christ who is the truth.

The gospel is truth, as Jesus Christ, who is the way, the truth, and the life indwells it. The indwelling of Christ is embodied in believers. So the gospel is inhabited culturally and socially by believers as they are formed into the body of Christ. This means that whilst accepting the partial and provisional nature of its expression the Church *has to believe that its message is true*. This is not an exercise in self-delusion; it arises, rather, from the necessity of generating the Christian faith as a way of life. Churches need to express and continually express the faith as they understand it, because this practice of communication is what brings life. It is only as the Church expresses the faith that this expression can be taken up by the Spirit and animated as truth. The Spirit then takes the cultural forms of the Church and continually acts to make Jesus Christ present and to vivify and make the Church ever youthful. The confidence that the Church has in the gospel comes from the work of the Spirit, rather than from the assurance that comes from any particular formulation or accepted theological framework. Belief can easily lead to delusion, however. The truth that is found in the expression of the Church can very quickly lead to the assumption that this truth is the possession of the Church and an inevitable consequence of right thinking, or a particular theological formulation, rather than being a fluid work of the Spirit bringing truth and life.

The way that gospel is carried in the life of the Church as convictions, i.e., as theology that is lived out and shared by the community, makes this possibility almost inevitable. In other words, the Church has an inbuilt predilection towards a misplaced and mistaken belief in its own expression as invariably and inevitably true. Part of the reason for this is that in order to become a way of life, the expression of the Church must be performed as action and inhabited as identity. This move into the lived necessitates commitment and conviction. Herein lies the paradox of the gospel and how it is made alive in the life of the Church. Paradox is a kind of Catch 22. It is not something to be avoided or even resisted, however. Paradox represents the way things are and it is because of paradox that the Church is called to a continual attentiveness to its life and to the gospel. This attentiveness is even more important when it is recognized that the gospel does not give rise to one way of life, but generates multiple ways of living. These ways are fluid cultural and social constructs in history. One of the paradoxical consequences of this is that *the life of the Church is always contested and open to challenge and revision.* So while the Church is led by the Spirit its journey into truth does not exclude the need for debate and difference. Difference comes about because Christian community is always on the move. As a result, the Church is fluid; fluid precisely because it is led by the Spirit. But it is also fluid because cultural forms are in process and on the move.

Remain in Light

The paradoxical nature of expression necessitates a close critical attention to the expression of the Church. There is nothing startling about this observation. Ecclesiology has always positioned itself in this critical theological position in relation to the historical and doctrinal expression of the Church. Liquid Ecclesiology suggests that empirical attentiveness can introduce significant elements into this critical conversation. In particular, it can shed light on the multi-layered and complex ways in which expression takes cultural form. The case study in Part II illustrates precisely these issues through an analysis of the expression and lived theology of contemporary evangelical and charismatic Christians.

The case study focuses on how the evangelical emphasis on communicating the faith has generated a particular understanding of the gospel. Through the practice of evangelism among young people, the gospel became closely identified with a series of very short and easily memorised doctrinal statements or propositions. The case study examines how this radically shortened expression of the gospel has paradoxically become a marker of identity and belonging, while simultaneously being largely sidelined in the lived theology of individuals and believers. At this point, it is worth taking what has been said about the gospel and convictions and making some observations with a direct bearing on what will be discussed in the case study.

When the gospel is reduced to doctrinal formulations alone, as (it is argued in the case study) in the contemporary evangelical Church, then conversion becomes a moment of acceptance. The problem with this approach to the gospel is that it can suggest that once an individual has accepted the truth, the gospel has done its work. The danger is that in some parts of the Church, the gospel brings conversion and establishes a relationship with God, but from that point it takes a less significant role in the ongoing life of faith. This is precisely what the case study sets out to show. Such developments are not deliberate or intended, but they have come about because of the fluid movement of culture and the lived. In evangelical Christianity, the gospel is the basis for Christian life and the starting point, but what I show is that it no longer has a central role to play in the everyday life of the Christian or the Church. This tendency is deeply problematic and it comes at a cost of failing to recognize the extent to which the gospel as the Life and Light of Christ is meant to always be the generative and revivifying force within the Church and the world. The function of the gospel in the Church thus cannot be reduced simply to a moment of comprehension and acceptance.

When the gospel is understood as having its being in Jesus Christ, it is clear that it *cannot simply be seen as propositions*. The case study shows how evangelical Christians have embraced a simplified expression of faith as an unchanging message and truth. The problem with this is not so much to be found in a debate about the content of these doctrines, but in the extent to which the propositions play a continuing role in the life of the Church. The point I make in the case study is that the simplified gospel of evangelicalism has lost a connection to the vibrant lived work of the Spirit in individuals and in the wider community. This lived (or operant theology) is evident in the worship songs and in personal spirituality. The problem that the case study seeks to explore lies in the possibility of the gospel of Jesus Christ reviving and renewing the Church when it has been reduced to a few very simple doctrinal statements.

This observation should not be taken as a rejection of the gospel as a message for the Church and for the world. Chapter 4 examines the Gospel as the expression of doctrine. By way of caution it should be said at this point that content, expression and doctrinal proposition are always the form that the gospel takes as message. To be message, it must be expressed, and this expression has a doctrinal form and content. Of course it can be conveyed both in narrative and in propositional ways, or indeed as a work of art, or as music. The point is that while as message it takes a doctrinal form, it is never simply propositional in the way it works in the life of the Church. Because the gospel is always the life of Christ and the Light of the World, it has to be received as transforming relationship. This means that although it can be conveyed through ideas or doctrine it does not function as ideas in the way that evangelicals might assume. To believe is not so much to understand, as to be understood. It is relational and fluid rather than a purely cognitive process. This means that the gospel does not operate in the Church as a theory or a purely rational expression of belief. This observation is fundamental to the complex, multi-layered analysis of the contemporary Church that is developed in the case study. By operate, what I mean is that it cannot be utilized in evangelism as information to be assimilated and accepted as truth, as many evangelical Christians assume is the case. The truth of the gospel is of a different character from other kinds of truth because it is the life and light of Jesus Christ the image of God. The truth of the gospel shines on and within those who respond in belief. The light that transforms through the reflected Glory of God is of a different order from other kinds of knowledge. This means that sharing the gospel has always been much more than a desire to impart information or to convince someone that these facts are true. This is not to say that the resurrection didn't take place, or that Jesus didn't die on the cross for the sins of the world. The truth of doctrinal statements is not at stake here; instead it is the assumption about how these doctrines work in the life of the Church. To say that they are not simply propositions is to challenge a reductive tendency that makes of the gospel something less than it is, by trying to make it into an idea. This characteristic evangelical reduction lies at the heart of the case study, but it is also a central argument in Liquid Ecclesiology, i.e., that expression needs to be examined in relation to the lived and the cultural. The case study explores this facet of ecclesial method through one particular section of the Church, but the basic methodological perspective is relevant to every ecclesial context.

CHAPTER 3

Making Church: Gospel, Construction, and Ecclesial Fluidity

The preceding chapters set out a theological framework for an empirically informed ecclesiology. This chapter marks a turn towards the cultural. This cultural perspective is also theological in orientation, but it has its basis in the recognition that the Church needs to be made and continually re-made if it is to be a meaningful way of believing in the present. In fact, Church needs continual reconstruction, because it is the construction of the past that has ensured that the Church is here in the present, and it is the construction of the present that will ensure its future. Another way of saying this is that the Christian faith has a continuity that is passed on from one community to the other, and yet each is charged with proclaiming the gospel afresh for each generation. So making "Church" also refers to the continual requirement to express the gospel in cultural forms, because it is the gospel that generates the Church as a way of life. Understanding what it means to make the Church demands attention to the way that theology and cultural forms interrelate, however. This cultural/theological orientation is fundamental to developing a Liquid Ecclesiology. In the case study, I explore what this perspective looks like in relation to the expression of a selected part of the contemporary Church. This chapter examines the basic frameworks that guide construction and expression in the Christian community which will shape the analysis developed in the case study. The focus here is on human agency in constructing expression and Church as a way of life. It should be stressed, however, that the paradox of the Church is that these activities are simultaneously, through the work of the Holy Spirit, made what they "are," i.e., gospel and Church, by the presence of Christ. This theological caveat means that while the focus here is on culture, there is no intention of reducing the Church to the human, the historical, or the social.

Making and Seeing

The Church is present at its own making, but this making takes place in the movement of the Trinitarian God. Making is always a project without guarantees. Making Church is a fluid movement of the Holy Spirit in cultural ex-

 | DOI 10.1163/9789004347359_005

pression. In Chapter 2 it was argued that the images of the vine and of the body of Christ both carry within them an assumption of human agency and movement. The biblical metaphors for the Church suggest that it is far from concrete.[1] Instead it is vibrant and full of movement and life. Thus construction, or making the Church in cultural forms, needs to be seen as an organic and fluid activity. This is because the being of the Church comes from union with Christ, but this union is moved and moving. Animated by the Holy Spirit, the Church is brought into being by sharing in Jesus Christ. By the same token, the cultural forms that are the expressive building blocks of the Church are also fluid and shifting. This interrelationship between the relational movement of the Trinitarian God and the fluid nature of social forms is not coincidental. They are related, the one giving rise to the other, such that attentiveness to the lived in Liquid Ecclesiology becomes a source for understanding and sharing in the divine.

Making the Church a cultural form rests on the continual return to behold Jesus Christ, the way and the truth. This is the basis for renewal and making in the Church. Seeing Jesus Christ therefore leads to the construction of the Church as a community on the way, and as the body of Christ. As Paul Fiddes says, seeing cannot rest on the distanced observer who has control over the "object" that he or she can examine and assess.[2] This separation between the seer and the world has been widely rejected as part of the problem of modernity. In its place, more participatory forms of knowledge are becoming commonplace. Seeing involves an acknowledgement that the seer is part of the world and that what can be seen is only partial. Fiddes' point is that this form of "epistemology" takes the believer deeper into the Christian faith. To see is to spend time developing disciplines of attention and theoretical construction, but all of this takes place in the relational being of God who is Trinity. To know, therefore, at whatever level, is to answer the call of Lady Wisdom, to be drawn into the complex life of God.[3] This complexity at one and the same time upholds the act of knowing, while making clear that any kind of comprehension rests in God. Seeing therefore takes the believer into the ultimate unknowability of the divine immensity. This moves the believer to wonder and the acceptance of an orientation or a relationship. It is seeing and participation that forms the basis on which construction takes place, for the Church is

---

1 This is as Healy, following Barth and Bonhoeffer, suggests. See Healy, *Church World*.

2 Paul Fiddes, *Seeing the World and Knowing God: Hebrew Wisdom and Christian Doctrine in a Late-Modern Context* (Oxford: Oxford University Press, 2013), 4.

3 Fiddes, *Seeing the World*, 199.

tasked with generating the body of Christ as a viable, and vibrant community, while simultaneously acknowledging the limits of its "seeing" and accepting the provisional nature of everything that is made. This is the deep learning that comes from the call to abide in Christ. It is not that the Church is simply confirmed in everything that it has made or that it is revealed how mistaken its construction has been. Attention to the presence of Christ in expression, making use of empirical and theological methods, takes the Church and individual believers into a place where there is an acceptance that making the Church is a calling and a divine vocation, but what is made is always conditioned by the infinite and contingent in the cultural.

To be the Church is to construct, to make pathways and to develop ways of belonging, expressing, and connecting. Construction is essential to the life of the Church. The Church must make itself in every age and it must continue to remake itself. Making is always provisional, however, always partly wrong, and partly right. This is the Catch 22 of theological construction. Making Church is a muddied reality. This muddied reality comes from the limitations of seeing, and yet it is also empowered by the dynamic participatory animation of the Holy Spirit that is present with the Church as the Church makes itself. The lived introduces elements of the random and the chaotic into Church life and it is this complexity that qualitative research is able to bring to light and introduce into theological discussion.

The fluid sphere of contemporary culture decisively affects the task of constructing and reconstructing the Church. Theologically, this complexity should not be a surprise. The God we worship is infinite and our comprehension of that God, and indeed of the creation that God has made, is limited. The complexity of human culture is just another aspect of the complexity of the God we worship. This does not mean that in seeking to make the Church in culture there should not be the attempt at disciplined reason and reflection. The point is that these take place not in order to be assured of the "effectiveness" of plans for Church and patterns for believing, but because such "work" is necessary as part of meaning-making and the construction of the body of Christ, but also as part of the movement of God who is Trinity. It is this dynamic that lies at the heart of Liquid Ecclesiology.

The Church as Sharing in Divine Communication

Empirically-orientated Liquid Ecclesiology rests on the realization that making Church or construction is basically an exercise in working with material forms. Materiality here might mean bricks and mortar, or music, but it may also mean the actual metaphors that are used in preaching or writing prayers. Materiality in this sense makes up the stuff out of which the life of the Church is made. This means that expression always assumes cultural forms. These forms are cultural and material, however, and as such they operate in certain ways.

Material Christianity

Colleen McDannell's ground-breaking book, *Material Christianity*, explores the various ways that the Christian faith in the United States has always taken material form.[4] The study of the material forms of religion does not limit consideration to objects, because these artefacts carry with them histories of human interaction and sharing related to faith. Religion that is seen as systems of symbols is deeply participatory, she argues. Symbols are not simply handed down from one generation to another. They are learned through touching, seeing, and doing. It is through a continual interaction with material forms and objects that Christianity is passed on and individuals and communities become religious in particular ways. This means that the material forms of religion—clothing, books, landscapes, ritual objects, music, and buildings—are not fully understood apart from a consideration of how they form part of a religious life.[5] There has been a tendency in the study of religion, says McDannell, to pass over or treat as superficial the way that religious communities make use of objects and landscapes. She argues that American Christian identity is closely related to material culture and that, "genuine" religion has always been expressed and made real with objects, architecture, art, and landscapes.[6] McDannell is reacting against the prioritisation of belief or doctrine as the primary form of discourse around religion. She is critical of the view that faith is mainly described in terms of theological ideas. Religious belief is not simply passed on through the communication of belief. Objects and materials form a key part in the sharing of belief. "Orthodox statements of belief and formal rituals are only one part of the complicated structure of religion."[7] This approach relocates theological communication as part of a much wider cultural system. Such a move does not privilege the theological or the doctrinal but sees it in some senses as also material.

4 Colleen McDannell, *Material Christianity: Religion and Popular Culture in America* (New Haven, CT: Yale University Press, 1995).

5 McDannell, *Material Christianity*, 2.

6 McDannell, *Material Christianity*, 272.

7 McDannell, *Material Christianity*, 272.

The Guitar as an Example

The materiality of expression introduces a number of central dynamics into the construction of Church. The first is that cultural forms are semiotically complex. This refers to the way that objects mean different things at different times. They are complex signifiers. A good example of the complexity of objects can be seen in something as everyday and commonplace as the guitar. In many ways, guitars represent a watershed in the development of the contemporary Church and the generation of worship that made use of the forms of expression of popular culture in the twentieth century. The introduction of guitars into worship presaged the influx of forms of music and ways of communicating that were drawn from the youth culture of the time. While in many Churches they are now the primary instruments used in worship, in some contexts guitars remain unacceptable. This is not anything to do with the instrument itself, but concerns the meanings that have become attached to the instrument. What the guitar means in the context of the Church can only be read through close attention to the fluid communicative practices of the Church, in other words, by dealing with ecclesiology as a form of cultural analysis. Such a move, it must be stressed, is not the reduction of the theological to the cultural, but arises from the theological insight that the being of the Church originates in Jesus Christ as he is made present in and through communication. Culture as a category therefore enables a shift from the concrete to the communicative in ecclesiology.

As it is performed in the Christian community, theological expression is lived in a culture. This cultural aspect of theology relates to every aspect of performance. It is culture as it is produced, represented, and made use of by the Christian community, but at the same time it is also indwelt by the community and indwelt by the presence of Jesus Christ in the power of the Holy Spirit. The cultural therefore mediates the presence of God. This presence may be elusive, but it comes in and through the communicative practices of the Church. Thus sharing in the cultural is also a sharing in the life of God. These insights draw directly on the cultural theories developed by Stuart Hall.

Culture is not primarily about things, argues Hall, *culture is about meaning*.[8] Culture, he says, is not located within novels or works of art; instead it is to be seen in practices that surround the material objects. These practices are concerned with the production and communication of shared meanings within society or between groups. Culture is not unitary, however, be-

---

8 Stuart Hall, ed., *Representation: Cultural Representations and Signifying Practices* (London: Routledge, 1997), 2.

cause meaning is diverse and varied.[9] It is people that give meanings to objects and events. Over time and between cultures meanings differ in what he terms their "codes."[10] "Things 'in themselves' rarely if ever have any one, single, fixed and unchanging meaning."[11] Meaning has to be shared if it is to be communicated. Those who share a culture, participate in shared understandings. Through these shared images, concepts and emotions they "interpret the world in roughly similar ways."[12] The guitar therefore does not contain within itself the meanings that make it so significant for some in worship, and so problematic for others. These meanings arise from the associations that gather around the object.

Meaning comes from articulation. Articulation, Hall argues, is the way that new meanings are generated by the connection of one thing with another. This connection does not have to be solid or closely linked. Articulation allows for movement and changing relations between different cultural forms as they shift in the flow of popular discourse. In the hands of a singer songwriter such as Ed Sheeran, or from an earlier era, Joni Mitchell, the acoustic guitar becomes a vehicle for personal expression. The guitar therefore acquires meanings that are linked to the intimate and the inner worlds that are shared by the singer in their songs. By contrast, the electric guitar carries a range of other meanings that might include power, sexuality, aggression, or virtuosity. As can be seen from this list, the electric guitar has generally had more male associations, while the acoustic guitar has been slightly less gendered. In 1965, Bob Dylan was famously booed at the Newport Folk festival when he appeared on stage for the first time with a band, and most significantly, with an electric guitar. For many in the crowd, the switch of instrument represented a betrayal of core values. This controversy was not necessarily concerned with the kind of guitar that Dylan used *per se*, but the sense that his change of instrument represented a move away from a political form of protest music. The guitar as a recognised "folk" instrument had become essential to the self understanding of many who were part of the folk revival and who saw it as a left-wing music of freedom and protest. For figures such as Dylan, the acoustic guitar thus operates as an articulation of those who went before, such as Woody Guthrie, Lead Belly, and Pete Seeger.

The strength of feeling that surrounded Dylan in the 1960s was replicated and continues to be replicated in the energy that surrounds the use of gui-

9 Hall, *Representation*, 2.

10 Hall, *Representation*, 61.

11 Hall, *Representation*, 3.

12 Hall, *Representation*, 4.

tars in churches. This energy goes two ways. For some the guitar and the kind of music that it enables represents a deep connection to the more affective worlds of popular music. This connection is not primarily related to the fact that a different type of music can be used in Church, but the associations that this kind of music brings to contemporary worship. The moods and inflections of popular music enable certain affective moves in the congregation as they sing. Put simply, playing like U2 or Coldplay in worship brings the affective associations of these artists into the Church by articulation. For others, however, the guitar signifies the thin end of the wedge. To use the guitar is to abandon canons of taste that have prioritised the organ and choirs over the guitar and the worship band. These judgements are not entirely theological, because they are also aesthetic, and as such they articulate structures of identity and belonging that complicate the construction of Church and form a fundamental part of the complex and muddied world of what it means to be and to make Church. Stuart Hall talks about these dynamics in cultural expression as the formation of identity in relation to discourse.

Cultural communication involves shared meanings and these shared meanings, Hall says, share in "linguistic codes."[13] Thus in the Church those who oppose the guitar appeal to shared understandings about what is valuable and what is to be preserved about the worship of the Church. Codes combine systems of language, and of concepts in relation to things.[14] Culture consists of systems of representation, Hall argues, and these work like a language. The meaning of facial gesture, media generated images, clothing, and musical sounds do not lie in themselves, but how they function in a system of communicating meaning.[15] Systems in turn operate in relation to wider discourses. "Discourses are ways of referring to, or constructing, knowledge about a particular topic or practice: a cluster (or formation) of ideas, images and practices which provide ways of talking about, forms of knowledge and conduct associated with, a particular topic, social activity or institutional site in society."[16] So the use of guitar in worship can be seen to have enabled whole ways of believing and being Church. These ways of being Church operate as sources of belonging and identity for believers. Identity is not a superficial style or a Church culture of taste so much as a deep way of life that is indwelt by the Holy Spirit as worship, and as such this way of life seeks to abide in the presence of

13 Hall, *Representation*, 4.

14 Hall, *Representation*, 21.

15 Hall, *Representation*, 5.

16 Hall, *Representation*, 6.

Christ. Identity is made in relation to the flow of discursive representation that the Church makes, for example, guitar-based contemporary worship music.

Identity is complex and multi-layered and negotiated between subjectivity and culture. Hall observes that "it seems to be in the attempt to rearticulate the relationship between subjects and discursive practices that the question of identity recurs."[17] With Foucault, he relocates subjectivity as a theory of discursive practice. "Identities are thus points of temporary attachment to the subject positions which discursive practices construct for us. They are the result of a successful articulation or chaining of the subject in the flow of discourse."[18] This in a sense is what McDannell is saying about the way that Christian identities are made by using objects and are passed on by practices of "doing" that make use of these objects. Hall's point deepens this insight, however, by indicating that identity has a relationship between the objects and the practices that are associated with them, and that there is also the level of identification. In terms of the Church, this points to the various ways that believers take up the objects that are around them and use these as ways of making sense of God and their own lives. Again this process should not be seen as entirely formed by human agency. Believing is a work of the Holy Spirit. So the complexity here is that it is in and through the activities of individuals as they take up cultural forms and shape their sense of self around them that the Holy Spirit is at work.

The Gospel and the Personal

The cultural and material forms of analysis found in the work of Colleen McDannell and Stuart Hall offer crucial insights for ecclesiology. They show how material forms are situated in fluid flows of meaning. A Liquid Ecclesiology sets out to examine these cultural and material dynamics and through close attention to both representation and the ways that material objects are used, individuals and communities construct identities. The case study in Part II develops these insights by paying attention to the discourse of evangelical churches. Central to this analysis is the observation that the contemporary Church has made a significant move towards forms of expression that focus on the experience of the believer. The move to subjectivity in the Christian Church has been formed through the process that Stuart Hall calls articulation. The case study shows how notions of a relationship with God have been

17 Stuart Hall, "Introduction," in Stuart Hall and Paul du Gay, eds., *Production of Culture/Cultures of Production* (London: Routledge, 1996), 2.

18 Hall, "Introduction," 6.

developed through linking this particular relationship to the dominant narrative of the subject in contemporary society. Relationship with God therefore takes on aspects of the present expectations and aspirations around relationships in general. In contemporary worship songs, this relational connection is given imaginative force through metaphors that connote the romantic and the intimate aspects of this relationship.

There has been a deep and long tradition of this kind of romantic and even sexualised language about spirituality in the Christian Church, which has deep roots in the bible and in Christian Theology. The patristic interpretation of the Song of Songs, for instance, and the development of bride of Christ imagery from Ephesians are clear examples of a more romantic or even sexualised understanding of the relationship between Christ and the Church. Contemporary worship songs, particularly those that are associated with John Wimber, are picking up on this tradition and giving it a contemporary inflection. This is construction, the imaginative generation of theological language that connects. In the case of worship songs, for a great many people these forms of expression facilitate encounter with Christ and lives that are lived as his disciples. These "fruits" are significant and they are not to be lightly dismissed. There are, however, limits to romantic and sexual images as articulated metaphors of the Christian life, for as much as believing is relational, this relationship is not entirely "like" romantic love. Relationship with God through the work of the Holy Spirit is as much unlike the kind of relationship that is being invoked as it is like it. God is the creator and people are always in a distinct relationship of being created. Jesus is not a boyfriend or a girlfriend, but the *Logos*, the Light of the World, the Lamb of God, and the Resurrection and the Life. The point is that relationship with Christ is not the same as having a peculiarly gifted lover. Articulation indicates the complexity of the construction of theology in the forms of expression that connect with popular culture. This introduces a classic theological dilemma and it is one that a Liquid Ecclesiology takes as central.

The turn towards the personal and the subjective raises the issue of the relative influence of theology and culture in ecclesiology. In the contemporary Church, the case study shows that the subjective and the personal operate as forms of expression through the use of metaphors. These metaphors have a double correspondence. On the one hand, they are meant to form a connection. They therefore need to have a rhetorical and an affective power, but they are also meant to convey truth. The truth is the truth of Jesus Christ. Here the issue appears to be quite straightforward: does the metaphor accurately represent the truth of Jesus Christ? There are two sides to this question. The first relates to the correspondence between expression and how it is taken up in the believing of individuals and communities. This correspondence is complicated for any kind of judgement or discernment in ecclesiology, however, by the ways in which meaning shifts over time and develops in representation within communal expression. So, for instance, an idea like relationship can develop in fluid forms such as the worship song, and it can generate a range of inflections and elaborations. As this creative force emerges, what might have been a cautious simile can become a more concrete metaphor. Hence in the expression of the songs, faith is sexual or Jesus is a lover. These small moves mean that symbolic language is fluid as it is expressed, but it is also fluid as it is taken up and used. Individuals will generate a variety of meanings from expression as they participate in the cultural expression of the Church.

The shifts in evangelical theology explored in the case study illustrate how fluidity comes about through a combination of changes in expression (or representation) of doctrine, and changes in how individuals and communities take up these expressions as part of believing. This insight is not simply meant as a critique of the contemporary evangelical/charismatic Church, however. The argument here is that this dynamic is true in all kinds of churches. The case study is introduced to illustrate a more general pattern in ecclesiology that is brought to the fore when qualitative empirical methods are used. So Hall's point about the way that identities shift in relation to the flow of representation, as people use what they see and hear to shape their own sense of themselves, has a much more general ecclesial relevance. Here the expression of the Church and the ways of being Christian that make up the life of the Church are seen as part of cultural flow. This fluid cultural nature of the lived theology of the Church makes judgements about what is true and what is not entirely true or even mistaken, highly problematic.

Theology in Three Dimensions

The fluid nature of ecclesial culture requires a form of discernment that is attuned to complexity. It is worth repeating that inspiration (the breath of God) is always carried in the cultural practice of fallible human communities. This means that it is never possible to filter out the work of God from the actions of individual believers, because the two are inter-dependent and contingent on each other. The Spirit works in and with communities and their expression, to make Jesus Christ present. The reference to communities here is not abstract. The presence of Christ makes the Church the Church in the particular, and in the local and this means in the everyday neighbourhood congregation and in the parish church. There are some implications for a theology of the Church here, and for the methods of enquiry and analysis that are most appropriate for Liquid Ecclesiology. For while it is relatively easy to make distinctions between different concepts of believing at the level of the ideal, these judgments become much more problematic in relation to the actual practices of communities and the ways that individuals believe. As a result, some means of taking account (or seeing) the lived complexity of communities is precisely what is required, because the Church doesn't inhabit the ideal of the doctrinal formulation. It exists in the cultural and the historical, and it is in this context that it seeks to fulfil its calling. So there will always be moments where it will be necessary to take stock and come to judgment, but discernment is far from straightforward because the mixture of divine life and cultural expression is part of the being of the Church. Hence to talk in solely theological ways or in solely cultural and historical terms, runs the risk of not really seeing the Church. The task of seeing requires that these elements be in some way combined.

A further complicating factor is that theological construction in lived cultural forms is quite different from doctrinal work in the academy or even in the pulpit. Ideas and the realms of theory are cultural and human constructions but they often bracket out the complexity of the lived. Thus theological work seen as theory might be regarded as a flat plane, or at least the equivalent of working in two dimensions. Theological construction in the lived culture of communities is, by contrast, more akin to working in three dimensions. Doctrinal discussion is altogether more straightforward, because it is able to restrict construction and therefore distinction, to the relatively limited field of the abstract. Construction and evaluation in the fluid cultural forms of lived ecclesiology is much more demanding. What is required of discernment, therefore, is an ongoing self-awareness. The ability to be reflexive needs to be more intentional and also more acute in its attention to how the Church is making itself in culture. This attentiveness has to develop into a more nuanced understanding of how contemporary culture is shaped, formed and moves.

Learning to See

Discernment in fluid ecclesiology must be attuned to see the work of the Spirit and the presence of Jesus Christ in cultural forms. Seeing here requires perspectives that take account of the dynamics that operate in the way that Church is made. Traditional discernment has been based on doctrinal definition, but this has severe limitations because it has a tendency to be drawn towards expression that it can recognise as theology. In other words, it focuses on forms of communication that appear to be more abstract or similar to doctrinal or theological discourse. It is possible, for instance, to read song lyrics or to analyze preaching in this way. Such analysis has some value, but it is not a methodology that can take the theologian into the heart of the lived experience of believing in the Christian community. What these kinds of analyses do is give the illusion of describing the theological communication of the community. So the content of the preaching is read as what people might believe in the pews, and the song lyrics are taken as the totality of what those who sing them believe. Qualitative methods of enquiry reveal that this approach is much too simplistic. All of these ecclesial forms of expression need to be read firstly for what they are, i.e., a construction in a cultural form, but also as the source of identity formation and the development of ways of living that are variously Christian.

The ability to see the Body of Christ in the lived expression of the Church therefore requires forms of attention that enable theologians, Christian leaders and members of the Church to see. This means that the actual experience and lives of believers are just as important as the things that are said in sermons, in the liturgy and in songs. Paying attention to the movement of the Spirit in the community thus becomes a crucial part of what it means to come to an evaluation of the cultural expression of the Church. This approach is not very far from the regular day-to-day practice of the Church, for instance in relation to the kinds of responses that are called for in the context of worship. Ministers and leaders pay attention to the numbers of people that come forward for prayer or healing at events. This kind of attention is habitual in the everyday practice of ministry, but it needs to become a more intentional form of paying attention. Everyday attention becomes intentional as it adopts more formal ways of seeking out the experience of believers at events and in the congregation, i.e., as it makes use of qualitative methods of observation and analysis. The point that is being made here is that theological construction necessitates forms of enquiry and curiosity that are drawn towards the way that expression is taken up in the lives of individuals and in the community. Such a perspective is not helped by the belief that abstract theology has priority over lived theology, and that abstraction is the purest form of communication. Nor is it helped by the requirement that, given the correct expression of theological forms, the lived and the everyday must conform to this notion of truth. Such a move ignores what has been argued at length so far: that the truth is a person, Jesus Christ, and that it is through the Spirit that the presence of Christ constitutes the Church. Christ's presence comes in cultural forms that both communicate and veil, however, and these cultural forms take shape in the life of the Church. The work of the Spirit in the Church is therefore taking shape, moving and vivifying the community as it shapes itself by forming its identity in Jesus Christ. The agency of the community in construction is not incidental to the work of the Spirit, but is the place where the Spirit is actively leading the Church into truth. The task of discernment is to pay attention to this lived expression for faith in the life of the Church. Discernment and theological judgement cannot be limited to forms of expression that appear to be abstract and therefore amenable to control. Rather, discernment should be expanded to the fluid and complex environment of the lived, and to the place that these more theological forms of expression take in these lived environments. This kind of discernment is explored in more detail as the practice of abiding in Christ in Part III.

CHAPTER 4

The Material Nature of the Gospel

In the previous chapters, the theological framework and cultural foundations for a Liquid Ecclesiology were explored. This leaves the crucial issue of what should, and indeed what can be expressed. In other words, what specific doctrinal content makes up the gospel message in the Church? This question is conditioned and also made possible by the paradox of the Church and its message. Paradox suggests that the discussion of the doctrinal shape of the gospel must proceed with caution because of the limitations of expression. At the same time, it is precisely because of paradox that such consideration is possible. As has already been argued at length, the gospel is a thing and yet it is not a thing. It is material and cultural and yet it is also made alive and indwelt through the power of the Holy Spirit by the presence of Christ. So the account of the gospel given by the Church does not operate separately from the embodied and present Christ in scriptures and in the Church. At the same time, the human and cultural form of the gospel in the expression of the Church is both necessary and operative. The gospel as message, i.e., as a thing or as materiality, is not an optional extra. Christ comes to the Church and the world in and through cultural forms of expression. This presence is not inevitable, nor does a particular form of words or ideas ensure it. Christ is present because of the freedom of the Spirit to reflect in and through the cultural expression of Christians, such that the light of Christ shines as presence, encounter, and transformation. The freedom of the Spirit does not nullify or negate the cultural form of the expression of the faith as message, however; it animates it, giving it life and making it young. The material nature of the message inevitably means that expression has limitations. Before examining the doctrinal content of the gospel, these limitations need to be discussed. The first relates to the nature of theology itself and the second to issues of culture, context and translation.

The Limits of Theology

The basic dynamic of expression and divine presence does not have its origins in the form of expression, but in the being of God. It is the nature of God that generates the limits of expression. But it is also the being of God that makes paradox the operative paradigm for the gospel and the Church. This is similar

 | DOI 10.1163/9789004347359_006

to what T.F. Torrance describes as the impossibility of objectivity in theology. For Torrance, the unique character of divine being fundamentally conditions all theological understanding. This means that the central concern of the theologian cannot be regarded simply as data that is given over to the control and the manipulation of reason. The gift and the giver, he argues, are identical. "It is God who has given and revealed Himself in Israel and in the Incarnation" to be understood, but he "remains the Lord God transcendent in His eternal and infinite Being who cannot be comprehended even when we apprehend Him."[1] God has given himself to us and yet in his giving there is something "unspecifiable." This gives the work of dogmatics "a rather baffling character."[2] Dogma is concerned with the ultimate ground and creative source of the Church. It focuses on the divine revelation in the incarnation as this communication "calls forth form and structure in the Church's existence and history."[3] Through continual revision and reflection, the Church advances in the depth and complexity of its knowledge, but this process is located in the continuing work of the Spirit. The "object," says Torrance, "proclaims, interprets and defines itself, and therefore instructs us in our knowledge of it, assimilating us in our knowing to its own activity and mission."[4] These formulations are not abstract theories or formulations through which the divine can be defined and encapsulated; these dogmatic frameworks are instead interpretative constructs or "hermeneutic media" by means of which the self disclosure of God is manifested in its own self interpretation and in our disciplined response.[5] Through this process in the Church, knowledge does not simply break through to us; it is also "broken up" in the activity of our knowing and articulating within the Christian community. "We cannot take these as transcripts of the Word of God but as orderly, scientific reactions of our relations with the Word through which we must allow the objective reality to reveal itself to us in its own essential harmony and meaning, yet always in such a way that it is sharply distinguished from our dogmatic constructs or dogmas."[6]

Torrance is talking about the particular task of dogmatics. In this task, reason, enlightened by the Holy Spirit, sets out to express theological "truth" in human categories. These observations by Torrance should lead to caution about the ability to "define" the truth of God in human categories. This does

1 Thomas F. Torrance, *Theological Science* (Oxford: Oxford University Press, 1969), 344.

2 Torrance, *Theological Science*, 344.

3 Torrance, *Theological Science*, p. 345.

4 Torrance, *Theological Science*, p. 346.

5 Torrance, *Theological Science*, p. 346.

6 Torrance, *Theological Science*, p. 347.

not mean that the task should not be undertaken. The opposite is the case. It is the crucial calling of the Church in every generation, in response to societal and cultural change, to seek to express the "truth" of God in ways that both communicate and correct the life of the Church and give witness to the presence of Jesus in the world. Yet at the same time, confidence in the forms of expression, in and of themselves, is misplaced. The divine being is always "beyond" the Church's attempts at expression, while at the same time through the freedom of the Spirit, Christ is able to inhabit the Church and the gospel that it shares.

Culture and the Translation Principle

The diversity in human culture increases the problems that are associated with the expression of the gospel. Doctrine, as Torrance makes clear, is always an approximate reaching towards God. This reaching towards is, however, contingent on the cultural differences in language, tradition, and thought. The Christian Church has from the very earliest period been characterised by differences in culture. This is evident in the New Testament itself, where the gospel message moves from the predominantly Jewish culture of the disciples and the Jerusalem Church, to the Hellenistic context of the gentile Church. Thus cultural translation is written into the texts of the Christian Church and is seen to shape the theology and practice of early Christianity. Andrew Walls speaks of the "translation principle" of the Christian Church. The Christian faith rests on translation, Walls argues. The Word is made flesh and dwells among us (John 1:14). This is the divine act of translation on which the ongoing translation of the Church rests. "Incarnation is translation. When God in Christ became man, Divinity was translated into humanity, as though humanity were a receptor language. Here was a clear statement of what would otherwise be veiled in obscurity or uncertainty, the statement 'This is what God is like'."[7] There are two crucial dynamics that flow from this. The first is that culture is particular and specific. The incarnation shows that it is the divine nature to inhabit and to be made known in the local language, or to borrow a term used by Lamin Sanneh, in the local vernacular.[8] The second is the distinctively Christian conviction that the original translation of the incarnation should lead to re-translation as

7 Andrew Walls, *The Missionary Movement in Christian History: Studies in the Transmission of Faith* (Edinburgh: T and T Clark, 1996), 27.

8 For a summary of the vernacular in Catholic and Protestant mission, see Lamin Sanneh, *Translating the Message: The Missionary Impact on Culture* (Maryknoll, NY: Orbis, 1991), 233.

the message is communicated across cultures. Through the translation principle, the Christian church takes different cultural forms in different places and in different times.[9] As Walls puts it, "the first divine act of translation into humanity thus gives rise to a constant succession of new translations. Christian diversity is the necessary product of the Incarnation."[10]

Lamin Sanneh develops a contextually-oriented theory of translation. He makes a distinction between what he terms diffusion and translation. Diffusion takes place where the Church seeks to share the faith in contexts that are culturally similar.[11] The problem with diffusion is that the Church can become accommodated to particular cultural norms and lose the ability to be prophetic. Sanneh argues that it is St Paul who set out the framework for translation. Paul, he points out, was the apostle who translated the gospel into Hellenistic forms of thought as he engaged in mission among the Gentiles. Sanneh identifies two leading ideas that shape Paul's treatment of the gospel and culture. Firstly, Paul resists any attempt to absolutize culture. Secondly, Paul treats all culture as being cleansed by the breath of God in such a way that it is not possible to view any culture as being in some way impure or inferior.[12] This dual approach meant that for Paul, culture is the means whereby the gospel is made known, but this message must never be subsumed by culture. "Paul's legacy to the church includes this exacting vigilance over the true nature of culture. Christian life is indelibly marked with the stamp of culture, and faithful stewardship includes uttering the prophetic word in culture, and sometimes even against it. Paul was a cultural iconoclast in his defiance of the absolutist tendencies in culture, but he was not a cultural cynic, for in his view God's purposes are mediated through particular cultural streams."[13]

The Church has a continual desire to halt the translation process, Sanneh argues, because it much prefers to absolutize its expression of faith. This desire leads to a preference for diffusion. Fixing the gospel message and the cultural expression of the Church gives reassurance and security. This temptation must be resisted, he argues. The Church must always seek to translate the message and hence resist the pull towards faith as a single ethnic identity. By continually embracing translation, the Church can keep a prophetic and self-reforming orientation.[14]

9 Walls, *The Missionary*, 27.

10 Walls, *The Missionary*, 27-28.

11 Sanneh, *Translating the Message*, 36.

12 Sanneh, *Translating the Message*, 47.

13 Sanneh, *Translating the Message*, 47.

14 Sanneh, *Translating the Message*, 48.

Kernel and Husk

The translation principle raises the question of continuity in the Church. If expression takes different cultural forms how can the gospel remain the same? The kernel and husk theory seeks to address this problem by reserving aspects of the doctrine as being above culture. It has been widely accepted that the Christian Church should not only be sensitive to culture, but it should also be contextualized in cultural contexts. The predilection towards contextualization raises problems about the truth of the gospel, however. If expression changes in different cultures, it is asked, "How can the gospel be consistent?" One approach to these worries about truth and consistency has been to argue that there is an irreducible core or essence of the gospel message that is supra-cultural, an approach that has been termed the kernel and husk theory. According to this theory, the essence of the gospel is like the kernel of a nut that is encased in the shell of the contextualized expression of the Church. The kernel represents the unchanging and unchangeable essence of the gospel message. This unchanging essence is encased in the cultural forms of expression that are necessary for it to be communicated and received in any particular culture and context. The casing or the shell can change, it is argued, but the essence or kernel must never change. It is to be preserved from dilution in culturally specific forms and norms. This is precisely the position advocated by many evangelicals in the contemporary Church, as will be discussed in Part II.

There are problems with the kernel and husk theory, however. As Stephen Bevans points out, there is no fixed agreement on what the supra-cultural kernel might be. For some, the irreducible core is simply Christ incarnate. For others, it consists of belief in the triune God, the bible, and the doctrine derived from the bible.[15] For Max Stackhouse, the supra-cultural gospel consists of four doctrines: 1) that humanity is fallen; 2) that God's revelation is in history as witnessed in the bible; 3) that the Trinity best expresses what God is like and what faith in God means for the world; and 4) that Jesus is the Christ and in him men and women can find the meaning of life.[16] Others might argue that the unchanging gospel approximates to something like the Four Spiritual Laws: 1) God loves you and offers a wonderful plan for your life. 2) Humanity is sinful and separated from God and therefore cannot know and experience God's love and plan. 3) Jesus Christ is God's only provision for humanity's sin. Through Him we can know and experience God's love and plan for our life.

---

15 Stephen B. Bevans, *Models of Contextual Theology*, 2nd ed. (Maryknoll, NY: Orbis, 2002), 40.

16 Max Stackhouse, quoted in Bevans, *Models of Contextual Theology*, 40.

4) We must individually receive Jesus Christ as Saviour and Lord; then we can know and experience God's love and plan for our lives. The Four Spiritual Laws are discussed in more detail in the case study in Part II, but at this point they are significant, because they offer a further account of what some might consider to be the unchanging heart of the Gospel that transcends culture. The diversity of opinion, however, about what constitutes the kernel, demonstrates the inherent weakness in this theory of the relationship between the gospel and culture.

That the unchanging supra-cultural essence of the Christian message is unsettled, and even perhaps a matter for dispute, suggests that far from being above culture, it too is subject to contingency. In other words, the guarantee that appears to come when particular doctrines are designated as unchanging and unaffected by culture is illusory. And yet this observation does not preclude the possibility that there might be a core message that could be identified as the gospel. The key issue that is at stake here is the assertion that this core is supra-cultural and therefore unchanging. The attempt to place doctrine outside of history and its embodiment in the Church is not only problematic from the theological point of view. It might also be argued that doing so ignores the role that the Church and tradition have played in the discussion of the reliability of the gospel that the Church shares.

Culture and the Rule of Faith

If the gospel finds its being in the being of Jesus Christ, then expression also has its orientation and its reorientation in Christ. This orientation has two aspects. First, Jesus Christ revealed in the scriptures, and secondly, Jesus Christ revealed in the Church. These two aspects together form the basis for the critique and for the reassurance about the truth of particular forms of expression. This dual orientation forms the basis for Irenaeus's rule of faith, where correct expression rests on the scriptures and also on the embodied teaching of the Church in the succession of bishops from the original Apostles. In *Against Heresies*, Irenaeus argues that the scriptures challenge wrong teaching and point to errors. The scriptures, he says, contain a repository of the faith and all teaching in the Church not only has its origins in them, but should not attempt to innovate and develop systems or patterns of thought that are not contained within them.[17] Thus he counteracts the "hidden mysteries" of the

17 Hans Von Campenhausen, *Fathers of the Greek Church*, trans. Stanley Godman (London: A.C. Black, 1955), 22.

Gnostics and other heretics, by appealing to the teaching that has been handed down in the Church.[18] The guarantee of this teaching, he says, lies in the succession of bishops that have handed on the teaching in the Church. This is the reassurance that the teaching in the Church is that of the Apostles.[19]

Apostolic succession indicates the importance of the embodiment of tradition. It is in the community that the scriptures have been interpreted, and through the expression of the community that they have been taught. This does not mean that doctrines and theology cannot be examined and discussed. There is a place for the critique of the content of expression and the correction of teaching on this basis. Reasoned argument about theology therefore has a significant place in the continual examination of the Church as it seeks to express the gospel, but this reasoning has its point of departure and return in scripture and in the continuity of expression in the Church. There are, however, complicating factors in a simple resort to scripture and tradition to regulate expression. Cultural factors mean that faith has been expressed in radically diverse ways. In an entertaining essay, Andrew Walls demonstrates these diverse forms of expression, but he also develops an argument for continuity that is similar to Irenaeus's rule of faith.

To advance his argument, Walls suggests that readers imagine an alien who can travel backwards and forwards in time. This "Professor of Inter-Planetary Religions" wants to study earthly religion empirically by observing a representative sample of Christians. With the advantages of time travel, the Professor is able to gather samples of data from different periods in the history of the Christian Church. First the Professor lands his time machine in *Jerusalem* around 37 CE. The people he meets are all Jews and they are worshipping regularly in the Temple. They sacrifice animals, keep the seventh day holy, they circumcise their male children and they are fully engaged in reading the old law books. They are differentiated from other Jews by their adherence to figures such as the Son of Man, the Messiah and the Suffering servant. The Jerusalem Christians, the Professor notes, have developed a practice of meeting in their houses for a communal meal. Leaving the Jerusalem church, the Professor next attends a great meeting of Church leaders at a Council in *Nicea* in 325 CE. Those gathered come from all of the Mediterranean, but hardly any of them are Jewish. In fact, they are rather hostile to the Jews. At the mention of animal sacrifices, they are completely horrified. Sacrifice for them signifies a meal of bread and wine, which seems to have parallels with the house meals in Jerusalem. They read the law books of the Jewish Christians, although

18 Irenaeus, *Against Heresies*, III.ii.

19 Irenaeus, *Against Heresies*, III.iii.

alongside these there is a new set of writings that are also revered. They are familiar with words such as Messiah and Son of Man, but they seem to use other titles, such as Son of God and Lord much more frequently. At present they are debating the distinction between *homo-ousios* and *homoi-ousios*, two words not found in either set of writings. This reflects the characteristic of this group, which seems to involve an intense intellectual scrutiny of their faith.

Leaving the group at Nicea, the Professor next meets a group of seventh century Christians on the west coast of *Ireland*, where he observes a number of monks gathered on a rocky shore. Some of them are up to their necks in the ice cold water reciting the psalms. Others are on the ground stretching out in the shape of a cross. A small group are setting off in a little boat bound for Scotland. All they appear to be carrying with them is a box of beautifully illustrated manuscripts. One or two others are sitting alone in small caves found in the rock face. The manuscripts are identical to those that were respected by the group at Nicea, and the monks, although they are not particularly interested in discussing theology, appear to be aware of the term *homo-ousios*. What appears to be of more interest to them, however, is the exact date on which they should celebrate their festival of Easter. The Professor is most impressed by the desire of the group for holiness of life and also their extreme austerity. The next time the Professor lands in his space craft the year is 1840, and this time he arrives at a meeting that is being held in Exeter Hall in *London*. Here he finds a large group of people who are excitedly listening to speeches advocating spreading civilization and the Christian message to the people of Africa. They are arguing that funds should be raised in order that they might send missionaries. These missionaries should be sent with bibles, but also with seeds to help develop agriculture. The group are also very interested in how they can pressurize the British Government to abolish the practice of slavery. They are raising funds so that pamphlets can be produced and meetings arranged to further this aim, and also seek to develop educational trades in order that they might train former slaves as mechanics. The meeting starts with a reading from the writings found in Nicea, which are the same as those that were revered by the monks in Ireland. Indeed, most of the people at the gathering are carrying bibles. All are familiar with the creed developed at Nicea, but they are horrified by the suggestion that they should pray while standing in water, or indeed that holiness might involve such practices. While the monks in Ireland were poor, this group appears to be very well fed, and indeed they give the impression of being quite wealthy.

The Professor returns to earth a final time, this time to *Lagos* in Nigeria. Here he meets a group all dressed in white and dancing and chanting in the street as they make their way to church. They tell the Professor that they are the Cherubim and Seraphim, and as they pass through the street they are inviting everyone they meet to come and experience with them the power of God in their worship service. They promise that they have messages for individuals from God and that they will be able to offer healing for those who need it. They also carry copies of the bible from which they quote regularly. They recognize the creed, but this does not seem to be central to their belief. Unlike the group in Exeter Hall, they are not concerned with politics or government, but they do practice fasting. The overwhelming impression left with the visitor is the interest this group has in preaching, personal faith and the power of God to change people's lives.[20] While it is a rather whimsical and selective presentation of Christian history, Wall's Professor of Inter-Planetary Religions serves to highlight the differences of expression in the Christian Church. The point is that cultural forms generate wildly different ways of life. These different ways of life have some common features, but they highlight the problem with any attempt to locate a fixed point in the gospel or indeed in practice, because the cultural forms of the Church are extremely significant.

The approach to questions of culture and ecclesial distinction that Walls advocates is echoed across a wide range of mission theologians. David Bosch, for instance, argues that Christian history should be divided into six periods: Apocalyptic: Early Church, Hellenistic: Patristic Era, Medieval: Roman Catholic, Reformation: Protestant, the Modern: Enlightenment, and the Ecumenical: Postmodern. Each of these periods, he argues, is characterized by a distinctive theological "paradigm." Paradigms, for Bosch, are an overarching thought world. "Each new macro-paradigm represents a reconstruction of the entire field of theology. Within one macro-paradigm the theologians indeed share, by and large one overall frame of reference and a commensurable perspective on God, humans and the world, even if theologians do differ substantially from each other in many respects."[21] The notion of paradigm shifts in relation to Christian mission is more developed than Walls' more popular illustration. The notion of different periods and paradigms, as developed by Bosch, can be criticized because it tends to smooth out continuities across time and make the movement from period to period more solid. This critique is particularly significant where Bosch talks about the shift to a postmodern paradigm in the present day. Where Bosch is helpful is in terms of the more general point that across time, cultural expression has meant that the Church has generated really quite different and distinctive ways of life.

20 Walls, *The Missionary*, 3-6.

21 David J. Bosch, *Transforming Mission: Paradigm Shifts in the Theology of Mission* (Maryknoll, NY: Orbis, 1991), 188.

The differences that can be traced between Christian communities across time are so acute that the temptation might be to conclude that what is being observed is not one religion but many. Walls, however, points to a common thread that runs between all of his groups. First, they all have the scriptures at their heart, and second, they share a focus on Christ. Third, they all appear to worship around the bread and the wine, and this focus on worship connects to a conscious continuity of a common Christian identity.[22] Stephen Bevans and Roger Schroeder also identify a pattern of cultural differences between churches across periods in Christian history, but they argue that these churches are nevertheless unified by elements that appear to be held in common. Building on Walls' suggestion of continuity across cultural diversity, they suggest six constants in Christianity. Bevans and Schroeder express these in the form of questions that the Church in each context needs to answer. The answer to the questions, they argue, will shape how the church will preach, serve, and witness to God's reign. The six questions are: "(1) Who is Jesus Christ and what is his meaning? (2) What is the nature of the Christian church? (3) How does the Church regard its eschatological future? (4) What is the nature of the salvation that it preaches? (5) How does the Church value the human? and (6) What is the value of human culture as the context in which the gospel is preached?"[23]

The work of these mission theologians is extremely helpful in that it serves to demonstrate the enduring and deep significance of culture in any consideration of the content of the Gospel. At the same time, while acknowledging cultural difference, they are able to point to important aspects of the Christian expression that have remained consistent. Churches have a familial affinity. These constants echo Irenaeus's rule of faith in that they point to the scriptures and also to the succession of teaching that has been passed between generations and indeed across cultures. For Irenaeus, the guarantee of the connection to the teaching of the Apostles was to be found in the succession of bishops. This structured account of tradition, it might be argued, has shifted in mission theology towards constants that have been handed on within and across cultures by the whole Church. This shift is also embodied and so the Church looks to Christ in the scriptures and in the practices of the Church as the framework for understanding the enduring content of the gospel. Andrew Walker further develops the idea that the content of the gospel should be understood and evaluated as the expression of the Church within culture and across time.

22 Walls, *The Missionary*, 6.

23 Stephen B. Bevans and Roger G. Schroeder, *Constants in Context: A Theology of Mission for Today* (Maryknoll, NY: Orbis, 2004), 34.

The Gospel and Story

Andrew Walker approaches the issue of the gospel and culture by developing a theory of story. The gospel, he argues, can be understood as a "grand narrative" that has been a consistent element in the history of the Christian Church. This grand narrative is expressed in different ways and at different times, but by taking an overview, a common pattern can be discerned. Walker argues that "historically, the gospel as a grand narrative was predicated—not overnight, but over a protracted period of history and experience—upon a number of interlinked Old Testament and New Testament narrations. This also included both the ordering of these narrations, and theological reflection on them by the apostles, Fathers, and doctors of the early church."[24] Walker summarizes this grand narrative of the Christian Gospel under nine headings:

1. Outside time and space there is God who is good and lives in loving and perfect communion as Father, Son and Spirit.
2. God calls time and space into existence with the creation of the cosmos out of nothing, and like its creator this universe is also very good.
3. Creation includes the formation of our world, where human beings are made in the image of God. This gives them power freely to follow God or reject him.
4. Humankind, however, wilfully rebels against God. This results in enmity between people and God and estrangement of all creation from its source—this is so because human beings, as matter made articulate, betray all of creation.
5. God takes the initiative to end this estrangement, because his nature is love. First he chooses a human tribe, the Jews, and establishes a special relationship with them in order to demonstrate his desire to restore communion with the human race. Second, after several hundred years of special relationship to the whole world, he enters the physical universe through the incarnation of his eternal son. He is joined to created matter—human nature—in the person of Jesus of Nazareth.
6. Jesus achieves God's desire to restores the broken communion between himself and creation through his birth, life, death, resurrection and ascension.
7. During his lifetime, Jesus Christ calls disciples as the authentic witnesses to and co-participators of his work. Through them he *institutes* a Church an *ecclesia*—the people of God. The people of God, in all generations, do

24 Andrew Walker, *Telling the Story: Gospel, Mission and Culture* (London: SPCK, 1996), 13.

not merely follow their founder, but are organically linked to him by divine favour, though not by nature. This is accomplished by the Holy Spirit, who is sent by Jesus from his Father after the resurrection. The Holy Spirit *constitutes* the Church.
8. The people of God, under the Spirit's guidance, are the bearers of the good news of God's restoration of the world through Jesus. They are bearers in the double sense that they are guardians of the apostolic "deposit of faith", and the tellers of the story.
9. The good news will not end like the final chapter of a book, because it is a never-ending story, which continues beyond time in everlasting communion with God. But it will reach its fulfilment at the end of time, when Christ will return in glory so that "God may be all in all."[25]

This account of the grand narrative, Walker argues, is not intended to be a definitive statement of the gospel. It is instead to be regarded as a guideline summary. This is because the story has been presented in different ways with various different embellishments and emphases. The purpose in setting out the main moves in the story in these nine sections is to show that there has been a pattern to the Christian understanding of the gospel that has persisted in the Church from apostolic times.[26] To talk of the grand narrative as story does not mean that it reads like a detective novel. It is not to be seen as a story in a plain factual sense. Yet this is a story that has consistently been regarded by the Church as objectively true.[27] Walker argues that his rendering of the grand narrative is a representation of Christ's relationship with the world. It is therefore a story that brings about encounter and that is itself a retelling of this encounter.[28]

The Grand Narrative as an Approximate Frame of Reference

The notion of the grand narrative is an important corrective to the problems that are inherent in the expression of faith within culture. Where Walls, Bevans, and Schroeder point to a cluster of sources of authority and community practice as constants in different cultural contexts, the grand narrative sug-

25 Walker, *Telling the Story*, 13-14.
26 Walker, *Telling the Story*, 17.
27 Walker, *Telling the Story*, 18.
28 Walker, *Telling the Story*, 16-17.

gests that more can be said at a doctrinal level that is consistent in the expression of the Church, whatever the cultural context. Walker's contribution here is that he accepts that the Gospel is subject to cultural contingency and he does not claim any particular authority for his presentation of the grand narrative. What he claims is that across cultures and contexts it is possible to see a roughly consistent Christian narrative. This narrative, whilst having different emphases and quite radically different forms of expression in culture, nevertheless remains recognizable as the same story of Jesus Christ. Yet despite this, it is important to understand that Walker is not claiming any particular doctrinal precedence for his version of the story. Neither is he expecting that the story should be presented in this form. The point of the grand narrative is to highlight the fact that the story of Jesus Christ has a content that has remained part of the Church's witness over centuries and that it is possible to offer an account of this story. It should be stressed that this concept of a grand narrative is distinct from the kernel and husk theory. There is no claim that the grand narrative is supra-cultural, or that it is unchanging. The grand narrative in Walker's thinking is pieced together from the culturally-specific expression of the Church and the assumption is that in each age there will need to be a new and culturally relevant contextualized expression of the gospel.

The dynamic that operates between culture and gospel leads to an inevitable problem with appropriate and inappropriate expression. This is part of the paradox of the Church. Nevertheless, it cannot be assumed that the work of the Holy Spirit in the Church offers a guarantee of inerrancy. Indeed, it is of the nature of paradox and fluidity that the expression of the Church can be prone to error, while somehow also being a place of divine presence and revelation. This conundrum does not, however, preclude the absolute necessity for the Church to be reflexive about its own expression and communal life. The call to abide in Christ is, I argue, an invitation to attentive self-critique, because of the possibilities of ecclesial error. The Gospel can be miss-spoken and misunderstood. In fact, even in speaking truth the expression of the Church veils Christ and generates a humiliation of the Word. It is in this context that the grand narrative can operate as a guide for expression. It should be stressed that the "truth" is Jesus Christ and not any theological system, but the grand narrative can play a role in helping the Church to remain faithful. It offers an approximate frame of reference. By approximate, what I mean is it can suggest what might be said and what might not be said. A similar role can be seen in Bevans and Schroeder's questions that they suggest are consistent in the life of the Church across time. The questions do not dictate the form of the expression, but they mark out the areas that need to be addressed by each community, whatever the cultural context. The grand narrative does something very similar. It does not offer a form of expression, but maps the area that the gospel should address when it is expressed in the community. So the idea of a grand narrative has echoes of Irenaeus in that the "authority" to evaluate a particular expression of the Gospel comes from Jesus Christ in the scriptures and in the Church.

The Gospel and Discourses

The grand narrative offers a pattern for the expression of the gospel, but it is important to note that this expression takes place both in the Church and in the wider society. Expression is thus operative in a fluid cultural sphere. This liquid arena does not consist of one voice or one expression, but many. The Church is made up of voices and these voices at times all speak at once. Similarly, in the wider society, issues of morality, ultimate worth, and even salvation, are continually at play. The Church is not immune to these voices; instead they form a part of the liquid flow of representation and contested identity formation of which the Church, or rather the churches, are a part. The reality is then that while there may be a grand narrative, expression within culture generates a complex field of different discourses. This notion of complex discourse can be combined with McClendon's discussion about convictions. Carried as convictions in communities and in the lives of individuals, the gospel is lived out in different ways. As a result, there is no single way of being Christian at a particular time and a particular place, but there are multiple ways. This does not mean that there can be no discernment of which is the better way, or what might be a more appropriate expression of the gospel, but it acknowledges the inherent fluidity and complexity that is introduced if the lived and the cultural form part of what is understood as the gospel. The grand narrative is helpful as a guide, but it can only operate as such if there is close and sustained attention paid to actual communities and actual expression, and even here its role can only be approximate.

Liquid Ecclesiology is based on the realization that the expression of the Church is a complex, and at times, contradictory mix of theology and experience, individual spirituality, and corporate expression. Making sense of this rich and varied mix requires the ability to pay attention to a range of different ways of sharing faith. In *Talking About God in Practice*, the authors introduce what they call the different theological "voices" that become evident through a careful examination of the practice of the church. These voices are mixed together in the everyday speech and action of communities, and as such they form a rich and living whole. In seeking to understand how theology is intertwined with action, Cameron and others have developed an interpretative typology that helps them to identify different strands of theological communication in the life of the Church. The authors are clear that their typology is at risk of oversimplifying the organic and interconnected nature of the lived situation. They see the voices typology as a "working tool." The tool is developed around the notion that in the lived practice of the Church there are four theological voices: operant theology, espoused theology, normative theology and formal theology.[29]

Operant Theology

Cameron et al. argue that the fundamental starting point needs to be the realization that the practice of the Church is "theological." As Clare Watkins puts it, "practices are bearers of theology."[30] This means that theology is somehow embodied in the practice of the Church. Embodied theology is not generally something that is easily explained or described; it needs instead to be uncovered and discovered by believers themselves. This is because operant theologies are often slightly hidden from view, or taken as "just the thing that we do." It is only when they are subjected to attention and reflection that these everyday ways of believing reveal their theological nature. This observation echoes the work of John Swinton and Harriet Mowat, who, as we have seen, suggest that the theology that lies embedded in practice can be elusive and hard to find. "Practices," they argue, "contain values, beliefs, theologies and other assumptions which, for the most part, go unnoticed until they are complexified and brought to our notice through theological reflection."[31] "Complexifying" might suggest creating an elaborate theory around practices. This is not exactly what is meant here. Swinton and Mowat are talking about the way that focused attention on action and belief in the life of the Church can reveal the layers of interaction and entwined meanings. The four voices method of analysis came about because the researchers found differences between the theology that is evident in practice and the theology that people articulate. The first they call operant theology and the second is what the group calls espoused theology.

29 Cameron et al., *About God in Practice*, 49-56.

30 Clare Watkins (with Helen Cameron, Deborah Bhatti, Catherine Duce, and James Sweeney), "Practical Ecclesiology: What Counts as Theology in Studying the Church?" in *Perspectives on Ecclesiology and Ethnography*, ed. Pete Ward (Grand Rapids, MI: Eerdmans, 2012).

31 Swinton and Mowat, *Practical Theology and Qualitative Research*, 2.

Espoused Theology

Very often when Churches are studied, belief and believing appear to operate in a way that enables and occasionally supports subtle, and at times, confusing differences between what is stated and the underlying operant theology that works out in practice. Watkins gives the example of a Catholic diocesan agency for evangelization, where the espoused theological position emphasized the responsibility of the Church for the wider society, and yet the practice was actually much more orientated towards catechesis and adult education within the Church. So the operant theology that lay behind these work patterns and strategies did not quite ring true with the theological position that the workers espoused or spoke about as their theology.[32] This example serves to show how espoused theology is always connected to other voices. It exists alongside operant theologies, but it is also drawn from formal and normative voices.

Normative Theology

Espoused theology has its roots in the wider tradition and expression of the Church. As Cameron et al. put it, "Espoused theologies come from somewhere." Churches and believers develop their espoused theological understandings in relation to the ongoing teaching and theological understanding of their churches. The theology that people speak about in relation to their practice is thus drawn from scripture or liturgy or other theological and spiritual writings as well as experience.[33] The normative theological voice is introduced to show how these varied sources are often utilized as a guide and a corrective alongside practices of both communities and believers. Here again it is possible to observe quite interesting and "complexified" relationships between the normative voice in a community and the espoused theologies of individual believers.

In his study of an evangelical church in the North of England, sociologist Mathew Guest traced the way that members of the congregation negotiated the official teaching of the Church in different ways. From his extensive observations and interviews made over a period of seven years, Guest was able to identify the different theological positions that co-existed in the church.[34] Perhaps surprisingly, given its reputation as a leading Anglican evangelical church, Guest found that a great many of those in the congregation appeared to hold quite liberal views. This liberalism extended to what he identified as

32 Watkins, "Practical Ecclesiology," 177.

33 Cameron et al., *Talking About God in Practice*, 53.

34 For methods, see Mathew Guest, *Evangelical Identity and Contemporary Culture*, 231.

central issues for this section of the Church, for instance, the kind of truth and authority that is to be found in scripture, and the place of women in the ministry of the Church. He also saw evidence that somewhere in the process of redrawing the boundaries of an evangelical world-view, there has been a move towards tolerance, universalism, and a general openness to spiritual exploration. This more open and experimental mindset brings with it a sense that it is possible and even desirable to engage in rethinking the Christian tradition. The result is that the congregation appears to support more individualistic forms of believing. The shift toward more open and exploratory forms of evangelicalism, however, was not universally welcomed in the congregation. Alongside the "liberals," Guest uncovered a number of conservatives who advocated a more traditional approach to evangelical theology. Interestingly, some of the leaders in the church welcomed the way that people with different perspectives were all able to be part of the congregation. Diversity in this sense became a value that they sought for the Church. Yet this shift towards a more open theology that overtly welcomed diversity was kept in check by the conservative members of the congregation and the sense that a move towards more liberal theology would result in censure from the wider evangelical world. As a result, the more open theological approach of some of the leaders and some in the congregation did not find itself reflected in the official theological statements of the church. What appeared to take place, therefore, was a complex set of checks and balances between the public voice of the church and more veiled private beliefs and convictions.[35] For Cameron et al., these correspond to the formal and the espoused voices, respectively. Guest traced this accommodation through a study of the sermons at the church.

From his study of just under fifty sermons Guest concluded that the preaching served to minimize conflict between the conservatives and the liberals in the church.[36] They did this by charting a middle path between the two groups, at times supporting one and then the other. Thus the public discourse of the church "appeared to function as a unifying force by keeping these two narratives in tension. It did this by avoiding the open endorsement of extreme positions and evading issues likely to provoke disagreement."[37] Guest found that within the congregation there were quite different perceptions of what it meant to be evangelical. The size of the congregation enabled different microclimates of theological understanding to co-exist. In this context, the formal

35 Guest, *Evangelical Identity*, 95-97.

36 Guest, *Evangelical Identity*, 98-102.

37 Guest, *Evangelical Identity*, 102.

theology of the church, as seen in the public preaching, on the face of it offered a point of unity, but this was not really the whole story. What Guest found was that individuals in the congregation heard and understood different things in what was being said by the leaders from the front of the church. "Conversations with individual parishioners revealed a vast diversity of responses to sermons, from boredom to incredulity, enthusiasm, emotion, deep reflection and an experience of being inspired to make life-changing decisions."[38] They found ways, therefore, to negotiate space for their own particular forms of espoused theology. It appears this space is in part supported by the preaching, and in part worked out as a mild form of resistance to what is seen as the party line. Guest sees these dynamics as the collective mechanism that enables the Church to maintain an evangelical identity while avoiding significant conflict, but also that they give a particular insight into the layers of theology that work together in the Church. Read through the interpretative lens of the four voices approach to theology, what becomes apparent is that an evangelical identity might encapsulate significant contradictions between formal theological utterances and more individually espoused theological positions. This contradiction may even extend to leaders, who consciously or unconsciously reproduce a party line in public, while holding different views themselves. Normative theological speech and espoused speech in this way may stretch in different directions when attention is paid to the lived expression of the Church.

Formal Theology

The final voice identified by Cameron et al. is that of formal theology. This refers to the contribution to understanding the practice and life of the Church by "professional" theologians. This formal voice is deeply entwined with the other three theological voices. Espoused and normative theology may draw on formal theology to varying degrees.[39] Good examples are the way ministers may continue to find inspiration from their studies at college when they preach, or the way believers may engage with academic theology when they attend Christian festivals and events. Normative theology contained in the liturgy of Church is often influenced by wider academic conversations that make up the formal theological voice. Alongside this embedded formal voice there is a particular role that Cameron et al. envisage for academic engagement with practice. Academic theology can offer a critical perspective on the

38 Guest, *Evangelical Identity*, 103.

39 Cameron et al., *Thinking About God in Practice*, 55.

lived expression of the Church. It is able, at its best, to "shine a light" on the actions of the Church and the state of believing.

Expressing the Gospel and the Four Voices

The four voices typology has been developed as a method for helping communities reflect on their own theological communication. It is helpful in showing how even in one community there may be competing and conflicting theologies that are given voice. This is extremely important in relation to the expression of the gospel in the Church and the world. The definite article used in relation to the gospel can mislead. "The" gospel is Jesus Christ. The expression of the Church is always in cultural forms and therefore partial, however. One aspect of this partialness is that the gospel circulates in the community and in the wider society in a variety of forms, and it can take on different "voices." The four voices theory describes the contested discursive field of the Church as different levels or forms of communication: espoused, operant, normative and formal. These distinctions are useful, but they have their limitations.

Espoused and operant voices very often overlap, for instance. Individuals and communities may talk about theology and also live it out. Operant theology is helpful in that it can identify how theology is often implicitly carried in practices. At the same time practices in the Church are often developed from, and carry within them, overt theological statements. The Eucharist would be a good example of this. Thus the distinction between espoused and operant is problematic. Where this distinction is perhaps helpful is that it can serve to highlight discrepancies between what is said within a community and how the community lives out the faith. In other words, espoused and operant can be used to describe a disconnection between the gospel that is preached and the way of life that develops in a community. It is perhaps less helpful in describing the many connections between practice and theology that shape the life of the Church. By contrast, McClendon's distinction between ideas and convictions might have more traction here. However, the problem with this is that "ideas" covers both academic theology and what members of the community might express. Having said this, the concept of convictions has merit over the espoused and operant distinction, because it allows for a mix of the spoken and the lived interacting with each other. There are similar issues around formal, normative, and espoused theology. A sermon may hold within it the influence of academic theology and the normative voice of the institution at the same time, so that it is hard not to see preaching as an espoused theological voice in a community. I have tended to use the term "expression" to refer to the cultural forms and communication of the Church. Expression works for formal, espoused, and normative kinds of theology. It also covers the embodied or operant. In the argument so far, expression has been contrasted and related to the divine presence. The four voices theory does not make any overt space to speak about the presence of God in the Church—a further limitation as an analytical framework.

These limitations to the four voices theory mean that it should be used selectively to help uncover the diversity of discourses in the Church. In the next part, the discussion of the fluid nature of the Church and the gospel is developed through a case study in which I use the idea of operant and espoused theology, but also make use of the terms "expression" and "conviction." Espoused and operant are helpful in shedding light on the connection between what is spoken of as the gospel and the way of life that the contemporary Church has generated. Conviction, on the other hand, is useful as a way of talking about the embodiment and practices that lie at the heart of the community and the ideas that help to sustain this life. Expression and the divine presence offer an overarching orientation to the paradoxical and fluid relationship that characterizes the Church.

PART II

Discerning the Liquid Church: a Case Study

CHAPTER 5

The Gospel and Change

There is a widespread assumption in the contemporary Church that the gospel is unchanging and yet the church must embrace change. Rick Warren typifies this position very well in *The Purpose Driven Church*. Warren is a significant advocate of finding the most "effective" way of communicating the gospel in contemporary culture. His vision for reshaping the Church, so that it becomes sensitive towards the dominant forms of expression in a particular town or neighbourhood, has made him one of the leading figures in the mega-church movement in the United States. Warren's vision is summed up in this advice to those who want to learn from what he has achieved: "Don't confuse methods with message. The message must never change, but the methods must change with each new generation."[1] These are sentiments that are shared by many in the evangelical Church. Central to this kind of reasoning is the assumption that the cultural forms that are adopted by the Church are simply the means to share the faith. In other words, cultural expression is seen as being theologically neutral. So it is almost immaterial how Christians seek to give form to the Church, or its worship, as long as there is clarity that the basic formulation of the gospel remains unchanged. If Christians are clear about their "purpose," i.e., communicating an unchanging gospel, then all kinds of innovation are given a licence to develop, and it is even an absolute necessity that they do. Herein lies a tension: conservative Christians have the freedom to continually reshape and remould the faith in the forms of popular culture, while at the same time believing that the central aspect of their faith, the gospel, has not been affected or compromised. The phenomenon of a Church promoting a faith that embraces the fast-moving world of popular culture and simultaneously holding to a gospel that is fixed needs some unpacking.

At the heart of this approach to gospel and culture in the contemporary Church is the phenomenon of the different theological voices that are found in the lived reality of the community. What appears to be happening in the contemporary Church is that the gospel has become fixed in a particular form. The gospel functions as a marker in the community and as such it is defended with considerable vigour if it is seen to be challenged. When asked about "the gospel," evangelical Christians will normally make a number of brief doctrinal statements covering the love of God, creation, sin and the fall, the coming

1 Warren, *The Purpose Driven Church*, 61-62.

 | DOI 10.1163/9789004347359_007

of Christ, his death on the cross for the sin of the world, and the necessity of repentance and faith for the forgiveness of sins and a restored relationship with God. This brief theology is seen as being a distinctive expression of what it means to be evangelical, and it operates as such within churches. At the same time, because the Church is oriented towards sharing faith in the forms that best communicate the faith in culture, alongside this fixed authoritative understanding of the gospel there exists a parallel operant theology. This operant theology will be set out in detail in the next two chapters, but it is much more rooted in a personal and experiential faith. The espoused theology of the fixed gospel and the operant theology that accompanies it are embraced by both individuals and by those in leadership. In fact, the two work as related, but distinct, theological voices. As such they are a natural and embodied expression of faith. The tension that I am seeking to explore in this case study lies in the way that the espoused and the operant do not appear integrated. In other words, while the fixed form of the gospel is seen as authoritative, it actually does not have much effect on the day-to-day life of the Church. At the same time, the operant theology of the contemporary Church has a slight connection to the specific theological formulations of the evangelical gospel. This is seen most clearly in the practice of worship and in worship songs. From the worship songs, what becomes clear is that the evangelical gospel does not play a crucial role in shaping Church. Liquid Ecclesiology is able to explore these kinds of tensions because it puts a priority on paying close attention to cultural forms of communication. At the same time, the fluid theological understanding of the Church, and notions such as the gospel as grand narrative, can offer a point of reference and correction. Liquid Ecclesiology, as this case study sets out to show, can be both analytical and also normative in relation to the expression of the Church.

Expressing the Gospel and Connecting to Culture

The relationship between the espoused theology and the operant theology that I am describing comes about through a dynamic that lies deep in the Church. The contemporary Church has been formed out of a basic drive to connect and express. Connecting and expressing are ways of referring to the evangelistic energy of the Christian community. Contemporary-style churches want to be effective in sharing the gospel. Being effective means finding a way to express the faith, while at the same time connecting with the cultural and spiritual worlds of those who are outside the Church. This has led to a dynamic where change is an evangelistic necessity. The drive to connect and express has given birth to new and vibrant churches. These are what Donald Miller calls the "new paradigm churches."[2] Rick Warren's Saddleback Church is a prime example of one of these new kinds of churches. Miller argues that a revolution has been taking place in the United States. Since the 1960s, while many mainstream churches are experiencing decline in membership, new kinds of independent churches are on the rise and many conservative churches have also found themselves undergoing a transformation. Miller calls this a post-denominational movement that is ushering in a radical reorientation in the religious economy of the country. "Appropriating contemporary cultural forms, these churches are creating a new genre of worship music; they are restructuring the organizational character of institutional religion; and they are democratizing access to the sacred by radicalizing the Protestant principle of the priesthood of all believers."[3] What Miller observes in the United States is equally the case in other parts of the world. The contemporary Church, with its adoption of popular forms of communication, including worship music, festivals, publishing, and in more recent times the use of Internet-based technologies, is a global phenomenon. The urge to share faith through expression and connection lies right at the heart of these developments. The dynamic of communication has actually had a deep effect on how the gospel is conceived and how it operates in the Church. Miller is correct that there has been a revolution in the Church, but this revolution is much more extensive than the new or independent churches. Churches across a range of denominations have experienced significant changes. The use of contemporary Christian worship, for instance, is very common in mainline as well as in non-denominational settings. Young people, and those who seek to reach out to them, have been the main culture carriers in the Church. The impact of youth ministry has generally been overlooked, but it has actually been one of the central agents in generating the particular shape of espoused and operant theology that this case study sets out to examine.

Youth Ministry and the Shape of the Gospel

Far from being an activity that is marginal to the life of the Church, ministry among young people has been, and continues to be, surprisingly influential. Youth ministry has been so significant, in fact, that it is not too much of an

2 Donald E. Miller, *Reinventing American Protestantism: Christianity in the New Millennium* (Berkeley, CA: University of California Press, 1999), 1.

3 Miller, *Reinventing American Protestantism*, 1.

exaggeration to say the cultural, social, and theological shape of the contemporary Church has largely been the product of work with young people. Most significantly, ministry among young people has generated the form of the evangelical gospel. By working with young people, evangelicals have developed a particular form in which the gospel should be expressed. This form has then come to be the normative understanding of the gospel. At the same time, it has also been the main source for the more personalised and worship-led theology that characterizes the lived expression of communities. In short, youth ministry introduces specific forms of communication into the mainstream DNA of Church life and these forms of communication have given rise to both the espoused and the operant theologies that are now predominant. The reason for this is that from the very beginning ministry among young people has been characterized by creativity and innovation. Starting with the Sunday School movement and then on into the various student-based organisations, through different kinds of student-based voluntary mission work, camping ministries, festivals, as well as all the huge variety of organizations, businesses, publishing houses, web sites and record companies, youth ministry has continued to generate new ways to express and connect.[4] It is youth ministry that has fostered and developed the forms of expression and cultural communication that Miller identifies and that Robert Warner calls entrepreneurial evangelicalism.[5]

Connecting with young people has made change inevitable. From its origins in the 1940s, *Youth for Christ* has had the motto, "Geared to the times but anchored to the rock."[6] Being geared to the times situates youth ministry in the rapidly developing arena of broader youth culture.[7] Being geared to the times necessitates a constantly shifting and flexible approach to ecclesial life. Culture is continually on the move. In the 1960s, it was common to think of this as a distinctive youth culture. Convinced that young people inhabited a different world, churches that felt the drive to share faith with them jumped into the fast flowing stream of popular culture. Hence it was generally felt that the Christian faith and message had to be presented in ways that made use of the

---

4 For more on this, see Pete Ward, *Growing Up Evangelical: Youth Work and the Making of a Subculture* (London: SPCK, 1996), and Ward, *Selling Worship*.

5 See Robert Warner, *Reinventing English Evangelicalism 1966-2001* (Milton Keynes, UK: Paternoster, 2007).

6 Joel A. Carpenter, *Revive Us Again: The Reawakening of American Fundamentalism* (Oxford: Oxford University Press, 1997), 161-176.

7 Quentin J. Schultze et al., *Dancing in the Dark: Youth, Popular Culture and the Electronic Media* (Grand Rapids, MI: Eerdmans, 1991), 14-45.

new youth-orientated forms of expression. The catalyst for this change came with the Jesus Movement in the United States. In the late sixties and early seventies, young people started to turn away from the counter culture and many of them became Christians. These young people, and those who sought to minister among them, forged a new kind of youth-orientated "hip" Christianity. In the process, new churches were started and old ones were transformed. The most significant and widespread result of this development was in contemporary worship. The current dominance of guitar-based forms of worship in many of our churches sprang in large part from work with young people. It was youth leaders who first adopted folk and then soft rock for worship. Contemporary worship music illustrates the transforming dynamic of connecting and expressing more clearly than anything else. Worship music started at youth camps and festivals, but it very soon made its way into regular Sunday congregational services. Once there, it became the everyday fare of contemporary Church life. The hymnbooks became dusty in the pews as screens and projected lyrics and images took over. This steady creep of contemporary worship songs into the blood stream is driven in the first place by a desire to connect and express, but this energy found real purchase for one simple reason: young people grow up. The fact that young people become adults means that what starts in youth ministry never stays there. We take what is most meaningful for us in our teenage years into later life. Adults in the Church who have been formed in youth ministry expect a similar style of ministry to that which they experienced as young people. The impact of this expectation is seen in the developing styles of the Church over the last forty years. The youth ministry of the fifties was imported into Church life, then that of the sixties and the seventies and so on. In the present day, the pace of this adoption has become much more immediate. As a result, what happens in youth ministry appears in the mainstream Church within a few weeks. This natural process lies at the heart of the spread of contemporary forms of Church.[8] Styles of expression are developed for work with young people, but in a few short years they become the standard fare in churches. What is true of congregational members is also true of Church leaders. Those who first learn about leading groups, speaking and leading worship in a youth context, very quickly start to exercise their ministry in the wider church. This is so commonplace that it is almost invariably the case that Church leaders who have been at the forefront of new developments in the contemporary Church have first learned their craft in ministry

8 Kenda Creasy Dean, *Practicing Passion: Youth and the Quest for a Passionate Church* (Grand Rapids, MI: Eerdmans, 2004), 14. See also Ward, *Growing Up Evangelical.*

among young people. The contemporary evangelical Church has been quite literally raised by youth ministers. Of course some people join churches later in life, but the Church they join has been deeply influenced by ways of connecting and expressing that were first worked out in ministry among students and young people. Youth ministry, while it has been very creative, has also been problematic. Some argue that rather than young people growing up and becoming adult members of the congregation, the Church has regressed into adolescent forms of communication and social life. There is some truth in this, but it probably needs to be set within the growing sense that what was at first seen as a separate youth culture has now morphed into a more widespread and universal popular culture. Young people and their parents increasingly share in the same world. At a very basic level, popular culture means that adults and young people can have similar tastes in music, entertainment, comedy, sport and fashion. So while it may be true that young people and adults often seek separate spaces for social life, style and the expression of musical taste, the way that these "spaces" operate is remarkably similar.

Youth Ministry and the Search for the Next Thing

The shared popular culture of young people and adults means that Church has reshaped itself around contemporary forms of communication. With its round of festivals, tours, training events, conferences and programmes, the Church has developed its own forms of cultural expression. This shift towards a faith that takes its shape in popular forms has its origins in youth ministry, but it has spread a great deal further than that. Youth ministry in a sense started the ball rolling, and it continues to be a major generative element in Church life. Churches that are shaped around connection and expression are always looking for the next new thing. The adult church has become much more attuned to the creative role that youth ministry plays. As a result, it is not at all uncommon for something that is first seen at a youth festival in the summer to appear in congregations before winter. New technology plays a crucial role in the spread of Christian popular culture. With the widespread use of Youtube, Facebook and Twitter, it is no longer necessary to be physically present to get the experience. Ministers can be in touch wherever they are. Trends can spread around the Christian world within a matter of hours. If a leading figure says something radical or publishes a book with controversial thoughts, the social media can explode. The media generated and sustained world epitomizes connection and expression. The fast-moving Christian culture has given birth to a more liquid form of ecclesial life that embraces communication by extension of the local congregation as part of what it means to be a lively and growing Church.

Those who have been given the responsibility of working with young people have always had something of a licence to experiment. Thus while ministry in congregations has often been tightly controlled, ministry with young people has been free to develop new forms of expression. Formal ministry in a parish requires training and ordination. Work with young people, on the other hand, has not been subject to any such demands. In fact most ministry with young people has largely been done by volunteers or by young people themselves. Student ministry, for instance, has operated for decades almost exclusively on peer leadership. Innovation in youth and student ministries has been justified by a basic assumption, i.e., that the faith should be expressed in ways that connect. This assumption has remained largely unquestioned, but its impact has been immense. Despite the commonalities in popular culture, the Church still assumes that it is self-evident that young people live in a distinct and different cultural world: a youth culture. It is argued that, like it or not, the fact that young people exist in youth culture means that to connect with them, the Church must change how it expresses itself. Consequently, when dealing with young people, even very conservative Churches have accepted that they must be creative and open to change. As Kenda Creasey Dean observes, young people have been meeting together to worship and study the faith in settings that are segregated from congregations. These separated spaces allowed a mindset that self-consciously sets out to do Church in ways that were different from their elders. "As a result," Dean observes, "youth ministry consistently challenged dominant ecclesiologies in American Protestantism by embodying alternative images of the church."[9]

Youth ministry did not just communicate with young people; it "re-imagined the Church." Dean points out that many of the leaders of non-denominational churches were first brought to faith through youth ministry. This is not simply a route into believing, because youth ministry then shaped the imaginative ecclesial world that led to the kinds of churches that these young people went on to plant. This is true, for instance, of Rick Warren, and also of Bill Hybels and the highly influential Willow Creek Church that he planted. John Wimber and the Vineyard Church likewise have their roots in the youth culture of the Jesus Movement in California.[10] Churches have experimented with separate youth worship and some have planted youth

9 Dean, *Practicing Passion*, 14.

10 Dean, *Practicing Passion*, 14.

congregations.[11] Connecting and expressing the faith among and with young people has led to a bewildering array of activities and ways of being and growing as a Christian. There is an irony here, because what is essentially a rather conservative impulse, i.e., to hand on an unchanging faith to the next generation, has actually built into itself a genetic predisposition for change. The story of youth ministry is not simply that of adopting different methods or means of expressing shared faith. It should not be assumed that it has generated only one side of Rick Warren's understanding of the gospel and communication. The truth is that the standardized form of expression that evangelicals regard as the gospel has itself been forged in ministry among young people. The unchanging gospel has undergone some quite significant changes as evangelicals have developed the most effective forms of communication.

The Origins of the Unchanging Gospel[12]

The evangelical understanding of the gospel itself arises from a tradition that has been decisively shaped by connecting and expressing. In one of the video sequences used in the Alpha course, Nicky Gumbel explains the gospel using a simple illustration. He lays the bible on his right hand and says, "There is a barrier between us and him which prevents us from experiencing his love." The bible plays the part of an imaginary blockage between God and sinful humans. Now showing us his left hand he explains that, "Jesus never did anything wrong.... There was no barrier between him and his Father." Then he lays the bible on his left hand, now leaving his right hand (sinful humanity) with no barrier, and as he does so he says, "On the cross, God transferred our wrongdoings (our iniquity) onto Jesus."[13]

These words and gestures reveal a theological pedigree that links present-day charismatic Christians with evangelicals of previous generations. This illustrative use of the bible may well date back to R. A. Torrey.[14] In 1912, Torrey led an influential mission for the newly-formed Cambridge Inter-Collegiate Christian Union (CICCU).[15] His visit to Cambridge took him into the place

11 Graham Cray, *Youth Congregations and the Emerging Church* (Cambridge: Grove, 2002).

12 The following section was first published as Pete Ward, "Union with Christ: The Subplot of Evangelical Soteriology," in *Journal of Youth and Theology* Vol 2 No 1 (2003) 84-93.

13 Nicky Gumble, *Questions of Life* (Eastbourne, UK: Kingsway Publications 1993), 61. See also *The Alpha Video*, Video II (Holy Trinity Publications).

14 R. A. Torrey, *Personal Work* (London: Pickering and Inglis, 1974), 33.

15 Douglas Johnson, *Contending for the Faith: A History of the Evangelical Movement in the Universities and Colleges* (Leicester, UK: Inter-varsity Press, 1979), 78.

where the future leaders of evangelicalism in England were not just learning the faith, but were also learning how to communicate the faith. It is highly likely that Torrey's characteristic use of the bible to share the gospel message was passed on at this time. A few years after Torrey's CICCU mission, the same illustration was regularly being used by Eric Nash (Bash), the founder of Iwerne Minster Camps,[16] or Bash Camps, as they were known, which nurtured the theological sensibilities of generations of evangelical leaders. Nicky Gumbel picked up the illustration from evangelical preachers who were schooled at Iwerne Minster Camps. The use of the illustration in the Alpha Course is not just an interesting case of cultural transmission; it also serves to show how a particular understanding of the gospel and how it works to save has characterised evangelicalism. Central to the gospel in evangelicalism has been the conviction that truth is communicated in a way that needs to be heard, understood, and then accepted. According to David Bebbington, this emphasis on rational acceptance of doctrine came to prominence in the last hundred and fifty years. For previous generations, conversion was often associated with a kind of emotional crisis. Accounts of these overwhelming experiences of the conviction of sin are quite common in Wesley's *Journals* and they are also discussed at some length by Jonathan Edwards.[17] In tune with modernity, the emotional crisis that was emphasised as an essential part of conversion in the eighteenth and nineteenth centuries, was replaced by a more rational and controlled conversion experience. Gradually preaching became a process where a morally corrupt sinner was led to Christ through a presentation of the "truth" and an act of the will.[18] Charles Finney's *Lectures on Revival* illustrate this shift towards conversion as a willed submission to the truth. "Human beings aren't converted by physical force or by God changing their nature by creative power, but by the truth made effective by the Holy Spirit. Conversion is yielding to the truth."[19]

In the 1950s, the chief proponents of this reasoned expression of evangelicalism were Billy Graham and John Stott. In *Peace with God*, Graham presents a soteriology that is based on moral choice, and the intellectual acceptance of Christ.[20] The result is a new relationship with God that restores the pos-

16 John Eddison, ed., *Bash: A Study in Spiritual Power* (London: Marshall Morgan and Scott, 1982), 50.

17 Jonathan Edwards, [1746] "A Treatise Concerning Religious Affections," in *The Works of Jonathan Edwards*, John E. Smith, ed. Vol 2 (Newhaven: Yale University Press, 2009).

18 David Bebbington, *Evangelicalism in Modern Britain: A History From the 1730's to the 1980's* (London: Unwin Hyman, 1989), 8-9.

19 Charles Finney, *Lectures on Revival* (Minneapolis, MN: Bethany House Publishers, 1935, 1988 ed.), 208.

20 Billy Graham, *Peace With God* (Surrey, UK: The Kingswork Limited, 1954).

sibility for right living and behaving through conversion. His starting point is the assertion that the sin of the first man, Adam, infected the rest of humanity. Adam had freedom of choice, and he chose to disobey God. Now as the "federal head" of humanity, his choice affects us all.[21] Adam's fall means that since that time we have all been infected with sin and we are unable to live as we should. God is loving and yet also holy. God's holiness requires that sin be punished. Yet Christ was sent by God to save us. He faced the same temptations as we do and he remained without sin.[22] On the cross, he was "made to be sin on our behalf," but because he knew no sin there was "value" in his death. This value was our salvation.[23] We are affected by Adam's sin, but we also fail to obey God. Conversion consists in repentance, faith, and regeneration. The first of these requires a decision and an act of will. The third is a work of God in the believer.[24] Graham describes the experience of being born again as an "infusion of divine life into the human soul," the "impartation of the divine nature" and we are "attached to God for eternity."[25]

John Stott is concerned to present a gospel that is "intellectually respectable."[26] *Basic Christianity* discusses salvation in terms that are similar to those used by Graham. Sin is seen as moral failure or the breaking of a law. "All men have broken their law. It is the same for us. What is our ethical code? It may be the law of Moses or the law of Jesus. It may be public school morality or white man's taboos, or the conventions of a decent chap.... We all stand self condemned."[27] Moral failure means that we are cut off from God, in bondage to sin and in conflict with others.[28] The gospel is a divine response to these problems: Christ died at Calvary for our sins, he rose again to give us a new nature and he founded a Church where we could enjoy true human fellowship.[29] Sin was a barrier between humanity and God, but Christ on the cross bridges that gap. At his death Christ bears the curse of sin, which is then transferred to him.[30] The Spirit works in the new believer to create a new nature. Christ

---

21 Graham, *Peace With God*, 34-35.

22 Graham, *Peace With God*, 35.

23 Graham, *Peace With God*, 83.

24 Graham, *Peace With God*, 95.

25 Graham, *Peace With God*, 124.

26 John Stott, *Basic Christianity* (Leicester, UK: Inter-varsity Press, 1958), 7.

27 Stott, *Basic Christianity*, 64.

28 Stott, *Basic Christianity*, 72-76.

29 Stott, *Basic Christianity*, 81.

30 Stott, *Basic Christianity*, 97.

dwells within and enables us to live our lives like Jesus.[31] All of this comes about when a personal decision is made.[32]

In John Stott and Billy Graham there is a presentation of the gospel based around notions of sin as wrongdoing and moral failure, substitutionary atonement expressed in forensic or legal terms, and the Christian life as the opportunity to start afresh and live life right. Rational conviction of these doctrinal truths is to be followed by a decision of the will at conversion, and assurance is to be found in the intellectual coherence of biblical truth. John Stott and Billy Graham do not simply share an understanding of the gospel and how it should be expressed, they also share a context where this particular expression has been formed: youth ministry. Billy Graham started his career working for Youth for Christ and John Stott came to faith through the ministry of Bash and was nurtured in the faith through CICCU and the Inter-varsity Fellowship. So the rational and propositional expression of faith that these two prominent evangelical leaders came to embody has its origins in the context of ministry among students and young people. The desire to reach young people with the gospel led to forms of theological expression that were even more distinctive. In the work of Stott and Graham, the gospel continues to be a relatively complex and sophisticated theological construction. In the drive to connect and express the faith with young people, there are radical moves towards simplifying how faith is expressed. It is this shift towards a form of expression of the faith in highly formulaic and simplified terms that fixes the gospel in a few easily-communicated theological propositions. By fixing the form of the gospel it then becomes possible to maintain that it is unchanged, while all around it there operates a fluid and highly adaptable state of believing.

Fixing the Gospel

As evangelicals have sought to express the faith among young people, their communication has taken a particular form. As a result, the expression of the gospel has become radically simplified into a few short statements. This "form" has a direct relationship to the preaching and teaching of figures such as Billy Graham and John Stott, and before them, D.L. Moody and Charles Finney, but it is distinctive in that it adopts a highly condensed style. This change was motivated by a desire to place the basic doctrinal elements of the message into people's hands. The method that was utilized for this was the gospel tract.

31 Stott, *Basic Christianity*, 101 and 105.

32 Stott, *Basic Christianity*, 123.

Tracts have a long history in political as well as religious controversy and debate. In recent times the tract has been most closely associated with a form of communication that is religious and evangelistic in nature and that often makes use of illustrations such as cartoons or diagrams. For those involved in youth ministry, tracts were a means of explaining the faith. Workers and volunteers would be trained to use a tract as a prompt when sharing the gospel with those they were hoping to lead to faith. The tract is important in this context because it illustrates how the gospel moves from the more theologically nuanced and relatively complex preaching of figures such as Billy Graham and John Stott, and becomes a much more rigid set of very short doctrinal statements. It is this shift towards simple doctrinal statements that can be memorized and communicated very easily that enables those in the movement to assert that the gospel is unchanging. In this radically shortened form this is of course much more plausible than it might be when comparing much longer theological works on the atonement, for instance, or even when comparing the sermons of different preachers where illustration and emphasis might allow for greater variation.

Dawson Trotman and the Bridge to Life Tract

The move towards the simplified doctrinal form of the gospel can be illustrated through two of the most popular tracts: the Bridge to Life diagram and the Four Spiritual Laws. These two tracts have their origins in American youth ministry. The Bridge to Life diagram is associated most closely with the work of Dawson Trotman, who founded the Navigators. The Navigators began in the 1930s in the United States when Trotman started to teach the bible to members of the US Navy. They took as their motto "To Know Christ and to Make Him Known." The Navigators practised intensive bible study and their main focus was on growing disciples who would be equipped to share their faith.[33] Trotman's work was well established by the time Billy Graham was starting out as a young evangelist with Youth for Christ, and Graham was anxious that Trotman join him in his ministry. Graham recognized that a critical element in evangelistic work was the need to help those who had come to faith develop as disciples. Graham saw in the programmes developed by Trotman the clue to effective follow up with those who were newly converted. Billy Graham's biographer, John Pollock, says that the Navigators' approach "depended on each

33 Lorna C. Sanny, *The Pioneer: A Condensed Life History of Dawson E. Trotman*, 14 (http://www.discipleshiplibrary.com/pdfs/dawson_trotman_more.pdf).

convert amassing such detailed knowledge of the bible by memory-training that he could win another who would repeat the process with a third."[34] Graham first met Trotman at Wheaton College in 1941 and later, in 1946, at a conference at the Trotman home, the young evangelist heard the older man talk on "The Miracle of Propagation—or producing the producers." Graham was deeply affected by what Trotman had to say and he convinced him to join forces with his fledgling organization. Thus began a long association that came to fruition in 1949 when the evangelist invited Trotman to provide support for his Los Angeles evangelistic crusade. William Martin describes the Navigators at this time as a "live-wire group of young people who emphasised personal evangelism, trained counsellors to help inquirers clarify their decisions and direct them to Bible-believing churches."[35] Central to the success of Trotman and the Navigators were the publications that they developed to enable this kind of evangelistic work.

The Bridge to Life illustration is a classic resource associated with the Navigators. The illustration presents evangelical doctrine in a radically simplified form. Essentially, it consists of a few words and some bible verses arranged as a diagram.

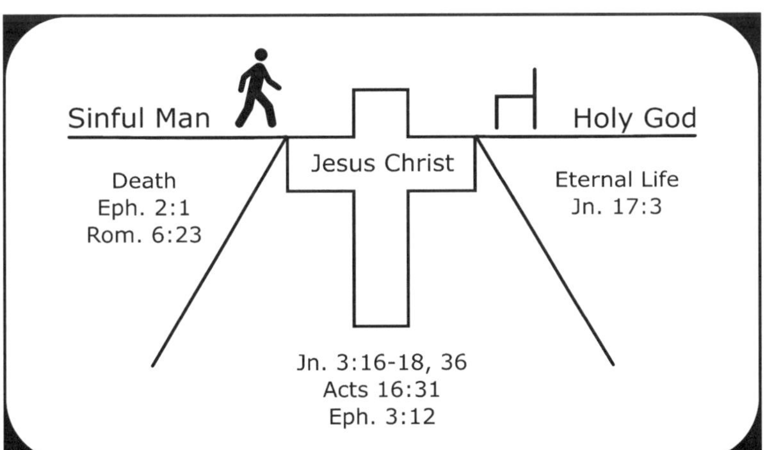

The intention of the illustration is that it should be used as a step-by-step guide to explaining the gospel in the context of personal evangelism. The tract

34 John Pollock, *Billy Graham* (London: Hodder and Stoughton, 1966), 73.

35 William Martin, *The Billy Graham Story* (London: Hutchinson, 1991), 113.

starts with a very simple cartoon of two sides of what appears to be a cliff. On the one side is sinful humanity and on the other is God who is holy. The divide between God and humanity has come about through sin. As the 2006 version of the tract puts it:

> This is especially bad news because there is no way for us to get across that gap on our own. We [humankind] have tried to find our way back to God and a perfect world on our own ever since then, and without any luck. We try to get there by being good people, or through religion, money, morality, philosophy, education, or any number of other ways, but eventually we find out that none of it works.[36]

The divide is overcome by the cross. Jesus, the explanation says, demonstrates the love of God by his death and thus wins for humanity peace with God and reconciliation. This is expressed in verse 3:6 from John's Gospel, "For God so loved the world that He gave His one and only son, that whoever believes in Him shall not perish but have eternal life." To come to faith and receive forgiveness and peace with God, the potential convert is instructed to pray a prayer that goes "something like" the following:

> Dear Jesus, I know that I am a sinner and that I need You to forgive me. I know that You died a painful death so that my sins could be washed clean. Thank you. I want to make You the Lord of my life, and I will trust and follow You. Everything I have is Yours now. In Your name, Lord. Amen."[37]

The connection to Graham ensured that the Bridge to Life illustration became widely-known and used in evangelical circles around the world. Speaking at his funeral in 1956, Graham said of Trotman, "I think Dawson Trotman touched more lives than any man I have ever known. We today are only representatives of thousands of many races and languages and cultures that have been touched by this great man."[38] Trotman's approach to evangelism typifies the approach of evangelicals of this period. He was an entrepreneur who was not constrained by denominational boundaries. In fact, Joel Carpenter makes the

36 The Navigators, "The Bridge to Life," http://www.navigators.org/Tools/Evangelism%20Resources/Tools/The%20Bridge%20to%20Life.

37 The Navigators, "The Bridge to Life."

38 Sanny, *The Pioneer*.

point that Trotman and other entrepreneurs were aided by the creeping secularization of American society because they could set up their operations in places like the military with much more freedom than recognized churches, which were restricted by the limitations that United States law places on religion in government-funded institutions.[39] As an entrepreneur, Trotman knew how to develop a culture of communication. He drew directly on the growing awareness of how businesses, and in particular advertising, worked in the United States, and applied these to his ministry context. His focus on bible memory and the production of tracts has significant roots in religious practice, but they were given a nuanced energy and direction through an understanding of what it means to "produce producers." This is a telling phrase, because it shows the extent to which evangelicals were willing to draw directly on the forms of communication that were being used in American consumer culture. What emerges is an evangelical form of persuasion that is motivated by the same kind of focus on numbers, market spread, and international significance as can be found in US business practices of the period. Here, however, the focus is on winning young lives for Christ. This is another deeply significant factor that characterizes the contemporary church: increasingly the new methods that were being generated to share the faith with young people found their inspiration in the commercial forms of popular culture, such as advertising or popular music. The same central dynamic elements are found in the ministry that gave birth to Campus Crusade and the hugely influential tract, the Four Spiritual Laws.

Bill Bright and the Four Spiritual Laws

The Four Spiritual Laws originated in the ministry of Bill Bright, who founded the US-based youth organization, Campus Crusade for Christ. Bright was deeply affected by a conviction that he should seek to obey the call of the Great Commission, "Go therefore and make disciples of all nations, baptizing them in the name of the Father and of the Son and of the Holy Spirit, and teaching them to obey everything that I have commanded you. And remember, I am with you always, to the end of the age" (Matt 28:19-20).[40] In 1951, following his theological training at Fuller Seminary, Bright set about trying to share the Christian faith with "every living person on earth." He chose as his

39 Carpenter, *Revive Us Again*, 239.

40 Bill Bright 1921-2003, http://billbright.ccci.org/public/.

starting point ministry among college students at UCLA. Success in California meant that the ministry quickly spread to other campuses and Bright soon found himself at the head of a growing international ministry.[41] Billy Graham paid tribute to Bright when he died in 2003 by saying, "He has carried a burden on his heart as few men that I've ever known. A burden for the evangelization of the world."[42] Bright exemplified the energy and creativity that gave rise to the contemporary Church. His ministry, which was eventually to become one of the largest, if not the largest, para-church organizations in the world,[43] was built on the drive that comes from a desire to connect with people and express the faith. Bright started to develop the Four Spiritual Laws as part of his preaching in the late 1950s.

The origins of the tract again serve to reveal the close links between the evangelical movement and popular culture. As Campus Crusade began to spread around the United States, Bright was influenced by Bob Ringer, who was a former salesman. In 1957 Ringer addressed Campus Crusade's annual staff conference, speaking on what he called "presentation fatigue." Ringer argued that effective salesmen, and by implication, effective ministers, learn how to "stick to one pitch."[44] What he meant by this is that the presentation of a product works best when the person selling it has learned a standardized way of selling. John Turner argues that Bright was significantly affected by what Ringer had to say and he subsequently wrote "God's Plan for Your Life," which was a twenty-minute presentation of the gospel message. Campus Crusade workers were then expected to memorize this as the way of introducing the faith, and use it as their entry point when they started to meet young people in universities and colleges. Workers were instructed to start conversations by asking, "Has it ever occurred to you that God has a wonderful plan for your life?" This would be the lead-in to the twenty-minute standardized presentation that Bright expected all of his workers to use in these kinds of encounters. This technique for evangelism had a significant weakness. The young workers found it hard to memorize such a long presentation. Bright then began to make the presentation much shorter and easier to memorize. In the end the gospel was condensed into four very short statements. Bright called these "the Four Spiritual Laws." He argued that, "as there are laws in the physical realm which are inviolate, so there are laws in the spiritual realm which are definite

41 Cru, "About Us," http://www.cru.org/about-us/what-we-do/milestones/index.htm.

42 Bill Bright, Campus Crusade for Christ International, http://billbright.ccci.org/public/.

43 Bill Bright, Campus Crusade for Christ International, http://billbright.ccci.org/public/.

44 John G. Turner, *Bill Bright and Campus Crusade for Christ: The Renewal of Evangelicalism in Postwar America* (Chapel Hill, NC: University of North Carolina Press, 2008), 99.

and true."[45] It wasn't until 1965 that the Four Spiritual Laws were made into a short booklet by a businessman from Toledo called Gus Yeager. Bright welcomed this resource and very soon ordered hundreds of copies to be printed. He incorporated the booklet and a new accompanying explanation of the tract into all of his organization's staff training.[46]

The Four Spiritual Laws provide an explanation of the Christian Gospel in four simple statements:

1. God loves you and offers a wonderful plan for your life.
2. Man is sinful and separated from God, therefore he cannot know and experience God's love and plan for his life.
3. Jesus Christ is God's only provision for man's sin. Through Him you can know and experience God's love and plan for your life.
4. We must individually receive Jesus Christ as Savior and Lord; then we can know and experience God's love and plan for our lives.

Bill Bright and Campus Crusade were born out of a cultural mix of business wisdom and ministerial practice that was familiar from the Navigators and also from Youth for Christ and other non-denominational evangelical youth ministries. The Four Spiritual Laws tract found its origin in the mix of entrepreneurialism and a form of ministry that focused on the most productive way to minister, and as a result was drawn from the methods associated with business and advertising. Turner makes the point that while Bright saw the Four Spiritual Laws as a distillation of theological truth, he was primarily interested in the booklet because it worked. As Turner puts it, Bright "verified it as an effective spiritual pitch by engaging in extensive market-testing."[47] In the next chapter these laws will be discussed in more detail, but it is important to make a few observations at this point. The first is that the Four Spiritual Laws are in effect very brief summaries of the more expansive and complex preaching of the evangelical Church. Of course it would be possible to trace the theology in the tract back to the preaching, and from there perhaps connect it to the various evangelical theological discussions of salvation and atonement theory. In terms of the four voices of theology developed by Clare Watkins and Helen Cameron, this would signify a journey from operant to espoused and on to formal academic theology. These voices are of course present, but they

45 Bright, quoted in Turner, *Bill Bright*, 100.

46 Turner, *Bill Bright*, 99-100.

47 Turner, *Bill Bright*, 101.

are not the most significant aspect of the tract that I want to focus on at this point. In fact, Bill Bright himself embodied a pragmatic suspicion of scholarly theological discussion of the gospel. At staff training events he was often critical of those who relied on their theological education. There was a simple choice, Bright felt, between complex and scholarly and the more straightforward and simple expressions of the faith. "The average person to whom you speak even on the college campus is not interested in the theology of Barth and Brunner, and Tillich and Niebuhr and the rest. You must be prepared to communicate in the most simple terms and I do not know a more simple way than The Four Spiritual Laws."[48] Bill Bright was motivated by a deep desire to share this gospel with young people. He sensed, however, that in order to communicate, he needed to adopt a form of expression that could be grasped quickly and easily. His solution was a formulaic theology based around short doctrinal statements.

The Four Spiritual Laws tract was intended to be used in a very similar way as the Bridge to Life Diagram adopted by the Navigators. In other words, both formed part of the process of personal evangelism. The Bridge diagram and the Four Spiritual Laws therefore have a dual impact. They were originally designed to communicate the faith to those who were outside the Church. They were given a very brief and easily understandable format in order to communicate. As a result, the tracts were taken up and used widely within the evangelical Church, but as they gained in acceptance, and as they were used, they had an effect on the espoused theology of evangelicals themselves. The way that this happened is very simple. The Gospel formula does not just communicate to non-believers; it becomes part of the belief system of believers as well. In these radically reduced forms, the statements of faith can be memorized. This in a sense is the intention. Within organizations like Campus Crusade and the Navigators, members were taught the basic outline of the gospel in order that they could share it with young people. Through this process of learning and then telling the gospel, these very brief doctrinal formulas became the absolutized and unchanging gospel of evangelicalism. The Bridge to Life illustration and the Four Spiritual Laws drew on the presentation of the gospel typified by Stott and Graham, but they simplified the message so that it could be more effectively communicated to young people. These simplified expressions of evangelical truth inevitably ironed out some of the nuances and complexities. They avoided any real discussion of what it means to sin or how faith relates to grace, or indeed the variety of ways that the New Testament and evangelical theology have presented the cross as atonement. These theological and

48 Bright quoted in Turner, *Bill Bright*, 102-3.

doctrinal issues have been part of a rich and ongoing theological conversation within evangelicalism ever since the Reformation. It is telling that even with two figures that had as much in common theologically as John Stott and Billy Graham, there were subtle differences of emphasis, illustration and application. Yet in the drive to express the faith and connect to young people, the nuances and complexities of theological expression were flattened out. The pursuit of effective communication combined with the adoption of methods of persuasion from advertising, led to the gospel being expressed in a particular form. It is this form that enables evangelicals to confidently assert that the gospel that they preach has not changed, whereas simultaneously, and in so many areas of their practice and lived faith, there is in fact enormous change, and what might be seen as accommodation to contemporary culture.

Seeing Christ and Cultural Transmission

This chapter has charted the development of the gospel in evangelical culture. It is not an account of the more academic debates among theologians. These discussions continue to play a part in the life of the Church and they have particularly come to the fore when controversies surrounding prominent evangelical figures such as Rob Bell, or in the United Kingdom, Steve Chalke, have flashed into the headlines. These more theological voices have for the most part not been as significant in the ongoing life of the Church as might be assumed. This chapter also set out how the flow of expression within evangelicalism has generated the cultural form of the Church. This form is not defined by a theoretical or ideal description of what it means to believe. There is no all-encompassing definition that states what contemporary churches consider belief to be. What I am suggesting instead is that believing is made up of the actions of individuals and communities who set out to express faith, and as they do so they make Church through their entrepreneurial creativity. This culture is fluid and complex in nature, shifting and moving over time. In this chapter, the cultural activity of the Church was traced through a range of different sources: historical, biographical and material. This range of sources has focused attention on the varied cultural communications and practices of the Church and the purpose of this discourse analysis was to trace patterns in expression.

An understanding of the gospel as a series of short doctrinal expressions has not come through the work of academics or theologians. It has emerged from the practice of the Church and for a large part it has been non-ordained entrepreneurs who have brought this about. Motivated by a desire to share the faith and see people come to faith, evangelicals, through their practice, have forged a way of talking about faith that has become highly stylized and simplified. Theology in this sense does not work in the way a kind of trickle down theory might suggest, whereby the most important thoughts are set out by theologians and then conveyed by the Church to the world. What is seen here is that in communicating faith, Christians actually shape the gospel. Ironically, this shaping has reinforced a conviction that the gospel that is being shared is unchanging, but this is not entirely correct, because the processes involved in expressing and connecting introduce a cultural dynamic.

The kind of cultural analysis that has been set out in this chapter is intended to make these developments more evident. What is thus made plain also needs to be set in the framework of discerning the body of Christ in the practices of the Church. This perspective values the passion and commitment of entrepreneurs and sees in their agency and creativity the work of the Spirit. So many Christians point to figures such as Billy Graham or John Stott or the ministry of Campus Crusade or Youth for Christ as the source for their own believing. There are thousands, perhaps millions of Christians in churches today because of these initiatives. It is not an exaggeration to say that the Church of today was built on the foundations that were laid at the start of the twentieth century by these important figures. This is not to reduce the work of Christ to a crude notion of success equals numbers or market share, although, as we have seen, this kind of thinking actually played a highly significant role in the creative thinking of evangelical Christians. Discerning Christ in these motivations and the effects that they brought about is not straightforward. The claim that the Church has sold out to consumerism is reinforced by the realization it was in fact born out of the methods and cultural logic of consumerism. There is nothing new in this observation, as Laurence Moore's work on the market and American religion has made clear.

Moore argues that the Church adopted the tools of a consumer culture and in effect made religion into something of a commodity. So while some attempted to maintain religion as high culture, "America's boom market in religion operated most effectively at the popular end of the market in cultural commodities."[49] He is talking in the first instance about religious publishing, including the production of bibles, and of course religious tracts, but also the development of non-profit organizations and the whole world of charitable causes and mission concerns. So before dismissing these as some kind of selling out, it is important to discern the ways in which the cultural activities of

49 Laurence Moore, *Selling God: American Religion in the Marketplace of Culture* (Oxford: Oxford University Press, 1994), 7.

entrepreneurs developed a vibrant and vital form of Church. At the same time it also has to be acknowledged that these cultural forms were in fact "selling." Nathan Hatch identifies similar traits in the origins of evangelical religion in the United Sates. Hatch concludes forms of communication that make use of ways of operating drawn from the media and advertising lead to a "democratization" of American Christianity.[50]

Discerning the body in these cultural forms requires the ability to accept the muddied and compromised nature of cultural transmission. Just as it is inadequate simply to accept market share and the bottom line as evidence of the work of the Spirit, it is equally mistaken to conclude that the widespread adoption of consumer culture and the "commodification" of religion is self evidently less than Christian. As we have shown in this chapter, cultural forms require close attention if we are to see what is happening. Patterns of communication, in and of themselves, do not tell the whole story. The cultural products of the Church do not reveal the whole truth. Tracts like the Bridge to Life diagram and the Four Spiritual Laws are good examples of this. At a purely theological level, whatever their creators might think, the tracts lack theological nuance and sophistication. It is thus possible to develop a line of argument that says that these forms of gospel communication are insufficient or academically lacking in terms of their understanding of theology and the bible. This approach might miss the point, however. This is not to say that the academic assessment of the gospel message that is expressed in the tracts is in any way mistaken. The point is that it seems that the Holy Spirit appears to have been quite content to use what are limited and perhaps flawed forms of communication to bring people to faith and into the Church. In other words, it becomes almost axiomatic that the actions of individuals and communities have been and will be both flawed and yet also capable of being inspired. As a result, the processes of communication that are adopted build the body of Christ, while simultaneously giving birth to unintended and unforeseen consequences that cause that body problems. The simplification of the gospel enabled those working with young people and others to share the faith. The unintended consequence, however, was that this focus on effective communication left the Church down the road with few theological resources to deal with the evident complexities of life. The version of the evangelical gospel seen in the tracts worked as a way to lead people to faith, but it has slowly become less important in the way that that faith is lived out. It is at this point that the

---

50 See Nathan Hatch, *The Democratization of American Christianity* (New Haven, CT: Yale University Press, 1989).

story of youth ministry and the development of new forms of Church and ways of worship associated with the Jesus Movement in America is so significant.

The motivation to share the faith and to find new ways of communicating the faith generated the energy that led to the development of new forms of ministry among young people, and also led to new vibrant churches around the world. This is the same energy and motivation that led to a distinctive understanding of the gospel. The desire to communicate the faith in accessible ways that connect to people's lives set the Church off on a parallel journey. The desire was to be "effective" in sharing faith. This drive to connect and express has brought unintended consequences, however. Chief among these has been a transformation in the way that the Gospel is understood and the way that it functions in the life of the community. The radical abbreviation of the gospel has enabled evangelism, but it has so reduced the "truth" of the gospel that it has become fixed, and the deep mystery of Jesus, who is the Way, the Truth and the Life, has seemingly been summed up in a diagram or a few lines of text. The confidence that believers find in Jesus Christ has become fixed in these forms of expression, such that they merge as one the experience and form of the gospel that gives rise to it. It is this merging that allows the assertion that the gospel is unchanging. The fact the believers come to faith through this gospel gives an enduring and robust support to the "truth" of the particular form that the gospel has taken in everyday expression. At the same time, in the operant theology of the very same churches, a much more dynamic theology is starting to develop. This theology has flourished alongside the more formal and abbreviated theological expression of the evangelical gospel. This operant theology embraces the "self" and the personal as a place of deep significance in the life of the Church. Interestingly, the seeds of the turn to the self are also contained in tracts such as the Four Spiritual Laws. The next chapter explores this turn to the self in evangelical operant theology in more detail, and this exploration involves further analysis of Bill Bright's Four Spiritual Laws.

CHAPTER 6

Personal Faith

The previous chapter set out how the communication of the gospel has led to doctrine taking on a particular form in the contemporary Church. This chapter continues the exploration by paying attention to how the communication of faith has taken a much more personal and subjective form. This shift towards a personal gospel has also come through the desire to connect with the cultural context of young people. This is the manner in which people have experienced the presence of Christ in their lives, but this vivid and dynamic form of experiencing the gospel has in turn shaped the contemporary Church in ways that are problematic.

A Personal Relationship with Jesus Christ

Nicky Gumbel, the leader of the Alpha Course, is being interviewed on national television. It is the run up to Christmas and this is the religious slot on a light and fast-moving early evening chat show. The interviewer starts by asking about declining numbers in churches. Gumbel responds by saying that he actually sees a "growing spiritual hunger among young people" and explains that in his church when they run the Alpha Course they get more than a thousand per session. "So why do people come?" asks the interviewer. Gumbel explains that people have an experience of God that changes their lives and they ask others to come and see. "People realise it's not actually about rules and religion, it's about a relationship with God that's the heart of it." He goes on to share how he had an encounter with Jesus that changed his life. As he read the New Testament, he says, "it was as if Jesus came alive and you actually could know this person."[1]

Nicky Gumbel is an accomplished apologist. His presentation of the faith is both accessible and profound. The analysis of his preaching found in the video clip from the Alpha Course discussed in the previous chapter shows Gumbel presenting the more formal framework of the evangelical gospel, yet in this quick-fire interaction he has to react immediately. This is live television after all. There is not much time for theological consideration. He just has to say what he thinks will make an impact. He is trying to connect with the viewers

1 http://www.youtube.com/watch?v=TfgwkN_-Jug.

 | DOI 10.1163/9789004347359_008

and express the faith in a way that he thinks they will understand. In this context Gumbel expresses the theology that is most frequently in operation in the contemporary evangelical Church. The particular terminology and turns of phrase that he uses reveal this theology. Jesus, he says, is someone you can "know." The experience of Jesus changes lives. We have encounters with Jesus and the heart of the Christian faith is a relationship with God. In his interview on the television, Gumbel tries to put some distance between what he is talking about and a religion that is based on rules, but interestingly he also omits to mention some of the things that might ordinarily be regarded as the gospel in evangelical churches. For instance, he doesn't talk about sin or the need for Jesus to die on the cross; he doesn't talk about the love of God, or grace; or about repentance and the need for faith. The interview takes place at Christmas time, but Gumbel does not even say anything about the incarnation. What he does instead is concentrate on presenting the Christian faith as an experience of encounter. Faith is a personal relationship with Jesus Christ.

This examination of a brief interview is not meant as a critique of Nicky Gumbel—far from it. In fact in similar situations I have said roughly the same sort of thing. The point is that, in his preaching and speaking, there is evidence of a complex and layered interaction between a more personal and subjective form of theology, and a more objective and doctrinally propositional theology. These two co-exist and they have an interconnected relationship in the expression and lived believing of the contemporary Church. In his various writings, Gumbel talks at some length about the gospel. In the materials linked to the Alpha Course, for instance, he sets out an evangelical understanding of salvation in doctrinal terms. So he is not only aware, but he is actually very comfortable with more objective kinds of evangelical theology. The point here is that in this interview we have a glimpse of what might be seen as his operant theology. It is important not to make too much of an isolated interview, but the theme of a personal relationship with Christ is remarkably common. It is, in fact, the dominant expression of the contemporary Church, not just among evangelicals but also more generally.

Subjectivization—the Turn to the Self

In the United States, the National Study of Youth and Religion that took place in 2002-2003 was based on over 3,000 telephone interviews and around 300 more detailed follow-up interviews.[2] The survey revealed some quite startling

2 Christian Smith with Melinda Lunquist Denton, *Soul Searching: The Religious and Spiritual Lives of American Teenagers* (Oxford: Oxford University Press, 2005), 292-307.

facts about young people and religion. According to one of the leading academics in the area of youth ministry in the United States, the survey shows that churches are very effective in their communication. Far from being out of touch, churches have actually found some very good ways of communicating with people. Unfortunately, what they are communicating is a version of the faith that can be seen as flawed and problematic. Christian Smith and Melinda Denton label this version of the faith "Moralistic Therapeutic Deism." Kenda Creasey Dean summarizes this expression of belief in five simple statements:

1. A God exists who created and orders the world and watches over life.
2. God wants people to be good, nice, and fair to each other, as taught in the bible and by most world religions.
3. The central goal in life is to be happy and to feel good about oneself.
4. God is not involved in my life except when I need God to resolve a problem.
5. Good people go to heaven when they die.[3]

What are described here are not the formal theological commitments of denominations, or the doctrinal formulas authorised and accepted by ministers and churches. The survey is based on the personal convictions of young believers. It is important to note that these individual beliefs co-exist with the more formal teaching of religious communities. This co-existence is part of the complex theological voices that exist in churches. However, Smith and Denton see "Moral Therapeutic Deism" as a form of belief that is universal across American religious traditions. "Such a de facto creed is particularly evident among mainline Protestant and Catholic youth, but it is also visible among black and conservative Protestants, Jewish teens, other religious types of teenagers, and even many non-religious teenagers in the United States."[4] This insight shows that there are more fluid forms of belief that appear to move between and within more formal traditions. Despite the different kinds of preaching and liturgies of churches and other religious groups, at a personal level believing appears to exist in what seems to be a common form. The one exception to this would be more conservative evangelical Christians, but even in this case there are significant features that echo the more general trends towards the personal. The themes that Smith and Denton have identified are therefore part of a much larger and more general shift towards the "self" in society and in religion. Sociologists Paul Heelas and Linda Woodhead refer to this as the

---

3 Kenda Creasy Dean, *Almost Christian: What the Faith of Our Teenagers is Telling the American Church* (Oxford: Oxford University Press, 2010), 14.

4 Smith with Lunquist Denton, *Soul Searching*, 163.

subjectivization thesis. The subjectivization thesis argues that there has been a "spiritual revolution" that takes the form of a reorientation towards the personal in religious life.

The contemporary religious environment, says Heelas, is characterized by a shift in religious sensibility towards "expressive individualism." The focus on the individual, he argues, leads to a collapse in the way that religious traditions are formed as distinctive and "different" forms of belief.[5] What this means is that more doctrinally-orientated religious traditions become subtly altered by the inclusion of perspectives that prioritize the individual and the sense of self.[6] This re-orientation around the personal is the subjective turn.[7] The turn is a move away from life, "lived in terms of external or objective roles, duties and obligations, and a turn towards life lived by reference to one's own subjective experiences (relational as well as individualistic)."[8] So the subjective turn is a shift from "life-as" to "subjective-life."

"Life as" is characterized by a sense of duty to perform a role as a parent, wife, leader, disciple etc, whereas "subjective-life" is framed around what Heelas and Woodhead describe as life "lived in deep connection with the unique experiences of my self-in-relation."[9] These changes in religious traditions come about with little reference to formal notions of belief or doctrine. The orientation to the self is simply added into the theological mix in a manner that is "de-regulated and un-policed."[10] Crucially, Woodhead points out that the self is particularly generated out of a more market-orientated entrepreneurial form of religion. Just as organized and more formal kinds of religion have been in decline, the subjectivized personal faith advocated by evangelical churches has increased in significance. "The new entrants to the spiritual marketplace," says Woodhead, "are more focused on supporting individuals in their everyday lives, fostering new kinds of identity and lifestyle, and linking the like-minded and like-hearted to one another in a vast plurality of different forms of religious alliance."[11] Central to these developments has been the growth in festivals, networks and events that generate and spread this more personalized form of believing.

---

5 Heelas, *The New Age Movement* (Oxford: Blackwell, 1996), 3.

6 Heelas, *The New Age*, 3.

7 Heelas and Woodhead, *The Spiritual Revolution*, 2.

8 Heelas and Woodhead, *The Spiritual Revolution*, 2.

9 Heelas and Woodhead, *The Spiritual Revolution*, 3.

10 Heelas, *The New Age Movement*, 4.

11 Linda Woodhead, "Introduction," in Linda Woodhead and Rebecca Catto, eds., *Religion and Change in Modern Britain* (London: Routledge, 2012), 27.

Selfation

The Dutch sociologist, Johan Roeland, has researched the way that evangelical groups have adopted forms of believing that embody the turn to the self. Building on the work of Woodhead and Heelas, he has coined the term "selfation." Selfation, he says, is a mix of salvation and self, and it refers to the way that the subjective has gained significance over more objective doctrine in the evangelical Church. This observation is in many ways a reversal or finesse on the idea of secularization. In the subjectivization thesis it is acknowledged that alongside decline (secularization) there are forms of more personalised religion that are starting to flourish.[12] Subjectivization refers to the modern idea that meaning, including religious meaning, is "relative to the individual." Religion therefore becomes more concerned with "individual experience, feelings and emotions."[13] In his research, Roeland finds aspects of subjectivization in the evangelical Church, but interestingly, he also sees a strong commitment to what he calls "religious realism." In other words, he does not go the whole way with Heelas and Woodhead on the theory that religion has been somehow taken over by the turn to self. What Roeland observes is a complex mixture of objective forms of gospel expression and belief and highly personal ways of orientating the individual to these formal doctrinal ways of speaking. This is the mix that gives rise to the term selfation.

Roeland's work is based on an extended ethnographic study of two churches that have active evangelical youth ministry. He finds much that might support Smith and Denton's notion of "Moralistic Therapeutic Deism." "Evangelicalism," he says, "not only embraces a subjectivist understanding of the good life, which is defined in terms of wellbeing, but it also provides the building blocks and the therapeutic means with which to achieve this. As a result, the evangelical moral life may be represented as turning the notion of subjecting oneself to the will of God around, with elements of today's culture of subjectivism being assimilated into this will."[14] He illustrates the turn to self through a description of an experience of worship with young people. The event takes place on a Saturday evening in 2006 in a renovated barn that belongs to the Netherlands Reformed Church in the town of Houten. The room is set up informally with tables and chairs rather like a café. The stage is lit up

12 Johan Roeland, *Selfation: Dutch Evangelical Youth Between Subjectivization and Subjection* (Amsterdam: Pallas Publications, 2009), 45.

13 Roeland, *Selfation*, 57.

14 Roeland, *Selfation*, 209.

with spotlights. Roeland says that the venue, with its dimmed lights, stage and background music, looks a lot like a pop or a party venue. The meeting starts with a young girl coming to the microphone and saying, "Please be yourself and do whatever you want."[15] A rock band starts to play charismatic worship songs. "One way, Jesus. You're the only one that I could live for. You are always, always there. Every how and everywhere. Your grace abounds so deeply within me."[16] Some of the young people begin to raise their hands and others begin to dance. After a little while a young man gets up and starts to give a message. It is based on the Old Testament Tabernacle. God is a camper because he lives in a tent, he explains, and he asks those gathered to start to explore for themselves this place of worship. Everyone is searching for God, but it is no good trying to jump up and look over the wall of the tent. In Jesus, the veil of the temple has been torn apart and now we can meet God. The speaker invites those gathered to come into the holy place to, "clamber onto God's lap" because God just wants to be with the people God loves.[17] After the sermon the band starts to play, but this time more quietly. "This is my desire, to honour you. Lord with all my heart I worship you." The lyrics go on to talk about giving every breath, giving heart and soul to God. The service ends with a time of ministry where young people pray for each other. At one point Roeland observes two girls praying for another girl. At the girl's request they pray and as they do so they place their hands on her shoulder. With her eyes shut the girl starts to tremble and then she begins to cry.[18]

The worship event gives a vivid picture of the lived expression in an everyday youth event. What Roeland's description highlights, however, is the way that through songs, preaching and spiritual practices such as prayer, charismatic Christians have developed a highly personal and subjectivized form of believing. At the same time, he notices the extent to which this conservative community retains significant elements of their Church tradition. There is a sermon, for instance, with biblical exposition. The tone of the service, he observes, combines a place where you can be yourself and do what you want with a real sense that there is a God and there are expected ways to respond to that God. Charismatic Christianity does not entirely follow the "turn to the self" that Heelas and Woodhead describe, then. Instead there is a kind of accommodation of a conservative Christian tradition to aspects of subjectivization. As he puts it at the conclusion of his study: "On the one hand, the self

15 Roeland, *Selfation*, 136.
16 Roeland, *Selfation*, 136-137.
17 Roeland, *Selfation*, 137.
18 Roeland, *Selfation*, 138.

is embedded in a number of arrangements that are defined by particular expectations and restrictions about how and what one believes, and how one lives, acts, expresses and displays one self. On the other, along with some of its moral notions of well-being and pleasure, the moral-ontological understanding of the self in today's culture of subjectivism… resonates in evangelicalism as well."[19]

Roeland's work highlights the complex relationship that exists between espoused and operant theology in the evangelical Church. It is not the case, for instance, that theology has been abandoned, or that there has been some kind of selling out to individualism. What is taking place is more nuanced and layered. Formal and more objective doctrinal theological expression appears to not only co-exist with more personalised belief, but seems to create and sustain an environment where subjective forms of belief can flourish. This observation is more complex again than Woodhead and Heelas seem to imply. As Roeland's work suggests, what is presented by the leaders within the Church as objective propositions framed in theologically realistic terms, is appropriated by the young people in very personalized ways. The same can be seen in Gumbel's presentation of the gospel, where objective doctrinal forms of expression are evident as well as the more personal expression of what it means to be a Christian. The traditional understanding of these two, the personal and the doctrinal, is that they have an intimate relationship with each other. What Roeland's research suggests, however, is that, in practice, the more doctrinal expression of belief is sustained by those who preach and teach, while ordinary believers appear to use this presentation of the faith as an arena for generating more subjective forms of personal faith. It is a fluid relationship between representation and the construction of personal identity that forms the basis for the growing disconnection between the gospel and the operant theology of the contemporary Church.

Four Spiritual Laws and the Shift to the Personal

The turn to the self has been embraced in evangelical preaching for quite some time. The desire to connect and express the doctrinal and theological understanding of the gospel has frequently been presented in very personalized terms. This can be illustrated by looking again at the Four Spiritual Laws. The small tract, as we have seen, is an example of the way that doctrinal forms

19 Roeland, *Selfation*, 209.

have become abbreviated and hence fixed in a stylized form. Alongside this process there is another dynamic at play. The brief objective theological elements of the gospel are articulated in the lives of young people and adults by a subjective orientation. Here the desire to connect to the contemporary cultural context has meant that theological expression has adopted the personal as a means to convey the significance of the faith. In the Four Spiritual Laws, the relationship between objective theological doctrine and personal and subjective orientation is very clear. Each of the Laws starts with a doctrinal statement, but it then adds the phrase "plan for our life" or "plan for our lives." This gives what are rather abstract theological statements a much more personal location.

1. God loves you and offers a wonderful plan for your life.
2. Man is sinful and separated from God, therefore he cannot know and experience God's love and plan for his life.
3. Jesus Christ is God's only provision for man's sin. Through Him you can know and experience God's love and plan for your life.
4. We must individually receive Jesus Christ as Savior and Lord; then we can know and experience God's love and plan for our lives.[20]

The idea of a plan for life articulates the gospel into personal narratives. It is intimate and quite engaging. God's love is made personal because it is located in the plan that God has for each person's life. Sin likewise is made more real because it hinders the plan that God has for life and so on. Each Spiritual Law therefore has two parts. The first part is what might be termed an objective theological statement, and the second part of the statement is more personal and subjective in tone. In the original booklet, the four laws are supported by a small number of biblical quotations and in the final section the reader is invited to pray a prayer of commitment. The prayer repeats in large part the theological journey that is contained in the four laws. In effect it is an acknowledgement of the truth of these laws, but in the prayer these are again given a personal orientation.

> Lord Jesus, I need You. Thank You for dying on the cross for my sins. I open the door of my life and receive You as my Savior and Lord. Thank You for forgiving my sins and giving me eternal life. Take control of the throne of my life. Make me the kind of person You want me to be.[21]

20 Cru, "Four Spiritual Laws," http://www.campuscrusade.com/fourlawseng.htm.

21 Cru, "Four Spiritual Laws" http://www.campuscrusade.com/fourlawseng.htm.

The prayer of commitment builds on the fourth spiritual law. Jesus Christ must be received individually. The door of each person's life needs to be opened and it is only then that they can experience God's love and the plan that God has for their lives.

In a later booklet entitled, "Would you like to know God personally?" The founder of Campus Crusade, Bill Bright, reworked the Four Spiritual Laws around the theme of relationship. He introduced the evangelistic booklet with a message to the reader:

> Dear Friend,
> Yes, you can know God personally, as presumptuous as that might sound. God is so eager to establish a personal, loving relationship with you that He has already made all the arrangements. He is patiently and lovingly waiting for you to respond to His invitation. You can receive forgiveness of your sins and assurance of eternal life through faith in His only Son, the Lord Jesus Christ. The major barrier that prevents us from knowing God personally is ignorance of who God is and what He has done for us. Read and discover for yourself the joyful reality of knowing God personally.[22]

In this version of the Four Spiritual Laws, the notion of "a plan for our lives" has been reframed in even more personal and intimate terms. The stress on loving relationship as the heart of the Christian experience reflects the cultural pre-occupations of the 1960s. In adopting this language, Bright is primarily motivated by a desire to connect effectively and to express the gospel. The orientation towards the personal achieves this goal and it resonates with people because it articulates significant trends in society. This extract from "Would you like to know God personally?" demonstrates how formal doctrinal elements such as the forgiveness of sins and assurance of salvation become linked with the more contemporary themes of loving intimate relationship. This is not to suggest that the idea of a relationship with God is not present in the Christian tradition. The point is that these theological perspectives are given a context and a correspondence in the present day by the adoption of notions of intimate loving relationship. They are in a sense made meaningful by making this connection into the ordinary understanding of the self and of intimacy that was in the cultural flow of the 1960s and that continues into the present day.

22 Bill Bright, *Would You Like to Know God personally?* 1965 (2007).

Expression and connection therefore introduce two quite different theological dynamics into the evangelical presentation of the gospel. On the one hand, the formal doctrine associated with the gospel becomes abbreviated and fixed. Alongside this, the shortened gospel becomes articulated, and a more subjective and personal kind of theology starts to develop. This personal theology makes the espoused operative in the lives of young Christians and it becomes the dominant framework for self understanding and this, as we will see in the next chapter, is particularly the case for corporate worship. In tracts such as the Four Spiritual Laws, there is a necessary relationship between the objective doctrinal proposition and the subjective reception of the evangelical gospel. The one leads to the other. In the Alpha Course and in Nicky Gumbel's regular writing and teaching, this relationship between doctrine and experience is continually affirmed. The two co-exist, but this co-existence is, I would argue, unequal at the level of practice. Thus while leaders such as Gumbel continue to make the connections explicit, as Roeland has shown, believers appear to accommodate the objective doctrinal elements into a more subjective lived theology. The espoused doctrinal theology does not disappear. It just appears to be something of a subplot or a deep background for everyday believing. So while in the contemporary Church the objective understanding of the gospel has not been abandoned and is regularly taught, it has started to become inoperative. It functions not so much as the source for faith, but as a kind of theoretical underpinning for believing. In the everyday lived expression of evangelical Christians, the personal and the relational has taken the place of the doctrinal, or we could say it has become the new doctrinal, or at least it is active as the conviction out of which people live their faith. The subjective is the operant theology of the community.

Themes and Testimonies

In the summer of 2009, Paul Fiddes and I conducted a small-scale research project into worship at a local church.[23] The study revolved around a single act of worship on Pentecost Sunday. During the service a small group of six students and young people were baptised. Actually three were not baptised technically because they had been christened as children, and so it was ex-

23 Pete Ward and Paul Fiddes, "Affirming Faith at a Service of Baptism in St Aldate's Church, Oxford," in *Explorations in Ecclesiology and Ethnography*, ed. Christian Scharen (Grand Rapids, MI: Eerdmans 2012).

plained in the service that those who had been baptised as children were renewing their baptismal vows and this would be symbolised by immersion in water. At the relevant point in the service each of the candidates came up to the podium and gave a short account of their faith. Then they went to the baptistery where they were immersed while their friends and family came around them and prayed with them. As this ministry was happening, the next candidate took to the stage and gave their testimony.[24]

A number of key themes characterize the testimonies, and together they offer an insight into the operant theology that this group shared. Nearly all of the candidates were actually from Christian families. In fact, only one appeared to have come to faith from a non-church background. Most of the students spoke very warmly about growing up in believing families. They were deeply grateful for the Christian ethos that they found in their families. Several of them used the word "privilege" about their Christian upbringing. The idea of faith as "privilege" is very interesting and it connects with another very strong theme in the testimonies. Three of the candidates spoke very enthusiastically about the church community and how Christian friends from the church had influenced their journey of faith. They also spoke about the Alpha Course and a Christian Union mission, but the impact that these evangelistic events had was set in the context of friendships and relationships. It was the warmth and fellowship of other Christians and the wider Church community that helped them come to faith. One of the characteristics that we observed at this church was the high value that was placed on a warm welcome and fostering the Church as a sociable environment.[25] This approach to making Church a welcoming community was reflected in the testimonies.

As might be expected in a testimony before a baptism, the candidates all spoke about faith as a change in their life or a conversion experience. Nearly all of them framed this idea as leaving their "old lives" and starting a new journey with God. They spoke about the Christian life as "trust in God." Three of the candidates described this new life of trusting in God in terms of God "having a plan for their lives." They shared their sense that this plan meant that they were setting out on an exciting journey of being a Christian. Several of them stressed God's faithfulness as a being a deep reassurance for their Christian life. God, they affirmed, was a faithful God, who would be with them as they took risks and "went for it as Christians." Above all, the candidates communicated a sense of excitement about a life lived with God, and also the

24 Ward and Fiddes, "Affirming Faith," 54.

25 Ward and Fiddes, "Affirming Faith," 67.

challenges and in some cases the sacrifices that this might bring. The emphasis throughout these testimonies was thus on the very personal nature of the Christian faith. Following Christ was generally set in the narrative of their own individual life journeys. What is most interesting is that with one exception, none of the students made any particular reference to any kind of objective theological expression of the gospel. The cross of Christ was hardly mentioned and there were no references to sin, or repentance, or even salvation in formal theological terms. Instead, these categories were recast in terms of the narrative of a personal relationship and the plan that God had for their lives. What appeared to be happening with these evangelical testimonies was that the operant theology of the self in relation to God had become the primary means for self-understanding and for communicating the Christian faith to others.

The testimonies at this Church were in the context of an Anglican worship service. As part of the service there were elements of Anglican liturgy and extended times of sung worship. There was also a quite lengthy sermon.[26] In the sermon in particular there was continual reference to the evangelical understanding of the gospel. The preacher that day was the rector of the church and the sermon formed part of an ongoing series preaching through the book of Philippians. The passage for the day was Philippians 2:1-13. In the passage, the Philippians are offered Christ as the supreme example of a sacrificial life of Christian service. "Let the same mind be in you that was in Christ Jesus, who, though he was in the form of God, did not regard equality with God as something to be exploited, but emptied himself, taking the form of a slave, being born in human likeness. And being found in human form, he humbled himself and became obedient to the point of death—even death on a cross" (Phil 2:5-8). Part of the intention behind the Pentecost service was that it would be evangelistic. Friends and family of those who were being baptized were invited along with others who might be on the fringes of the church. The testimonies of the students were therefore intended to be a witness, not simply of their faith, but also a form of outreach to the guests who had been brought along to the church that evening. With this general aim, the sermon took the form of an apologetic for Christ and an explanation of the good news of the gospel.

The first part of the sermon focused on Jesus Christ. The preacher drew on a number of different figures in history and philosophy and spoke about how Christ was both attractive and deeply significant. Above all, the challenge was put to the congregation in general to embrace the Christian faith as a journey of sacrificial and costly service in the wider society and world. The basis for

26 Ward and Fiddes, "Affirming Faith," 52-56.

this kind of discipleship, it was explained, was to be found in the cross of Jesus Christ. The heart of the sermon came in an explanation of the cross as the sacrifice for sin and the salvation of humanity. In his exposition of the cross, the rector made use of the illustration that we have already discussed in the previous chapter, where the bible is passed from one hand onto the other hand symbolising the transferring of the sin of humanity that is passed onto Christ on the cross. So in the sermon the unchanging evangelical gospel is preached; in fact it is so unchanged that the exact same illustration used by preachers for more than a hundred years gives a graphic form to the message.

The presence of the evangelical gospel in the service is significant. It shows that while the students may not have felt the need to speak directly of an objective doctrinally-based faith, and instead framed their testimonies in more personalized terms, this expression has not entirely supplanted more objective theological expression. The espoused and the operant co-exist in the lived. This is very akin to what Roeland's research has highlighted. The evangelical Church appears to consist of a complex mixture of different theological voices. The more objective and theological has not given way to the subjective in the way that Heelas and Woodhead appear to want to claim. Instead it has shifted from the operative to the espoused, or perhaps more accurately, the objective continues to function as a root to conversion, but it may not operate as a lived theology of the everyday. It continues to be preached when conversion is the main focus, but as such it seems to simply provide the context or the pretext for a more personalized form of believing. Thus the young Christians have come to faith in a context where this message is preached and yet they appear to have selectively internalized and made operant in their lives the more individualized forms of expression. These are the aspects of the faith that "work" on a day-to-day basis in their lives.

The group was made up of intelligent and articulate students, and if they were questioned it seems highly likely that they would be able to repeat the espoused theology of the evangelical gospel. What they are not doing, at least as far as can be ascertained from these testimonies, is choosing to make a direct connection between these theological statements and their everyday lives. There is a reason for this. They don't need to, because the God they have experienced is so vivid and engaging. They are taken up in God's life and energy and as long as the gospel is preserved in some form as collective memory there are no real problems. Issues begin to arise when the lived faith of believers no longer sustains or nurtures them. When this happens the disconnection between formal doctrine and the operant theology of the personal can become more problematic and even less plausible. What happens, for instance, when the God with whom you have a personal relationship appears to go silent, or when the plan that God has for your life appears to involve tragedy and suffering? Or even, what happens when the welcoming family of the Church is experienced as abusive? In these circumstances the disconnection between a simplified gospel and the personalized fast-moving operant faith of evangelicalism becomes a significant issue. Yet simply pointing out that there is a problem is not enough. Discerning the body here requires close attention to the way that theology and believing are present in the lived expression of the Church. It is only by paying close attention to the multi-layered nature of believing that a constructive theology can be developed.

Making Sense of the Personal in Believing

Evangelical believing is complex and nuanced. The turn to the self can be traced in the expression of the Church where it functions as a primary operant theology. As such it has not replaced the more traditional objective theology. Instead, the gospel has become a more specific and formulaic pattern of theological propositions. The propositions in this shortened form have become fixed. As such, they operate as an assurance of faithfulness and of a rootedness in tradition. At the same time, the more personalized operant theology has become highly adaptable and open to frequent re-expression and new articulations. These developments have come about as the Church and its leaders have sought to communicate the faith, and in particular, as they have tried to make a connection to the perceived cultural world of young people.

There is a symbiotic relationship that exists between the espoused theology of the evangelical gospel and the turn to the self in operant theology. Talk of a personal relationship with God, or an encounter with God, arises out of, and has its supporting theological framework within particular doctrinal perspectives. Similarly, talking about the Christian life as a part of God's plan or as a journey with God also rests on doctrinal connections. The Four Spiritual Laws make this connection very explicit, as do other more structured evangelistic programmes such as the Alpha Course. Roeland's research also indicates that it is the mix of objective and subjective that characterizes the evangelical and charismatic form of religious expression. At the same time there are hints this connection might have a tendency to come adrift. The personal is perhaps slowly losing a connection to the doctrinal. This has parallels with "Moral Therapeutic Deism" as described by Kenda Creasy Dean, who suggests that a counterfeit faith is being spread by the churches, so much so that the more subjectivized forms of believing become the dominant form of operant theology. This tendency can be seen, for instance, in the testimonies of the young people who were being baptized in the church that Paul Fiddes and I studied. Their explanation of the faith seems to suggest that while they may not disagree or even challenge the kind of message presented by the rector in the sermon, what they have appropriated into their lives and made operational is the more subjectivized form of the faith.

The two sides of the subjective and the objective that are held together in the Four Spiritual Laws have become more distant and even perhaps separated at the level of practice. In the Four Spiritual Laws, the objective doctrinal elements: God's love, human sinfulness, Christ as the "provision" for sin and as Saviour and Lord, are each connected to the personal through the notion that God has a plan for our lives. In the testimonies of the students, the love of God remains as a central organising framework, and with it the strong conviction that they are called to live their lives for God as Christians. The specifics of sin, the cross and salvation, have receded into the background. Again this is not to say that this theological infrastructure is not in some sense still "present." It is there in the theological capital of the wider expression of the Church and it is almost certainly there in the understanding of the faith that each of these young people would espouse if asked. The point is that the theological framework has ceased to be the primary or even necessary part of the explanation of what it means to be a Christian. Theology in this fixed doctrinal form has ceased to be the means by which the message of the Christian faith is conveyed. Instead, what has emerged is a return to the personal as what connects and expresses the faith. This shift in effect splits the two parts of the Four Spiritual Laws. In the more traditional evangelical setting, the doctrinal is the basis and the substance for the personal. In the contemporary context, the personal has quietly been unhooked from the doctrinal and started to float as a free agent in the community. It has become the operant voice of the community.

Changing the Unchanging Gospel

The personal in the Christian faith is what is effective—so much so that the personal becomes the operant theology. This is what people relate to and what they live out of. In the example from Nicky Gumbel's interview, talk of a personal relationship with Jesus connects and expresses, but it does so without any requirement or necessity for more formal or theological communication. Whereas in the past, theology would be the means to share faith, now it has become the explanation, the supporting rational framework for communication. The gospel set out in doctrinal terms has become something that people might need to know at some point, but it is no longer necessary as the only means of sharing faith. At the same time, the subjectivized operant theology has become the dominant means of communication and of self-understanding. But this operant theology, freed from any necessary connection to the theological specifics of the objective, has now become much more fluid. This fluidity is evident in the links that are made to the self as a process of construction in life.

The plan is not simply a reference to divine providence. It also connects to the widespread shift in society towards the personal as a task for self-improvement, self-enhancement, and self-fulfilment. These are powerful and omnipresent themes in wider society, and by incorporating this language into their operant Christian theology, evangelicals are not simply connecting and expressing, they are subtly making changes in Christian theology. These changes are legitimized, however, because at the same time the gospel is seen as continuing to be present and believed fully. The gospel is unchanging. This more complex manoeuvre is made possible by the split that begins to develop between espoused and operant theologies. The espoused becomes fixed in a highly abbreviated form. In this form it functions in limited ways as an explanation of the experience of believing and also as a marker of group identity. As espoused theology, it can be used as a point for policing the boundaries of the community. This conservative appeal to doctrine as an unchanging marker of faith that should be defended at all costs marks the boundary between evangelicals and others, but it does not tell the whole story, because at the same time in the lived expression of communities, a very different theology holds sway. Thus evangelicals are able to generate versions of the Christian faith that are highly subjective in form, while maintaining that they have made no change to the gospel.

The relationship between the unchanging espoused theology and the operant theology of evangelicals is therefore highly complex, and at the heart of this complexity there are tensions and even contradictions. One of the most significant aspects of the contemporary Church is that it has embraced an environment where change has become part of the life of the Church. Nicky Gumbel, like Rick Warren, argues for flexibility in the cultural expression of the faith, while maintaining that the gospel is unchanging. In *Questions of Life*, he talks about the need for the Church to seek to worship and witness to eternal truths through the use of contemporary forms of expression. "God does not change," says Gumbel, "neither does the gospel." The Church should therefore not be prone to simply following any passing fashion, but at the same time, "the way in which we worship and the way in which we communicate the gospel must resonate with modern men and women." In order to communicate, it will often be necessary to make changes in the kind of music that is used in worship and also the kind of language that is most appropriate.[27] This is basically a balancing act. Gumbel is not being disingenuous here, but I think he underestimates the extent to which a commitment to communicating the faith in the terms and categories of contemporary popular culture itself brings about change. At the most basic level, as we have seen, connecting with people has led to prioritization of the personal and the self in relation to believing. This operant theology has become increasingly important as it has been communicated, and the charismatic worship song has been one of the main reasons why it has spread so rapidly. The gospel has not been rejected, but it has become somewhat marginal to the ways that the Church talks, both to its own members and also to those outside. Contemporary worship has played a vital role in these developments. It is important because it has become the main focus of the liturgy for contemporary Churches, but the way this has been done has made the singing of songs a deeply participatory activity. Songs position the worshipper in a narrative of personal encounter with God. What is perhaps even more important is that these narratives of personal encounter appear to be fluid. In other words, they are subject to a significant level of theological innovation. This fluidity means that over a period of time the theological imagination of the Church shifts and changes in subtle but significant ways. While these changes are taking place, the fixed gospel remains in the consciousness of the Church, although it plays a less and less important role in generating or regulating these new forms of expression. This theological dynamic forms the basis for the next chapter.

27 Gumbel, *Questions of Life*, 216.

CHAPTER 7

Narratives of Encounter

A split between espoused and operant theologies characterizes the contemporary Church. This split has led the espoused and the operant to take divergent and quite different courses. The gospel in its radically abbreviated form has become fixed, and as a result is seen as unchanging. This "fixing" of the gospel means evangelicals are reassured that no-one has altered the central ingredients of the faith. Believing is what it has always been. At the same time, alongside this fixed point, the more subjective and personal operant theology has been free to adapt and change with every new theological and spiritual trend. This means that the contemporary Church is deeply rooted in the flow of culture, while maintaining what is seen to be the traditional and eternal message. In fact, a commitment to change has become something of a core value. As we have seen, Rick Warren expresses this very clearly. "The message must never change but the methods must change with each new generation."[1] There is therefore an imperative to change that comes from the desire to communicate the faith in the context of a changing culture. Expressing the faith and connecting with people in the context of contemporary culture has led to rapid innovation in the Church. This innovation is seen in the way that digital technology has been adopted and embraced and in the creation of new kinds of entrepreneurial activities, such as festivals, courses and events. There has also been an explosion in new kinds of churches ranging from huge mega churches to small missional communities. All of these activities have been sites for the generation of a fast changing and adaptable evangelical culture. Right at the heart of these developments has been the worship song.

Worship songs are the most distinctive and omnipresent features of the evangelical/charismatic Church. They have become the primary source of encounter with God for most Christians. Songs have not replaced the sermon or the sacraments, but they have, according to the leader of Soul Survivor, Mike Pilavachi, become the "main event" in Church life.[2] Songs are the main event because it is in worship that the presence of God is experienced and embodied. Songs have their source in a Christian cultural industry. The Christian

---

1 Warren, *The Purpose Driven Church*, 61-62.

2 Craig Borlese and Mike Pilavachi, *Live the Life: The Soul Survivor Guide to Doing It* (London: Hodder and Stoughton, 1998).

 | DOI 10.1163/9789004347359_009

worship music business comes with all of the promotional and production paraphernalia of popular culture. The contemporary Church has been deeply influenced by the collective activities of worship music artists, Christian publishing and recording companies, and all of the associated publicity generating vehicles that form part of the logic of popular culture. These activities do not simply ensure that songs are being sung, they also introduce a dynamic of continual change. Worship artists need new songs to sing, record companies need new material to sell, and churches have become used to an ever-shifting worship environment with album launches, promotional events, music awards and even a worship song chart, based not simply on sales, but on the use of songs in churches. The worship industry therefore leads to a fast-paced circulation of songs within churches. This culture of innovation and exchange has had a significant and enduring effect on the operant theology of the Church. In short it has made it fluid. Over a relatively short period of time, the operant theology that is found in worship songs has gone through a series of changes. These changes are such that the ways of talking about God, salvation and Christian self-understanding and mission in the world have been radically re-imagined. In a context where the worship song has become the primary means for meeting with God and experiencing God's blessing, these changes are deeply significant. They mean that the evangelical of forty years ago lived and worshipped in a theological world that was almost entirely different from what is commonplace today. Songs have therefore been the main driver in theological innovation in the evangelical Church.

Songs and Hymns—Exploring the Difference

The worship song differs from the more traditional hymn in a number of ways. Hymns have usually been seen as a congregational response in the liturgy. This is why hymns are generally placed at specific points in the liturgy. They bring the congregation together as if they are using one voice to affirm what has been taking place in the service. Hymns also have another very significant role: in a traditional Church setting, they are seen as a means of instructing the congregation. In the Methodist tradition John Wesley spoke about hymns as a way of learning the great doctrines of the Church. Through singing hymns, he argued, Methodists received a theological education.[3]

3 Lionel Adey, *Hymns and the Christian Myth* (Vancouver: University of British Columbia Press, 1986), 4.

The modern worship song functions in a very different way from the hymn. Songs are used as part of a "time of worship." Here the word worship is being used in a telling way, and it reveals a significant aspect of the operant theology of the Church. Singing is not simply a part of a worship service. In the contemporary Church, singing is the worship. In other words, it is in singing that something special and distinctive is taking place that can be designated worship. As has already been noted, it is very common to be in a Church service and after thirty or forty minutes of liturgy and prayers have a person stand up with the guitar and say, "Now we are going to enter a time of worship." What follows is an extended time of singing worship songs. This can last for an hour or more, but more often it takes between twenty and forty minutes. One song will lead into another. There will be times where the singing is very loud and praise orientated and there may well be times where songs are broken down into very quiet and more reflective moments. In this way the songs develop a dynamic or a series of waves of praise and intimacy that are repeated. This can happen within one song, where through repetition and a dynamic of crescendo and diminuendo the wave pattern can be developed, or it may come about through the use of different songs one after another.

The time of worship signifies a particular moment in a Church service. This is a time of encounter. In more traditional churches, encounter has been seen in one of two ways. In Protestantism, God is encountered primarily through the preaching of the word. In more Catholic traditions, God is encountered sacramentally, i.e., in the Eucharist or baptism. For the charismatic, however, encounter with God takes place through the practice of singing. Songs form a liturgy of coming into the presence of God. They do not so much teach doctrine as enact it. This does not mean that the songs are not theological, but they do not teach in the objective way that Wesley sees with traditional hymns. Songs enact encounter with God by situating the individual within a theological narrative.

Contemporary worship began to take its current form in the 70s and the 80s. Deeply influenced by the charismatic movement, it also drew on the forms of musical expression popularized in the Church by the Jesus Movement. The dynamic of expression and connection legitimized the use of first folk music and then rock music in Church worship. The connection to the wider popular culture has become less and less evident as Christian worship music has increasingly developed as its own distinctive genre. The soft rock style of most worship bands is now hardly heard anywhere except in the contemporary Church. Yet while the musical feel of the worship song has become somewhat set in stone, the lyrical content of the songs has continued to develop and change.

Our God is a Great Big God

The Christian worship charts give a strong indication of the extent to which particular songs are being taken up and used by churches. The charts don't count sales. Instead they are based on the frequency with which songs are sung in local churches and at events. This means that they give a snapshot of the theological world that is being generated by the songs, and which theological images and metaphors are forming the way that communities and individuals journey into the presence of God. In 2012, the top three songs on the chart had remarkably similar themes.[4] Number three was "Our God," which starts by talking about incidents in John's Gospel. Jesus is referred to, as is most often the case in contemporary worship songs, as "You." You, the song says, turned water into wine and opened the eyes of the blind man. You are a light that shines in the darkness and so from the ashes we rise. These events are then celebrated by the repetition of verses that talk about the greatness of God. God is greater, stronger, and higher than any other. God is a healer who has "awesome" power. With this God on our side no one can stand against us. If God is for us, the song explains, no one can stop us. "Our God" was composed by a group of songwriters and worship leaders, including Matt Redman and Chris Tomlin. Chris Tomlin also wrote the number one song on the 2012 chart. Like "Our God," this song follows a similar theme of the greatness of God. "How Great is our God" talks about the King robed in splendour, who wraps the light around him so that the darkness must hide. All the earth sings and rejoices at this King. God is Trinity and also the Lion and the Lamb. Time itself is in the hands of this God and the worshipper is invited to join in the song of celebration. When together we sing, "How Great is God," then everyone will see. The worship song that was at number two in the chart, "Mighty to Save," came from Hillsong and it used remarkably similar themes to "Our God" and "How Great is Our God." "Mighty to Save" talks about the power of God that can move mountains and can save. The song sets out how everyone needs love and healing and compassion. Jesus rose from the dead and rose again and God takes us as we are with all our failings and gives us life again. This is the work of the mighty Saviour.

These three songs mix more objective theological statements with subjective elements. The theme of God's greatness and power are illustrated by images and metaphors drawn from the bible. God is enthroned and robed in

4 CCLI Top 25 songs reported by churches in their Copy Activity Reports, as used for the August 2012 royalty payout.

power and it is this God who is able to save and also to move mountains. These ideas are mixed with non-biblical themes such as the Trinity, which comes from later Christian theology, and interestingly, the pre-Christian image of the phoenix rising from the ashes. The greatness of God is focused in the narratives of individual worshippers through very personalized language. Everyone, says "Mighty to Save," needs help and compassion. Salvation takes us as we are and helps us to rise above our problems. So the doctrinal orientation of the song is located in the personal in such a way as to draw the worshipper into the experience of worship. At the same time the subjective elements in the songs provide the dominant narrative. The subjective is so significant that personal belief sets the tone for the song and also for the whole act of worship. This is what Lionel Adey calls "reflexive worship." What he means by this is a type of worship that pays particular attention to the act of worship itself.[5] In "Mighty God to Save," the song enters a reflexive mode in the third and fourth verses. These invite God to "take me as you find me" and the worshippers offer themselves to God as followers, and crucially the verse uses the word "now." In other words, the lyrics position those who sing as being in that moment, in the "now," giving themselves to God. This kind of wording shifts attention from the objective to the subjective. The mighty God is spoken about, but this God is personalized by an act of surrender that is taking place in the worship time itself. "Our God" does not move towards the reflexive, but it does place the power and authority of God in a personalized narrative. God is for "us," we are told in the lyrics of "Our God" and so nothing can stop us. The use of "us" and "our" in these songs is also significant. Our God appears to be juxtaposed against other Gods. "Who can stop us?" and "Who can stand against us?" the song asks. The song locates the divine as being on our side and consequently not on "their" side. "Our," in this sense, designates those who are singing together and hence the contemporary Church. "Nothing can stop us," locates the divine in the story of those who are gathered for worship. Invincibility comes from the greatness of God the creator and healer, but it finds expression in the aspirations of the community. "How Great is Our God" focuses throughout on a theological expression of the divine power and glory as a focus for worship. It is in this sense primarily objective in tone. It says what God is like and invites praise, but this doctrinal tone shifts with the last refrain. Here the worshipper is invited to sing of God's greatness because in and through their singing "all will see" the greatness of God.

Christian hymnody has always contained a mix of more theological songs and those that are subjective or even reflexive. In some cases, as has been seen

5 Adey, *Hymns and the Christian Myth*, 5-10.

here, songs shift between these modes so that a verse may be more theological and descriptive of God, with the chorus containing a response. Occasionally hymns will be written that are mainly reflexive, inviting the worshipper to enter into the act of worship as a moment of deep significance. Objective, subjective and reflexive elements in hymnody are familiar, but what has changed in modern worship songs is that the subjective, and in many cases the reflexive, have become the most prevalent forms of lyric. What this means is that the focus of the songs has shifted from being specifically theological, i.e., lyrics that talk about Jesus, God, salvation or creation, and has become much more focused on the personal and the worshippers as they are in the presence of God while they worship. The objective has not gone away, however, but has become fragmented and finds its location in the more subjective flow of what I term a *narrative of encounter*.

Shifting Narratives of Encounter

A narrative of encounter refers to the way that the songs position the worshipper in relation to God and offer a framework for meeting God in the act of worship. It should be stressed that this kind of encounter is connected to the evangelical gospel, but it takes the form of a more nuanced and free flowing improvisation on doctrinal themes. The enduring feature of these narratives is that they are located in the personal and the subjective. The songs therefore develop extended metaphors that enable individuals and communities to come to God and experience God's presence. These narratives are not fixed or static in any way, however. So in contrast to the evangelical gospel, the songs have evolved as a more free form and a fluid personalized theology. Having said this, it would be wrong to try to set the objective gospel over and against the more personalized narratives of encounter in the worship songs, because the objective and doctrinal elements continue to play a part, although this part has become less and less significant over time.

Changes in narratives of encounter in worship songs can be traced over a much longer period in such way that it becomes clear that the operant theology of the Church is constantly on the move. In *Selling Worship*, I set out in detail how the theological imagery most commonly used in worship songs has changed in quite significant ways. My research was based not on the Christian Worship Charts or on individual acts of worship, but on songbooks from the days before the internet, times when songbook collections were the primary means for disseminating songs. Actually, they are still very important, because they are still the most convenient way for local worship bands to gain access to music, and most importantly, the guitar chords, although the internet has now become a significant alternative source to the books. My research took the most popular songbooks used in the United Kingdom during the 1960s, 70s and 80s. During this thirty-year period, a new songbook came into popular use roughly every five years. I analyzed the lyrical content of these songbooks to trace the pattern of theological expression that was evident in the songs. What emerged was a theological voice characterizing each of the songbooks. These voices generated a distinctive narrative of encounter. In other words, each songbook had a particular theological framework within which communities and individuals were led into a worship-based encounter with God.[6]

In the thirty years from the mid 60s to the mid 90s, the theological language used in song lyrics in worship songs went through a number of significant changes. In the late 1960s, the songs portrayed encounter with Christ as closely linked to the experience of conversion. The songbook, *Youth Praise*, published in 1966, and used throughout the United Kingdom, has a number of examples of these conversion-orientated songs. One example is the song, "If you want joy." The song speaks of conversion as taking away sins and hearts being "made over anew." At the moment of conversion, Jesus will "come in to stay." If the believer lets Jesus into their heart they will also experience joy. Joy in *Youth Praise* represents a total life-changing event, often expressed as Jesus coming into the life of the believer. Another song popular in the 1960s, "Life is Wonderful,"[7] says that nothing will be the same after Jesus has "come in." Jesus is portrayed as "knocking, patiently waiting/Outside your heart's closed door."[8] In the song "Jesus is the Saviour," individual sinfulness is linked to a more contemporary youth-orientated language.[9] "Sometimes when you're feeling all alone and blue, Jesus can come in and help you to pull through."[10] Here the discourse of adolescent anxiety articulates with a theology of redemption. The focus on conversion leads on to a concern for those who have not yet "let Jesus in." This period is interesting because the songs give a very full account of the evangelical Gospel. They often read like a version of the Four Spiritual Laws that rhyme and have been set to music. Many of the lyrics are built around the rather neat pattern of "free, me, tree and Calvary" that enables them to give an evangelical

6 What follows is a summary of the key changes in the theology of worship songs since the 1960s. For a fuller account of these changes in narratives of encounter, see my previous work, *Selling Worship*, 121-16.

7 *Youth Praise* 1966 London: Falcon, 46.

8 *Youth Praise*, 73.

9 *Youth Praise*, 61.

10 *Youth Praise*, 61.

version of the atonement that fits into the conventions of popular songwriting. The close link between the songs and the evangelical gospel changes, however, as the charismatic movement increasingly shapes the lyrical content of the songs in the 70s and into the 80s.

In the 1980s, a new wave of charismatic churches began to emerge in the United Kingdom. At the time they were known as house churches, and the songs that came out of these churches were gathered together in the songbook *Songs of Fellowship*. Strange as it may seem, the first volume of *Songs of Fellowship* contained very few references to the earthly life of Jesus. One quite remarkable song seems to suggest that the historical Christ is something of a distraction from spiritual experience in the present. "Jesus, Come Closer to Me," speaks about an encounter with Jesus in the present moment.[11] To emphasize the immediacy of the experience, the lyrics say that Jesus will no longer be just a historical or factual figure because he can be known in the present.[12] The humanity and the life of Jesus are bypassed in favour of a vision of the risen and ascended Lord who reigns on high. "He is Lord" speaks of the risen Christ to whom all people will bow and confess that "Jesus Christ is Lord."[13] In "The Name of Jesus is Higher Than Any Other," the writer recounts the names of Jesus: Lord, Counsellor, Prince of Peace, Wonderful, Mighty God.[14] These names again emphasize the transcendent powerful nature of Christ. The worship of the people, however, is also said to, "build a throne" for Jesus the King. "Jesus we Enthrone You" speaks of the praises of the people raising Christ onto a throne built from worship. Worship in this sense builds a throne for Christ.[15] The people of God are those who "enter his gates" and "enter his courts." This is a vision based upon the Jewish temple.[16] To be in the "House of the Lord" is to be purified, refined like gold.[17] The people of God are pictured in worship as being in this spiritual temple. The servants of God stand and serve at night in the temple. Here in the House of the Lord they lift up their hands in the holy place and bless the Lord.[18] There is a mystical encounter with God in the temple, for here it is that the "royal priesthood" worship, and it is, "within the veil," where they can look upon the face of God.[19] Here again they are

11 *Youth Praise*, 61.
12 *Songs of Fellowship*, 67.
13 *Songs of Fellowship*, 36.
14 *Songs of Fellowship*, 37.
15 *Songs of Fellowship*, 86.
16 *Songs of Fellowship*, 62.
17 *Songs of Fellowship*, 70.
18 *Songs of Fellowship*, 15.
19 *Songs of Fellowship*, 155.

portrayed as lifting holy hands and blessing the Lord.[20] The royal priesthood is also described as a "holy nation."[21]

Alongside the temple imagery, there is a strong emphasis on God as Father. The song "Abba Father"[22] asks that God will let the believer be "yours and yours alone," that his or her heart may never "grow cold." "Father" represents a dependable relationship into whose hands family, friends, our past, and our future may be placed.[23] Outside of this secure relationship with the Father, outside of the temple, and outside of the city, the royal priesthood is ringed by fire and what are called "the nations." It is primarily in these terms that *Songs of Fellowship* deals with missiology and the wider non-christian world. The nations will eventually come to Mount Zion and offer their praise to God.[24] The nations are in need of healing[25] and they are thirsty.[26] Closely related to the nations is the use of the metaphor "the land." The people of power will "move through this land by my Spirit."[27] In the land, the Church will be built by God, and it will be strong and ready. Eventually the Church will "march upon the land." God's own army are the children of God's Son. When it moves as a body this army will be able to claim the land, which God's mighty hand has set before it.[28] The Promised Land is right at the feet of the Church, and they are to take it, and build a new Jerusalem upon it, according to "The Promised Land."[29] This conquering metaphor is taken further in, "I Hear the Sound of Rustling."[30] This song portrays the present time as one in which the Church, which was once asleep, is now starting to awake. The watchmen on the towers are ready to answer the call. The climax is an apocalyptic encounter, where the Church is likened to a body of soldiers prepared for war. With the lead of the spirit, believers will be commanded to rise as a mighty army and the devils will "see and hear for their time is at hand."[31]

By the 1990s, images of warfare and the temple give way to a language of intimacy. Intimacy in charismatic worship is most closely associated with the

20 *Songs of Fellowship*, 16.
21 *Songs of Fellowship*, 14.
22 *Songs of Fellowship*, 1.
23 *Songs of Fellowship*, 21.
24 *Songs of Fellowship*, 91.
25 *Songs of Fellowship*, 48.
26 *Songs of Fellowship*, 48.
27 *Songs of Fellowship*, 25.
28 *Songs of Fellowship*, 142.
29 *Songs of Fellowship*, 126.
30 *Songs of Fellowship*, 48.
31 *Songs of Fellowship*, 48.

ministry of John Wimber. Wimber's songs drew on romantic imagery. A typical example of this kind of romantic worship song is "Thank You for Being,"[32] where the worshipper expresses him or herself by singing, "Thank you for being just who You are."[33] "Lord, I'll seek after You"[34] speaks of the Lord as "the only one that satisfies," as "I draw near to you," I, "Turn to kiss your face." The intimacy of worship is the arena where the relationship between the believer and Jesus is celebrated and enacted. Jesus is "always near, when we call."[35] Praise is a sacrificial gift and this involves offering ourselves in love to God, falling down upon our knees before him. In turn, the worshipper meets with God in the intimate space. The Spirit "moves upon" the believer. With hands lifted to the throne, God meets the deepest need.[36] In worship, the encounter with the Spirit brings healing and the meeting of needs. The believer can speak of God's power being "on me now."[37] "I Receive You" is a song about the moment of worship. God's touch is felt "right now." It is at the very moment of worship that encounter and personal transformation take place.

Intimacy continues to be one of the main themes in the songs that emerge in the early years of *Soul Survivor*. A key metaphor in these songs is the idea of heart. There is a heart to worship. This is what happens when the music fades and the believer comes to God.[38] This heart is located in acknowledging that worship is all about Jesus. Heart here relates to the essence or the deepest truth of worship. It is possible to drift from this "heart" and to be distracted even by worship itself. We can make worship something that it should not be, but this is a mistake, because the pure, essential nature of worship relates to Jesus. This is its heart.[39] At the same time Jesus also has a heart. The heart of the Lord is something that we should search for.[40] Knowing God's heart will help us to steer our lives. Heart in this sense relates to the feeling, sensing, willing nature of God. To approach God's heart is to experience the grace of God who gives and gives.[41] This is the Heart of the Father, the merciful graciousness of the Lord. God's Heart has a centre and it is this heart that we must continually

32 *Songs of the Vineyard*, 45.
33 *Songs of the Vineyard*, 45.
34 *Songs of the Vineyard*, 34.
35 *Songs of the Vineyard*, 16.
36 *Songs of the Vineyard*, 18.
37 *Songs of the Vineyard*, 20.
38 *Soul Survivor Songbook*, 181.
39 *Soul Survivor Songbook*, 181.
40 *Soul Survivor Songbook*, 104.
41 *Soul Survivor Songbook*, 25.

seek.[42] The language of the heart is thus the language of an embodied feeling. The God who "has our heart" receives the emotional centre of the believer.[43] Searching for God's heart is the response of one lover to another. God holds our heart in his hands and we are committed to seeking after him. To this end our heart is fixed after his emotional and gracious "heart." The believers focus the eyes of their hearts towards the object of their love.[44] The hearts of the believers can be described as full and burdened. "Here I am Once Again" says that no matter what state the believers' hearts may be in, through the encounter of worship they will approach God. The heart is then said to be "poured out" in love to God. Pouring out the hearts as well as speaking of the love of the believers also expresses that they need God and they are thankful to God. Pouring out hearts to God is not just offloading problems, it is also an act of praise. We pour out our hearts to God when we say that he is wonderful.[45] This heart of worship sings with praise as the believers offer all of themselves they offer their hearts.[46] The Vineyard song, "Hungry: Falling on my Knees," describes the believer as broken, empty and hungry. Acknowledging this need, the believer "runs" towards a God whose arms are open in welcome. The believer may be weary, but God's love does not run dry. With an attitude of waiting, believers fall to their knees. Here believers offer all of themselves. Here in the moment of encounter, honesty and intimacy, the confession is made. Jesus is all the believers' hearts are living for.[47] Intimacy relates to encounter with God in the present. In "I Come Too: Here With Me Now," the believer approaches the "Lord of all hope." He is the giver of life, the Prince of peace. The believer is to draw near and to feel the presence of God. Although it is acknowledged that God is always present, there is a desire to know that this is so "here and now."[48] Reference to the present moment locates this intimacy within the act of singing. In this sense, the "now" connects to the experience of those currently singing the song. Today those singing the song are coming to God.[49] This is immediate and made present by those who use the song in worship.

This brief survey of the lyrics in worship songbooks demonstrates that the operant theology of the evangelical church is subject to a steady evolution.

---

42 *Soul Survivor Songbook*, 25.

43 *Soul Survivor Songbook*, 104.

44 *Soul Survivor Songbook*, 17.

45 *Soul Survivor Songbook*, 31.

46 *Soul Survivor Songbook*, 52.

47 *Soul Survivor Songbook*, 37.

48 *Soul Survivor Songbook*, 41.

49 *Soul Survivor Songbook*, 42.

This is in contrast to the widespread perception that the gospel is fixed and never changes. The point is that these two realities, the fixed gospel, and the more fluid subjectivized theology seen in the worship songs, co-exist. The theological elements in the songs become more fragmented and doctrinal as the central Christian story becomes less and less evident. The objective gospel is replaced and repositioned with a subjective narrative of encounter with God. The self moves to centre stage. It is important to see that this "self" is a self in relation to God, a self that is positioned in relation to God in praise and intimacy. It would be wrong therefore to speak about the self as supplanting the divine in worship in some kind of idolatrous way. One aspect of contemporary worship that would caution against this is the continued presence of objective theological elements throughout the songs, but also the songs seen as part of a much wider ecology of worship: liturgy, preaching, as well as the ongoing conversation that makes up evangelical life. The analysis of the songbooks in and of themselves is therefore slightly artificial, because in practice churches pick and choose from a range of sources. To identify the theological content of the singing, two worship services will be looked at in more detail. The first is again the baptism service that I studied with Paul Fiddes, and the second is a worship service in Thurso, Scotland, that I analyzed with Heidi Campbell as part of the SCOT Project.

Examining the Practice of Worship

The baptism service that I discussed earlier in the chapter echoed the theme of the greatness of God seen in a number of the more recent worship songs. In the service there was also an extended time for singing. This lasted for around fifteen minutes and it was led by a young male worship leader playing a low-slung acoustic guitar and backed by a full rock band featuring a bass guitar, drums, keyboards and two female backing singers. The worship started with a traditional hymn, "How Great Thou Art,"[50] which focuses on the awesomeness of God, but does so by first talking about the beauty of creation. Then the hymn speaks of the incarnation and the sacrifice of Christ. The cross takes away sin through the shedding of blood. All of these theological themes are made personal. It is when "I see" the beauty and it is for "my sin" that Jesus dies on the cross. Eventually the singer is transported to heaven where there will be shouts and acclamations declaring "How great thou art." The second song

50 Copyright 1953, Stuart Hine Trust.

picks up on similar themes, although it was written by one of the worship leaders at the church: "Come Hear the Thunder of a Victory Cry."[51] The lyrics speak about the saving work of Christ as a victory that has been won. The third song in the set was a slightly older worship song, "There is a Redeemer,"[52] which gives a quite detailed account of the work of Christ and offers a song of praise. Jesus is the one above all names who the believer will meet in glory. The final song featured a refrain, "Fire Fall Down," taken from Hillsong.[53] Here again the power of God is emphasized, but it is also located in a personal narrative of salvation. Through Jesus's death we will never be the same. Our broken lives have been fixed. We are blessed and we walk in the light. This is what it means for the fire to fall down on the people of God.

The worship time at this church demonstrated how songs from different periods and even hymns can be woven together to form a liturgy of praise and encounter. The service took place on Pentecost Sunday and so the tone of praise and also the theme of the power of God falling on the worshippers seemed highly appropriate. At the same time the song choices, although they ranged across different styles and periods, did tend to focus in a similar way as "Our God," "How Great is Our God" and "Mighty to Save," not only on the greatness of God, but the ways in which this power is experienced in personal salvation. God is "awesome." Awesome refers to the sense of wonder that comes from the experience of this God in the daily lives and struggles of individuals. There is another very significant insight that can be gained by looking at this group of songs that formed the worship set in the service. Although this is a slightly shortened worship time (the curate later explained to me that they would normally have a longer time of singing, but in order that they might accommodate the testimonies and the baptisms, they had cut it a little), it is still possible to see some significant theological trends. Each of the songs makes isolated references to Christian doctrine. The most obvious of these is the reference to the Trinity, but there are several that mention Jesus, his death on the cross and the resurrection. The doctrine of creation is there and also a number of references to glory and the life to come. This material is scattered throughout the different songs. Doctrinal material does not generally form the main focus of any of the songs, but comes as a passing reference, a brief metaphor. Thus while the songs might not be an instruction in doctrine they situate what is a very subjective and personal narrative of praise and encounter in relation to the gospel story. The personal narratives operate as a consistent pattern of

51 Copyright Rich White.

52 Copyright 1982, Birdwing Music, Melody Green.

53 Copyright 2000, Matt Crocker, Hillsong.

narrative across the songs, but the emphasis on the personal is tempered in these songs by significant theological elements. What is interesting is that the theological is much more prominent in the older worship songs than in the newer ones. This shows that choice in a worship service can balance the subjectivizing tendencies of a diet that consists only of the most recent songs. This worship service also shows how in practice, the expression of the Church is quite fluid and made up of a mix of different voices and traditions that mingle together as choices are made between hymns and more contemporary songs. Having said this, the flow of theological expression has a shape and a direction. The subjective remains a strong current in the life of this particular church. The intermingling of different theological voices and emphases is also illustrated in the analysis of the worship service in Thurso.

In 2002 and 2003 Heidi Campbell travelled around Scotland recording evangelical worship and prayer meetings.[54] She called her work the SCOT Project ("Scots Cry Out Together") and as part of the project she recorded around forty hours of youth prayer at fourteen events. Analysis of this material showed that particular phrases and metaphors were repeated at several of the events. This made it possible to see how a kind of vernacular form of theological expression was held in common by these groups of Scottish Christians.[55] The research offers a snapshot of typical turns of phrase, ways of speaking, and styles of prayer at a particular time. The most common theme found in the words spoken at these events was "God's presence" and this theological metaphor had two related aspects. First was the use of language acknowledging God as present in the meeting. For example: "Thank you for being with us and for giving us words of redemption, hope, light and peace." Second, there were instances of young people highlighting a desire for "intimacy with God," and having some tangible experience of this presence, such as "Please meet with us, we want a glimpse of your glory." Perhaps reflecting the fact that the events were prayer and worship related, prayer itself was another important theme. Linked to prayer were two further themes: worship, and forgiveness. The themes of God's presence, worship, prayer and forgiveness seemed to represent a core theological style or sensibility among the young people. This might be termed a *narrative of intimacy*, but alongside this there was another cluster of metaphors, which could be called the *narrative of revival*. The narrative of revival is seen

54 The following sections were first published as Pete Ward and Heidi Campbell, "Ordinary Theology as Narratives," *Journal of Contemporary Religion* Vol. 24, No. 2, May 2009, 217-234.

55 Heidi Campbell, Gordon Lynch, and Pete Ward, "'Can you Hear the Army?' Exploring Evangelical Discourse in Scottish Youth Prayer Meetings," *Journal of Contemporary Religion* 24/2, May (2009): 217-234.

in the four remaining themes that were most frequently found in the prayers of these young people. In eleven of the fourteen sessions, we found prayers that made reference to a specific geographical location in Scotland. One-third of the prayers related to this theme focused on praying for specific cities, such as, "May Aberdeen come to know you." Central to the narrative of revival were two closely related themes, the Church as an army, and the significance of young people as a "generation." Examples of the army motif included references to youth being in a battle, requests to "Give us wisdom to know when to take up the sword," or the need for a Church of holy warriors to arise for God's purposes, and "Father make us a Church of warriors."

At one of the events that Campbell observed and recorded, songs and prayers were interspersed with extended periods of prophetic movement and dancing. This act of worship took place in Thurso, Scotland, in February 2002. The event was run under the auspices of New Wine Scotland. In what was an extended worship service of over three hours, there were two "times of worship." These started and ended the service. In between there was a sermon, a message from a visiting speaker and a quite unique and unusual period of prophetic dancing. During the dance, which took place for more than an hour, there were militaristic elements present. In particular, there was a moment where the worshippers were encouraged to march around the room as the army of God. These prophetic actions pick up on the metaphor of warfare and the Church as the army of God in the other recordings that were made. In the dance at Thurso, being an army was also explicitly linked to the idea that God would do a unique work in the nation of Scotland. These revival type motifs were set alongside the emphasis on God's presence and ideas of intimacy.

The theme of intimacy can be illustrated by a summary of the lyrical content of the first period of worship at Thurso. There were five songs used in this worship set. These were nearly all drawn from the *Soul Survivor* group of songs and were: "Open the Eyes of My Heart Lord"; "The Happy Song (I Could Sing)"; "Holy is the Lord Holy is his Name"; "We Exult Thee; and "O Sacred King." The lyric in the first song, "Open the eyes of my heart Lord, I want to see you," prepares the worshipper for encounter with God. This is picked up in some of the other songs, for example in the line, "I could sing unending songs of how you saved my soul," from the second of the songs, "The Happy Song," which focuses the worshipper on the present and the act of singing. The worshipper is called to embody what is being sung and enact this embodiment in the act of singing. The next two songs, "Holy is the Lord," and "We Exalt Thee," focus on moments of praise. The worshipper is drawn to acknowledge the holiness and transcendence of God. With "O Sacred King" and "Breathe on Me," the dynamic shifts. Sung in a quieter and more reflective way, the worshipper is drawn through the instrumentation and the lyrics towards an encounter with the suffering Lord. The "Breath of God" invokes the transforming and enervating action of the Spirit.

Intimacy in the songs is articulated throughout with doctrinal expression. With the exception of "O Sacred King," and "I Love You For the Cross," few of the songs are built around an extended reflection upon what could be termed traditional doctrine. These doctrinal elements are present, but they are spread throughout the songs in occasional references to doctrinal themes, bible verses and theological terminology. For instance, the songs speak of Lord ("Open my eyes"), God ("Happy Song"), Christ ("Holy is the Lord"), and Father ("O Sacred King"). Biblical themes are explored, for instance, in "Open My Eyes," where the lyric states, "To see you high and lifted up, shining in the light of your glory," which combines references to Isaiah's vision of God in the temple with John's reference to Christ on the Cross as being lifted up in Glory (Isaiah 6; John 3:14). The song, "We Exalt Thee" is based around a quotation from Psalm 97:9. "Praise the Lord Oh My Soul" has the line, "As Far as the East is from the West so far has he removed our transgressions from us," a direct quotation from Psalm 10:12. The doctrine of salvation in particular appears in a number of the songs, and while a clear statement of atonement theory is not laid out in any systematic way, the references throughout the songs used in the event may be used to develop the key elements in the doctrine. For example, "O Sacred King" speaks of disgrace and the saving action of Christ's death on the cross.

These studies of evangelical expression in Scotland suggest that narratives of encounter may vary. The idea of the greatness of God is present, but it does not assume the high prominence it has in more recent songs. Intimacy and subjective frameworks for structuring encounter with God are present across the two worship events. What is also clear is that while there may be different theological themes that come to prominence, the songs taken as a whole carry a range of doctrinal content. The link between the more objective doctrinal elements and the subjective narratives of encounter appears to shift and develop even over a relatively short period of time. When song lyrics are looked at in a longer time frame, then the relationship between doctrine and the changing focus in narratives of encounter becomes even more evident.

Doctrine and Narratives of Encounter

Contemporary worship songs are a vital piece of the puzzle in thinking about the developing and complex relationship between espoused and operant theologies in the contemporary Church. The songs have had a huge impact on individuals and congregations, and worship songs exemplify the way that evangelicalism has generated momentum within the Church. One of the unforeseen consequences of this is that the split between espoused and operant theologies has become more of a feature. The theological fluidity of the Church is in many ways something that has gone under the radar of formal theological reflection. Hymns and hymn books have often had an official place in Church life. The Methodist hymn book and the Baptist hymnal are specifically linked to denominations, for example. Other hymn books, such as the Anglican *Hymns Ancient and Modern* have evolved through the work of editorial groups closely linked to the Church. Worship songs, in contrast, have managed to become the mainstay of the contemporary Church with little if any scrutiny. They have become the liturgy, and yet they have never been subject to any kind of official Church review or sanction. Even in a local context it is not at all unusual for the songs used in each individual service to be selected by the worship leader rather than the senior pastor. Thus worship songs have become part of Church life almost by default. As they have been adopted they have introduced a dynamic of change. It is this change that continues to shape the operant theologies of individuals and communities.

Worship songs represent something of a quiet theological colonization of the Church. This development is by no means inconsequential, because it goes to the heart of the relationship between the gospel and culture in the Church. It is worth recapping the theological themes that have been found in the songs at different periods. In the 1960s the songs offered an evangelical message of salvation set to music. The objective or doctrinal aspects of the songs were much more explicit and central to the lyrics. These songs shared a similar purpose to Wesley's hymns. They were a means of instruction and teaching. At this point there was a strong link between the operant theology of the songs and the espoused theology of the evangelical gospel, as seen in the tracts and preaching of figures such as John Stott and Billy Graham. The objective theological doctrine was therefore seen as the "means," not simply to come to faith, but to continue on in the faith. The objective "gospel" was therefore both the espoused and the operant theologies of the Church.

The advent of the charismatic movement heralded the eventual split between the operant and the espoused. Charismatic spirituality, with its emphasis on the experience of the Spirit, reinforces those elements of the evangelical gospel that were being articulated with the personal and the subjective. The personal relationship with Jesus and the plan that God has for every Christian's life takes central stage. They become the focus for the Christian project of the self. The objective aspects of an evangelical gospel do not disappear entirely. Rather, doctrine becomes more fragmented and scattered throughout the songs. So instead of instruction or teaching, doctrinal elements are hinted at or referred to in passing. The songs therefore seem to assume a certain level of Christian understanding in the worshipper, but they do little to develop this, particularly if they are the standard fare for young as well as not so young churchgoers.

The specifics of the evangelical gospel are now replaced in the songs by narratives of encounter. These narratives appear to move and develop over time and also between different groups. So for instance, the focus on the greatness of God in some of the more recent songs is not necessarily a new departure. The greatness of God would not have been unrecognizable to believers in previous periods, but it is actually a significant move away from the more romantic imagery of the Wimber songs and early *Soul Survivor*. At the same time, ideas of intimacy with God are clearly carried through into the present. Yet the language of the heart of God and the broken heart of the worshipper seem to represent a very different world from the more militaristic ideas of the Church as an army marching on the land. In the Thurso worship event these narratives seemed to exist alongside one another. The point is that the songs exist in a free-flowing environment where different ideas are picked up at different times. This picking up is seen very clearly in the prayers that were recorded in the SCOT Project. Here young people drew directly on the language of the songs in the way that they prayed. The prayers offer an insight into the way that the song lyrics are internalized and then used as the framework for a continued relationship with God.

Subjectivized Improvisation

The songs are a powerful theology that is operant in the lives of people and in communities. It is important to realize that the narratives of encounter do not replace a more formal or structured understanding of the Gospel, however. They operate as a subjectivized improvisation on the gospel. They are not a substitute theology; they are instead an aspect of the gospel that is expressed in a form that allows it to be performed or enacted. The narratives in this sense are pathways that enable the worshipper to come into the presence of God. Another analogy might be to speak of the songs as creating a world or a space where the worshipper can journey towards God. So for instance, the idea of worship as a sacrificial gift that brings worshippers to the foot of the cross where they can meet with the gracious and loving presence of Jesus is not meant to replace formal doctrinal expression. The point is that this world makes a place where worshippers can move into the forgiving embrace of God. Interestingly, theological expression in the songs ranges well beyond the confines of evangelical understanding of the gospel. So, for instance, the songs we have examined contain the idea of a phoenix rising from the ashes, or of Jesus as a lover whom we kiss and who kisses us. In the Thurso event, aspects of the Church militant are mixed with themes that evoke Scottish nationalism. In the more formal communication of a theological text or even a sermon, these kinds of ideas might be seen by evangelicals as rather risqué and possibly even shocking, but in a song lyric with a good tune and a great band such ideas are perfectly acceptable. Change is thus a feature of the operant theology of the Church, but this is supported by a simultaneous belief that the gospel is eternal and remains fundamentally unaltered. Belief in the unchanging gospel therefore offers cover for what are in effect quite promiscuous borrowings from the wider culture. The two co-exist and are part of the one lived dynamic. At the same time, what appears to be taking place is that while the liturgical expression of the Church contains a rich mix of different theological elements, it would be wrong to interpret this as being indicative of individual believing. So while in the practice of worship through preaching and the reading of scripture the more formal doctrine continues to be significantly present, what is taken away and internalized by believers appears to be primarily a more personal theology. In a sense, the worship songs offer a clue as to the general trend or direction of flow. In the songs, the personal has become the dominant narrative of encounter. Encounter here is particularly significant, because formally it is the gospel in evangelical theology that shows the way to God. The idea of an unchanging eternal gospel rests on the sense that the expression of this way has become fixed. In the songs the way appears to be in flux, however. Through articulation with a range of metaphors and images, the way to encounter with God is restructured. Taken as a whole, either in the songbooks or in individual worship events, what emerge are patterns of theological expression that enable believers to journey into praise and intimacy with God. These patterns of encounter are fluid and in many ways rather indiscriminate in the links that they make between evangelical theology and a range of ideas and images drawn from popular culture. These connections do not come from any sustained theological reflection, but arise from what feels right for the songwriter.

Songs, Culture and Flow

Songwriters do not operate in a vacuum; they are part of the ebb and flow of the evangelical scene. They read the latest books and listen to the teaching and preaching of evangelical leaders. The evangelical worship culture is therefore part of an ongoing discourse that is shaping the Church and being shaped by its own expression. This in a sense is the complexity and the paradox of the Church understood as cultural expression. Attentiveness to the cultural forms has the theological purpose of discerning the Body in and through this complexity. Theological discussion without reference to the performance of communities and the lived experience of individuals does not encompass what is actually taking place. Attention to the lived reveals the muddied and often contradictory nature of ecclesial life. Communities share in a range of different theological traditions and forms of expression, and these co-exist and intermingle in acts of worship and in the habituations of individuals as they set about what it means to live the life of a believer. Discerning the body requires a focused attention on the diversity of expression in the Church. What is evident in worship is the way that through the creativity of individuals and the thousands of choices that are required to construct contemporary worship, the Church has become alive as a dynamic and meaningful part of communal life. So the work of the Spirit appears to be mediated in the collective practice of creating and performing and participating in worship. The patterns of theological expression in the songs, and in their use in worship, are an indication of the ongoing theological life of the Church. This analysis is much more than an account of ideas or theology. The songs are actually sung by communities as part of their worship. In nearly all of the examples given, I have sung the very same songs myself. By my own participation I know that these songs can be a means to journey into the presence of God and I can understand how they might operate in exactly the same way for other people. It is not unreasonable to talk about the way that Jesus Christ has been present in and through these songs and to see and to value the way that his presence, through the Spirit, has thereby transformed communities and individuals. This is the reason why the songs exist, and in fact it is the reason why there is a continual flow of new songs. The practice of making worship and sharing in worship is alive and well in the Church precisely because it is experienced as a vivifying practice. It is out of this cultural complexity that is indwelt by the presence of Christ that the new songs are generated.

The songs give rise to new ways of participating in worship and yet, as they do so, they innovate theologically. Discerning the presence of Christ in and through these practices is fundamental to any claim to see. Such seeing does not imply that there are no problems or limitations to the expression of the Church. The point here is that there should be an expectation that expression, even as it is meaningful, will need correction and adaption from time to time. This notion of correction is significantly already there in the practice of the

Church. The gradual development of imagery and theology in the songs shows how the organic expression of the Church has built into it processes that allow for change and evolution. This observation is also of crucial importance in discerning the body. The fluid theology of the worship songs raises the central issue of discernment. If the worship songs are theologically fluid and continually on the move, how is the Church to make any kind of judgment about what is a right development and what is a wrong development? It is one thing to participate in the flow of evangelical culture. It is another to be aware of this flow to the extent that it is possible to form a critical evaluation of the culture which a believer might share. Creating such an awareness has been one of the purposes of this present work.

Seeing involves making some kind of judgment. The observation that worship songs introduce a theological dynamic is an indication that the cultural flow of the lived Christian community may contain within itself a self-correcting dynamic. The Spirit might be seen as leading the Church forward into ways of expression that connect in new ways. What is interesting here is that this self-correction operates at the level of creativity and the combined actions of the individuals and communities. There is no one authoritative voice or theological commission. Instead, what appears to happen is new ways of speaking about God and what it means to come into the presence of God in worship, which then play out at personal and corporate levels. This generative and creative theological life of the Church is actually deeply significant. It is fluid theologizing in practice that has kept the evangelical Church in touch with cultural expression, and has meant that it has been able to adapt and renew itself by connecting and expressing. Technological developments have helped this fluid Church culture to evolve. The move towards digital projection, for instance, has meant that hymn books have become less important for the churchgoer in the pews. Before the projector and the computer, there was the more basic technology of the overhead projector, and before that, the photocopied song sheet. These technologies have allowed contemporary Churches to embrace a much faster moving hymnody, where new songs can be incorporated into worship very quickly, in some case immediately after they have been written. Whereas in the past songs would have to wait for the next hymn book, and then once a Church had bought an expensive set of books they would be in use for at least ten years. New technology has had the effect of speeding up the rate of change. Paradoxically, this fluid environment has meant that evangelical Christians simultaneously participate in a highly adaptable and creative operant theology, while also holding that their core beliefs have not changed. It is the form of the unchanging evangelical gospel that enables this slightly paradoxical self-understanding to persist.

The gospel is not entirely left behind in the new and more fluid theological world of the worship song, however. One way to view the songs is as a kind of freestyle improvisation on the evangelical gospel. While it is seen as fixed, the gospel can become a source for creative expression in certain circumstances. It is permissible to work with and around ideas such as the cross or relationship with Christ in ways that draw on a wider range of theological metaphors than those that are contained in the very limited ideas of the evangelical gospel. This improvisation is not seen as being a particular threat to the gospel or indeed any kind of drift away from orthodoxy. This is an interesting insight into how operant theology plays out in the lived expression of the community. So while theological innovation expressed in more formal ways will almost invariably be read as a challenge to evangelical identity and the very being of the community, similar ideas may well be quite happily expressed in more lyrical ways in the songs. The songs seem then to be a mechanism for flexible and adaptive theologizing, where academic theology or even preaching, or the publication of similar ideas in books may be highly problematic. At the same time there is an issue with this arrangement, because the very limited expression that is generally seen as the gospel is not a good basis to correct or review the freestyle improvising of the fluid operant theology. The abbreviated form of the gospel makes it slightly redundant in effect. This is why improvisation is necessary, because it generates a theology that is rich enough to sustain a vibrant and ongoing faith.

CHAPTER 8

Evaluating the Case Study

The case study has so far explored the complexity that arises when the gospel is expressed in culture. As the gospel generates a way of life, the paradox of presence and partiality is revealed in the split between espoused and operant theologies. This chapter explores the dynamics that have been set out in Part II in relation to theological and cultural currents set out in Part I. Evaluation needs to be conducted carefully, however, because of the divine being and the fluid nature of the Church. This chapter divides into two main sections. The first sets out some considerations that should precede a critical evaluation in a Liquid Ecclesiology, and the second is the evaluation itself.

A. Before Evaluation

Reflexivity

The organic images for the Church of vine and body are clues as to the way that evaluation should proceed. For just as an objective and disconnected approach to the study of the environment and biodiversity has become unacceptable, it is similarly inappropriate for the theologian to position him or herself outside of the living and growing organism of the Church and hence to make it a distanced object of study. This does not mean that judgment is not possible. Actually the reverse is the case. The Church has a responsibility to always be self-critical. Criticism needs to be self-aware, however. For my part, this kind of reflexivity requires a consideration of how I have been formed in my own Christian journey by the contemporary Church.

In many ways, the case study of the contemporary Church traces my life as a Christian. I first came to faith at a youth meeting where the evangelical gospel was preached in much the same form as it is found in the Four Spiritual Laws. My memory does not allow me to say that the Bridge to Life diagram was actually used, but I would not be at all surprised if this were the case. I certainly became acquainted with it through my local evangelical Anglican church, where the "Journey Into Life" tract was displayed on the bookstall. From the early 1970s until the present day, I have sung the songs that I analyze in the case study. They have not simply been a source of academic research, but have formed a significant part of the liturgical diet that I have been nourished by, and it must be admitted, at times also frustrated by. In fact, this book and the

 | DOI 10.1163/9789004347359_010

research that lies behind it came about as a direct result of my sense of unease with the contemporary Church and its gospel presentation. My journey embodies the tension and indeed the problems that I have described. The contemporary Church has been the source of my Christian life and yet it has also been a cause for reflection and criticism. Just saying this is an important move. It recognizes the organic and participatory nature of the Church. I write not as an objective academic observer and analyst, but as an insider who is grateful for what the Church has given him and concerned to help the Church to fulfil what it is meant to be. This kind of reflexivity is an essential aspect of Liquid Ecclesiology.

Humility and Discernment

As well as a commitment to reflexivity, the process of evaluating requires caution and also humility. To set out to evaluate a theory or a theological argument is one thing. To evaluate a Church is something else. In Part I it was argued that the "being of the Church" is Jesus Christ. This has significant implications for the way that theological reflection can be constructed. If the being of the Church and the gospel is Jesus Christ, then discerning the presence of Christ is a matter of faith and prayer as well as critical reason. Churches cannot be debated about or objectified in an argument in the way that is possible with theological ideas. However imperfect they may be, churches are places where the Holy Spirit is bringing life and transformation. Evaluation in the first instance requires a gift of discernment. Seeing the Church in the lived is a theological discipline of attention and contemplation. This situates empirical work in a theological epistemology. Such an approach is necessary, because, as has been said, the Church is the Church because of the presence of Jesus Christ through the power of the Holy Spirit. It is also necessary because seeing in this empirical/theological context should be regarded as an act of reaching out towards God through the use of human observation and reason. Seeing is sharing in a divine vision. Seeing the Church therefore requires a spiritual methodology. Such a methodology needs to be God breathed because it is an act of seeing Jesus Christ in the social and the historical.

Paul Fiddes defines seeing as wisdom. Wisdom, he argues, does not locate the one who is seeing as above or beyond what is seen, but embraces embodied forms of knowing. These forms of knowing do not repeat the problems associated with the distance between the object and the subject and the consequent issues of power, or the claims to "comprehend" that characterize enlightenment forms of knowing. Thus wisdom is a discipline of reflection and a kind of knowing, but it transcends both of these. Seeing the world (through reason and knowledge) can be a means of knowing others in a truly relational way, and finally knowing God. In the biblical tradition, wisdom is personified in female form. Thus to see is to respond to the call of Lady Wisdom. "Does not wisdom call, and does not understanding raise her voice? On the heights, beside the way, at the crossroads she takes her stand; beside the gates in front of the town, at the entrance of the portals she cries out" (Prov 8:1-3). The figure of Lady Wisdom represents the dancing and travelling of divine self-giving.[1] This understanding of Lady Wisdom transforms the act of seeing (knowing and rationalizing) from the distanced gaze of the detached but powerful modern observer that has been problematized in more recent thought, into a relational movement within the life of God. The call of wisdom, says Fiddes, is to see the world and thereby know God.[2] Yet for wisdom there is a paradox that combines transcendence and immanence. As it is written in the Wisdom of Solomon: "For wisdom is a kindly spirit, but will not free blasphemers from the guilt of their words; because God is witness of their inmost feelings, and a true observer of their hearts, and a hearer of their tongues. Because the spirit of the Lord has filled the world, and that which holds all things together knows what is said" (Wisdom 1:6-7). Here, says Fiddes, wisdom is identified as the Spirit of Yahweh and this identification contains both the notion of observer, and also wisdom as the means of coherence in the world. These two are held in paradox. Wisdom is therefore both a "faculty of mind and the field of investigation that lies outside in the world.... Wisdom as the faculty of God is also there in the world, drawing near to her devotees on the path of daily life; she offers them communion with her, inviting them to walk with her on her own circuit through the cosmos. This is observation that it is also sympathetic participation."[3] Such wisdom cannot be pinned down. It is not to be found in a particular location. Wisdom is a riddle that points to a journey. Wisdom is not hidden away in a place where she might be found if we knew the secret. "Wisdom," says Fiddes, "transcends or goes beyond the grasp of the human mind," because God alone grasps the complexity of inexhaustible Wisdom.[4] Thus the personification of wisdom is an invitation to participation in a kind of investigation and knowing that is shared with God. Seeing, even seeing in God, is not entirely straightforward. The Wisdom tradition speaks of the immensity of creation and the unknowability of the created world and this invokes the "elusive" quality that exists alongside the possibility of exploration. Wisdom is

1 Proverbs 8: 22-31.

2 Paul Fiddes, *Seeing the World*, 188.

3 Fiddes, *Seeing the World*, 199.

4 Fiddes, *Seeing the World*, 239.

there to be enjoyed but can never be possessed.[5] What Fiddes terms the "no place" of wisdom represents a check on the assertion that to be "wise" is to have control over the world: "it affirms a hiddenness at the heart of reality."[6]

The figure of Lady Wisdom, the personification in the tradition, is picked up in John's gospel in the person of Jesus Christ. In the prologue of John's gospel Jesus is introduced as the *Logos*. "In the beginning was the word and the word was with God and the word was God" (John 1:14). The *Logos* terminology in John's Gospel, Fiddes points out, echoes the personification of wisdom.[7] The implication is that wisdom is made manifest in the person of Jesus Christ. The divine wisdom or *Logos* is incarnate in Christ and this is the "glory" that is seen by believers. "And the Word became flesh and lived among us, and we have seen his glory, the glory as of a father's only son, full of grace and truth" (John 1:14). The revealing of wisdom in Jesus Christ, the *Logos*, does not lead to an escape from complexity and ambiguity, however. The plethora of names for Christ in the New Testament, even in this opening passage of John's gospel (light, life, son, lamb, word), are an indication that in Jesus Christ there is the "fullness" of God. This personification (or incarnation) is the revelation of complexity. It is precisely for this reason that the Christ of the gospels is elusive, even as he is revealed.[8]

For Fiddes, seeing is not confined to the Church. Seeing encompasses the ways of God in the world. Discerning Jesus Christ and the work of the Spirit therefore becomes a more fluid business, where the presence of Christ passes between the Church and the wider culture. This fluidity challenges a solid notion of the Church as containing the work of God and defining by its actions all that God might be and do. The presence of Christ in the Church is instead a clue to the further discernment of the work of the Spirit beyond the solid meetings and worship activities of the community. This fluid nature of the work of the Spirit is a call to reach beyond the Church that is to some extent embodied in the concern to express faith and connect, but is also a continual challenge to be drawn into and participate in the work of the Spirit beyond the solid boundaries of the Church. Such fluidity is a parallel to the cultural adoption and adaption that mark the life of the contemporary Christian community. The contextualising of worship and ways of experiencing faith through the use of the forms and ways of communicating of popular culture is a further

5 Fiddes, *Seeing the World*, 239.

6 Fiddes, *Seeing the World*, 250.

7 Ben Sirach 24: 6-10.

8 Fiddes, *Seeing the World*, 345.

clue that the Spirit, the world and the Church have porous boundaries. This is what I call Liquid Church.

The Trinity as Relation

God is seen by Fiddes as a complexity that matches the complexity of the world. The Trinitarian God for Fiddes subsists as persons in relation. The Trinity, he argues, is "not a mathematical puzzle. It is all about a God who lives in relationship and is in movement."[9] The persons of the Trinity are not to be seen as formed by relations, but as actually being relations. "The Trinity, then is a vision of God as three interweaving relationships of ecstatic, outward-going love, giving and receiving."[10] The persons in relation move within and between each other in movements suggestive of a dance. This movement is expressed in the term *perichoresis*, where the persons in the Trinity "co-inhere" with each other "without confusion."[11] This is a development of the words of Jesus in the Fourth Gospel: "Believe me that I am in the Father and the Father is in Me" (John 14:11). So for Fiddes, "The hypostases are 'distinct" realities as relations and the *perichoresis* is an interweaving of relations."[12] This language about God is not generated out of the position of the distanced observer, because to see in these terms is to share in the relations of God. God makes sense as we are involved in God's life. "Talk of God as Trinity is not the language of spectator, but the language of a participant."[13] To see God in this sense is to be taken up in movements of being glorified, being sent and being breath. As Fiddes puts it, "Talk about God begins from encounter with God."[14] It is this God that opens a space in the interweaving and dancing movement for relations with human beings. "In creation and in redemption God opens a space within the interweaving movements of relation, so that the created universe exists 'in God',"[15] and to speak of God in this way is not to "describe God" or to claim to see God. The language of relations "describes what it is like to engage in God."[16] Relation with God is like the intermingling flow of water. The Trinity is the fount, the spring and the stream, "three currents or movements of 'delight', which intermingle and can nevertheless be distinguished from each other."[17] The Trinity

9 Fiddes, *Seeing the World*, 256-257.
10 Fiddes, *Seeing the World*, 150.
11 Fiddes, *Seeing the World*, 151.
12 Fiddes, *Seeing the World*, 151.
13 Fiddes, *Seeing the World*, 152.
14 Fiddes, *Seeing the World*, 153.
15 Fiddes, *Seeing the World*, 153.
16 Fiddes, *Seeing the World*, 257.
17 Fiddes, *Seeing the World*, 259.

seen as relations opens the space for understanding the world as being within the movement of God. So to see is to share in the divine movement, to see "in God." This form of knowing is particularly appropriate for ecclesiology, where cultural forms and theological expression are seen as being that is in movement. The liquidity of the Church is therefore to be seen as arising from the being of God, but just as God is being in relation and movement, so is the Church. Yet in so saying it is always acknowledged that the ability to "see" this movement and hence to discern the Church arises from relation. Seeing is participatory rather than structured by modern notions of subject and object. There is an appropriateness to this approach to epistemology as the basis for an ecclesiology that takes account of the lived in coming to discernment and also construction.

Discerning the Body

The investigation into believing in the contemporary Church requires the wisdom of God. But seeing is complex and discernment is not straightforward. The reality of believing is to be found in the work of the Spirit and in the presence of Jesus Christ. To see the Church therefore is to see God. At the same time, this seeing requires the ability to discern Christ within the particularity of lived expression. Seeing is thus problematic and relates to the wisdom that Fiddes describes. To see is not simply an academic exercise, however. Seeing, and the attempt to develop discernment, is a responsibility for every believer in the Church. Christians are called, says Clare Watkins, to continually be attentive to the presence of Christ in the practices of the Church. She calls this "discerning the body."[18] Her starting point for understanding what it means to discern the body is found in the eucharistic passage of 1 Corinthians 11: 27-29:

> Whoever, therefore, eats the bread or drinks the cup of the Lord in an unworthy manner will be answerable for the body and blood of the Lord. Examine yourselves, and only then eat of the bread and drink of the cup. For all who eat and drink without discerning the body, eat and drink judgment against themselves.

This passage has traditionally been interpreted in Catholic circles as having to do with Eucharistic reception, says Watkins, but it might also be seen in light of the wider argument of the letter as a commentary on the life of the Church. In particular, 1 Corinthians 10 and 11 are an extended discussion of

18 Clare Watkins, Recorded Address, King's College, London, 2014.

the ethical behaviour of the Church and the way that worship is conditioned by communal life. First Corinthians 11: 27-29 comes at the conclusion of some of these arguments. As a result, discerning the body becomes an admonition about what it means to be the Church, i.e., the body of Christ, and how by not discerning the body, individuals may effectively put themselves outside the community by taking part in meals in inappropriate ways. The appeal to the words of the Lord and the discerning of the body, says Watkins, thus take on a particular meaning. Believers are called to pay attention to the practice of the Church and to be aware of their own participation in these practices, because to share is to partake in the "body." For all members of the Church there is, Watkins says, a constant task of discerning the body of Christ, not simply in the sacraments, but also in those practices and ways of living together that form communal life.

Discerning the body means paying attention to Christ in and through the practices of the Church, seeking out and being conditioned by the presence of Christ in the community. Discernment is also a task that involves an ability to be self critical and reflexive about the life of the Church. Seeing in this sense involves a call to share in the life of the Church, while being attentive to the possibility that practices and communal expression may be less than the "body." This kind of discernment is a call to take responsibility for the imperfections of expression and the social forms that constitute the Church. Such attentiveness does not mean separating oneself from the Church in order to be objective, or indeed adopting the role of the critic, but instead accepting that participation in the Church always involves the contingency of cultural expression and as such discernment remains necessary, even as Christ might be made present in the sacrament, in preaching, or through the singing of contemporary worship songs.

The significance of Watkins' approach to discernment is that all Christians are called to be continually attentive to the life of the Church. Discerning the body is an ongoing responsibility, a call to faithfulness. It is in this context that the work of the theologian should be understood. Theologians, says Watkins, are seeking to discern the body of Christ when they start to take seriously what is taking place on the ground. Such attention is a demand on theologians, but this kind of discernment is itself complex, because there are different layers of meaning within communities. She calls these "Christ's various and layered presences in the practices of communities." Discernment is therefore a human activity that is spiritual, pastoral and intellectual. Discerning the body needs each of these areas if it is to be possible to encounter what she calls the mysteries of Christ's presences in practices. Discernment therefore requires an empirical engagement with ecclesial communities and the ways in which they express faith in cultural forms. So for Watkins the Spirit is out there doing the work of God and the task of the theologian is to catch up with what God is doing. An ecclesial practice is a response to the work of God in the world. The theologian articulates what is taking place. The role of the theologian is therefore to articulate how God might be at work in relation to the empirical. For Watkins, this approach rests ultimately on a particular understanding of the work of God in the world drawn from Catholic theology. She points out that Vatican II argues scripture makes "progress" in the Church with the movement of the Spirit. This includes all of the work and teaching of bishops and priests, but it is also concerned with the believing of individuals.

> This tradition which comes from the Apostles develops in the Church with the help of the Holy Spirit. For there is a growth in the understanding of the realities and the words, which have been handed down. This happens through the contemplation and study made by believers, who treasure these things in their hearts[19] through a penetrating understanding of the spiritual realities which they experience, and through the preaching of those who have received through Episcopal succession the sure gift of truth.... The words of the holy fathers witness to the presence of this living tradition, whose wealth is poured into the practice and life of the believing and praying Church. Through the same tradition the Church's full canon of the sacred books is known, and the sacred writings themselves are more profoundly understood and unceasingly made active in her; and thus God, who spoke of old, uninterruptedly converses with the bride of His beloved Son...[20]

Here revelation is seen as developing in the Catholic Church, both through official teaching and through the ways in which individual believers take up the words of scripture and inhabit them as part of who they are. Seeing the Church therefore involves paying attention in order to "see" the work of Christ in communities and in practices. Watkins likens this process of discernment to the revelation that comes upon the Apostle Peter in the book of Acts when he sees the Holy Spirit descend upon the gentile Cornelius and the members of his household. Peter expresses his own transformation to Cornelius with these words: "I truly understand that God shows no partiality but in every nation anyone who fears him and does what is right is acceptable to him" (Acts

19 See Luke, 2:19, 51.

20 Second Vatican Council, *Dei Verbum* 8.

10:34-35). Even though he says these words of acceptance and welcome, it is only when he witnesses the Holy Spirit descending on these gentiles that he discerns Christ at work. Astonishment then quickly turns to acceptance and these new believers are welcomed into the community through baptism (Acts 10:44-48). Discernment in this context is complex. Peter is a participant in the events that are unfolding, but his understanding seems to grow as he sees the work of the Spirit. This kind of participatory discernment is the responsibility of every member of the Church, Watkins argues. The call is to seek to discern where and how God is at work. And in order that the work of God might be discerned, it becomes essential to engage with practice. In order to know what God is doing in the world, there is an imperative to engage in attentiveness. This means that there is a requirement that theologians who study the Church develop the skills and ways of paying attention that are found in empirical work. It is important to stress that such attention is not a reduction of the theological to the social and cultural, but precisely the opposite. The point that Watkins is making here is that these theological insights generate an approach to seeing and discernment that means that empirical methods are not simply an option, but a necessity. Seeing in these terms is participating in the complex and contested conversation in which there are many voices.

B. Evaluating the Case

Problems and Their Correction

Churches generate problems for themselves by doing the right thing. This may seem contradictory, but there is a simple logic to this idea. The logic rests on the idea that movement and life bring complications. Growth causes tensions and as a result sometimes takes the Church in directions that it does not quite intend. Thus doing the right thing can sometimes require that Christians periodically take stock and pause. Blessings give rise to dilemmas. So the social and expressive activity of the Christian community makes Church in cultural forms, and like all culture, it is not static but fluid. Fluidity is in the way that expression changes over time, and it is also there in the different ways of believing and being Christians that individuals and communities construct and then inhabit. This is what I call Liquid Church.

In the Liquid Church, forms take on a life of their own and generate a momentum. Life and energy thus lead to movement and change. In the contemporary era, ecclesial change has been significantly accelerated by the use of forms of communication that are common in popular culture. These forms have given rise to a plethora of events, festivals, publications and organizations, all dedicated to resourcing and renewing the Church. This is what Rob Warner calls entrepreneurial evangelicalism.[21] In a study on the impact of an evangelical festival in the United Kingdom, Warner demonstrated how it became the site for a new kind of theological and spiritual experience. This was based on conservative bible teaching and an orientation towards personal lifestyle issues. These themes were brought together in the rapidly spreading new forms of song-led charismatic worship. Warner argues that as these conservative evangelical Christians started to embrace the entrepreneurial activity facilitated by the use of popular culture as a means of worship and developed a festival-based culture, there were unintended consequences.[22] Warner calls this "acculturation." What he means by this is that the conservative evangelical form of Christianity began to take on board notions of personal choice and the priority of the individual. "Entrepreneurial evangelicals," says Warner, "habitually experiment at the level of popular religion with dialectical re-articulations of Gospel and Church, and this trend can be expected to increase within the ferment of cultural change in post-modernity."[23] Personal encounter with God and the utilization of popular culture in generating new ecclesial forms are intimately related. This interrelationship is complex and contradictory, but understanding something of the fluid cultural shape of the Church is fundamental in developing a theological evaluation of the expression of the gospel.

The Heart of the Problem

In seeking to express the faith in contemporary cultural forms, the evangelical Church has generated a significant problem. The problem is a split that has opened up between the gospel and the everyday lived believing that operates in the Church. This disconnect is not at all straightforward. It is not as simple as saying, for instance, that the Church has through its entrepreneurial activities sold out to the wider culture, as Rob Warner seems to suggest. Warner is nevertheless pointing to a crucial issue when he says that entrepreneurial activity with its accommodation to the wider culture brings about an inherent tension with the more static doctrinal roots of the movement.[24] The disconnection, I want to argue, is not primarily between doctrine and entrepreneurial activity,

---

21 Warner, *Reinventing English Evangelicalism 1966-2001.*

22 Robert Warner, "Autonomous Conformism—the Paradox of Entrepreneurial Protestantism Spring Harvest: A Case Study," in *Religion and the Individual: Belief, Practice and Identity*, ed. Abby Day (Aldershot, UK: Ashgate, 2008), 101.

23 Warner, "Autonomous Conformism," 101.

24 Warner, "Autonomous Conformism," 101.

but between the personalized lived faith of relationship with God and the understanding of the gospel that has developed in the contemporary Church.

In seeking to communicate faith, the contemporary Church has come to think of the gospel in a particular form. The form of the gospel has come about through the desire to find the most effective way to communicate faith. Evangelistic practice has therefore generated a radically foreshortened expression of belief that is based around a small number of short doctrinal propositions. This form of the gospel has enabled communication in ways that help non-believers to quickly grasp the basics of the faith, and by accepting the facts of the gospel, to find Christ through turning to him in prayers of acceptance. These prayers in essence repeat the gospel formula and become the doorway into relationship with God. Thereafter believing takes a form that is personalized and experiential in nature. The seeds of this personal faith have always been deep in the evangelical understanding of the gospel. Alongside the presentation of the gospel as a series of doctrinal propositions there has also been a more participatory and relational understanding of what it means to believe.

At conversion, it is typical for believers to invite Jesus to come "into their hearts" or "into their lives." This invitation carries the idea of being indwelt and builds on the way that evangelicals have always regarded faith as in some way being a relationship with Christ. A personalised faith is supported and enabled by the doctrinal formal of the gospel at conversion. The one is dependent on the other. What I argue in the case study is that what has started to happen in the lived expression of the Church is that the theological expression of the gospel has become less and less significant in the day-to-day walk of faith of Christian communities. While the doctrinal form of the gospel continues to function as the means to conversion, it appears to play a less significant role in faith as it is lived and experienced in communities. It is important to note that while it may not be central to the regular walk of faith for individuals, the gospel has not gone away. In fact it has become enshrined as a key identity marker that must be defended when challenged, and preserved at all costs. Hence the gospel is believed, and it is seen as being unchanged by culture, and yet paradoxically, or perhaps as a consequence, it appears to play a marginal role in what it means to live as a Christian. As a result there is a disconnection at the heart of the state of believing.

The Consequences

The first consequence is that there is *widespread amnesia about the Gospel.* Many Christians struggle to see the connection between their everyday life in the Church and any kind of formal doctrine that might be seen as the gospel. In a recent interview that I conducted with a youth leader in a national role, the widespread nature of this forgetting of the gospel became clear. The youth leader spoke of a training event for a large charismatic festival. They were training leaders who were regularly involved with the Church and the festival and most were between eighteen and twenty years of age. Some of these leaders were employed as youth ministers in their churches. The training session was preparing them to counsel young people who had made a commitment to Christ at the festival. When speaking with the leaders, my interviewee encountered a distinct reluctance to explain the gospel to the new Christians. Many, she felt, were unable to articulate what she described as the basic three point message of sin, the cross, and repentance and faith. To address this failing, the leaders were given a pack of literature that included a gospel tract. This pack gave them the confidence to meet with converts after the event, where, instead of explaining the faith, they planned to simply pass on the pack and say it was all covered in the literature. This was not an isolated incident. During the interview the national leader commented: "I spend my life explaining the gospel to Christian youth leaders. Nobody has the confidence to share the message. They just can't articulate their understanding of the gospel, they haven't got the language to do it. They haven't been taught it in their church."[25]

The reason many Christians now struggle to articulate the Gospel is that *it is no longer central to the life of the Church*. The case study demonstrated the importance of narratives of encounter in contemporary worship songs. Encounter is set within a highly personal and subjectivized account of the faith. Where doctrine is present, it is fragmented within a narrative about the individual meeting God. In the contemporary Church, this encounter is enacted in the context of worship and ministry times. The worship services build towards times when individuals come forward and teams of volunteers pray for them at the front of the church. This is the climax of the worship in contemporary church settings, in particular those that have been influenced by John Wimber. Ministry times have become a focus for an intense and deeply significant meeting with God and they have been life transforming for many. This practice has an unintended consequence, however. Such is the focus on what will make a difference and help believers to respond and receive what God has given in ministry, that anything that does not serve this practice of personal encounter is downplayed. Ironically, this might also include the gospel, because in the contemporary Church, the truncated gospel has been reduced to the prayer that is prayed when a person becomes a Christian. It is not held at the level of conviction. The personal narratives of encounter are the operant convictions

25 Interview with the author, May 21, 2015. Source anonymous by agreement.

of the Church. As my interviewee explained to me, the overriding interest of leaders within the Church is to present something that leads towards ministry, i.e., something that can be prayed into people during ministry times. So talk of the gospel or doctrine is reduced to the personal, because leaders are always asking: "What are we going to pray for? It has to go to a ministry moment where the person can connect with God." If this connection doesn't happen, then whatever is shared as teaching has little point or purpose. My interviewee went on to explain, "We have said feeling is enough, it is all about encounter with God."

The evangelical Gospel has become a method for evangelism in the contemporary Church. It is not at the heart of belief or practice. Again my interview with the national youth leader showed how this comes into effect. She explained how becoming a Christian is enacted by going down the front at a festival and encountering God. This involves praying the prayer that summarizes the three point gospel. "The place I encounter God is one of these large festival gatherings and I am prayed for and then I take God out." With this basic pattern *the Gospel is only for sharing faith with your non-Christian friends*. The gospel therefore becomes a vehicle to convert others. The problem with this is that the Christian message has been reduced to its bare essentials in order that it can be communicated. My interviewee was clear that the festival culture and ministry time had had a detrimental effect on the Church. "The gospel has been reduced to one dimension, because it is easy to sell." Yet even in this form, many Christians lack the confidence to articulate the theology of the Church. The main reason for this is that the gospel has ceased to be the operant theology in the contemporary Church. So the gospel in its short and unchanging form is not part of the deep convictions of the community in the way that it should be.

A Different Diet

In the contemporary Church, everyday faith comes about through an acceptance of the gospel, but thereafter it is sustained by a quite different diet. This observation comes from an analysis of the lived faith of believers and the observation that the contemporary Church is characterized by a highly fluid Christian culture. The most significant feature of this fluid Church life is the worship songs. The songs are the main cultural carriers and the central distinguishing mark in the contemporary Church. Singing is more than a moment of communal feeling or even theological assent. The songs are meant as a place for divine encounter through praise and through moments of intimacy. The songs frame this encounter in increasingly personalised terms. An examination of the theological content of song lyrics demonstrates how the more objective doctrine of the evangelical gospel has been largely replaced in the worship songs by the language of relationship and encounter. The Jesus of the scriptures has become the more intimate, but less well defined "You" of contemporary worship. The worship songs point to forms of believing that are less wedded to specific doctrinal formulation, while being articulated by a theology of the self in relation to God. It is important to note that this theology of the self in an intimate and ongoing relationship is of deep significance and meaning. This orientation means that the criticism that the contemporary Church lacks theology is misplaced. Believers have rich and highly rewarding theologies that sustain in many cases vibrant faiths and lively churches. At the same time these personal theologies appear to operate with only a slight relationship to the kind of doctrine that most evangelicals would identify as the Gospel. In other words, there are in effect two kinds of theologies that exist simultaneously in the churches.

The description of a disconnection between the evangelical gospel and the personalized theology of everyday worship and spiritual life highlights the complexity of contemporary believing. The significant point here is that close attention to the lived expression of faith in the Christian community is able to identify how it is possible for Christians, and indeed Church communities as a whole, to believe one thing at an almost theoretical level and to live their Christian lives in ways that have little or no meaningful connection to these beliefs. When asked about the gospel, individuals will be quite convinced that it is a true and unchanging statement of the faith, and yet in their songs and prayers and even in their daily lives, these "truths" may not play any significant role. The Gospel is true and must be preserved, but that is about the sum of it. It is important to note that this is not at all to say that people are dishonest or that they have "sold out" the gospel. All of these criticisms of the contemporary Church misdiagnose what is actually taking place, because they do not adequately account for the complexity of lived believing. It is also important to note that such an observation is by no means meant to support the idea that there are no problems in the Church, because there are. The disconnection between the gospel and lived theology is deeply problematic, but it has not come about through unfaithfulness, or through a desire for the wrong things, or even through theological neglect or ineptitude. It has come about through the Church trying to do the right thing.

Activity brings tensions. In the case of entrepreneurial evangelicalism, the drive and the energy has come from a desire to remake the Christian faith and Church life into a form that connects with people. For Rob Warner these developments are a kind of accommodation to culture. The irony is that through such accommodation, thousands of believers have been encouraged in their faith, and the churches that have participated in this renewed form of Christianity have flourished. In other words, without accepting wholesale the idea that numerical success equals blessing, it seems obvious that the Spirit has been at work, even as evangelicals have seemingly incorporated aspects of popular culture into the life of the Church. It is this use of cultural forms that brings tensions. But the problems come from life and movement. They are a symptom of the work of the Spirit, rather than an indication of its absence. Believing, as a result, is an expression of faith lived out in cultural forms. It is what is made that simultaneously becomes a place of divine encounter. Jesus Christ is present through the power of the Holy Spirit, in and also through, the cultural activity of Christians and of the Christian community. All culture is fluid, including Church culture. Yet it is the Spirit that is the life. The Spirit is the water that wells up in the Church to eternal life. The fluidity of cultural human expression means that as it moves, it changes shape and inflection. Movement therefore, even movement that is generated by and infused by the Spirit, throws up problems rather than closes them down.

Expression of belief in cultural forms is simultaneously a place for revelation and also a place for the veiling of God. God is beyond all expression, but the Church is charged with the task of communication. This is the deep cultural paradox of ecclesiology. For without expression there is no life. Yet it is a communication that is always limited and contingent. At the same time it is as the Spirit takes up the expression of believing that the Church is vivified and made alive, but this expression is always limited, and an honest assessment would be that it is very often mistaken. The mistakenness of the Church does not preclude the activity of the Spirit, since the revealing of the presence of Christ is always predicated on imperfect culturally-bound expression. Imperfect expression and the fluidity of ecclesial culture together ensure that Church is always provisional, and provisional in the sense that it is necessary to accept that it carries imperfections along with it as it shares in the work of the Spirit. These imperfections mean that the expression of the Church requires periodic attention, as in attentiveness, but also as in correction. The analogy here might be that of a car. Cars need work because they are driven about. Mobility brings wear and tear. We might resent repair bills, but they arise because of use. Driving is in most cases not aimless, for it is how people do their business and spend their leisure time. We drive because we have purposes. Vehicle repair is thus the by-product of our "life."

The Problem with the Kernel and Husk Theory in Practice

The kernel and husk theory sets out to reassure a fast-changing Church that it has not let go of its essential theology. The case study suggests the belief that the Gospel is unchanging and yet the fact that the Church must always change to communicate the faith in cultural forms has within it significant problems. These problems are the unintended consequences of trying to "preserve" a form of the gospel while living in a dynamic and ever youthful Church. In Part I these issues were discussed in relation to the theological currents in Liquid Ecclesiology. What was argued was that the presence of Christ in the Church through the work of the Spirit is fluid, but this fluidity is matched by the way that culture works. Cultural forms shift their meaning across time and within communities.

The case study shows how cultural forms shift over time. This includes the expression of the gospel. When the evangelical Gospel was developing in its shortened form, it operated as an effective means to help young people come to faith. As culture changed and the expression of the Church adopted more subjective forms of expression and these came to predominate, the unintended consequence was that the evangelical gospel moved away from being central to the life of the Church. It was no longer part of the convictions of the community as it once was. The case study therefore demonstrates how in the lived expression of the Church, the kernel and husk theory is highly problematic. The fluid nature of culture bypasses the attempt to preserve the faith by a refined theological definition. What has actually transpired has been that the Gospel has become all but marginal in the life of the Church. People are living off the husk rather than feasting on the kernel.

The Grand Narrative and a Foreshortened Gospel

There is a further, and perhaps more profound problem that arises from the case study. The contemporary Church has developed an understanding of the gospel that has been developed primarily to communicate quickly and effectively with young people. This highly abbreviated form of the faith has been effective in the limited purpose for which it was first devised, but again there is an unintended consequence. In Part I, the "grand narrative" was discussed as a means of evaluating the communication of the Church. The shortened gospel is theologically quite limited. When it is put up against the grand narrative that Andrew Walker has suggested as a measure for gospel communication, it has some significant gaps.[26] The grand narrative represents the gospel in the broad perspective of creation, the Trinity, and eschatology. These crucial elements of the Christian narrative are missed in the evangelical gospel. There is good reason for this: they complicate the telling of the message. Simplification is required to communicate with young people and indeed with wider

26 Walker, *Telling the Story*.

society. This is not necessarily a problem, but when this shortened expression becomes "The" Gospel, in other words, all that is said or all that it is possible to recall, and when it seems that even recalling this can be a challenge, then there is a real issue. Here the idea of a grand narrative might serve as an important corrective.

The grand narrative is a corrective not because it is theologically more sophisticated or more complete, but because it offers a vision of the fullness of Christ. The gospel should be an attempt to express Christ if it is to be termed "the" gospel. The foreshortened evangelical message and the personal narratives of encounter do not represent Jesus Christ in his fullness and indeed his complexity. This is why there is a problem. To make this observation is not to say that Jesus Christ is not present and real to people in the expression of Church, however. This is the paradox that is discussed in Part I. Jesus is present in the particular and in the culturally-bound expressions of the Church.

That Jesus is present does not mean that the expression of the Church is adequate. This is where the pragmatic concern of the contemporary Church for growth and the numbers who come to faith at events misses the mark. Through the power of the Spirit, Jesus is present to people, but this should not be taken as a total affirmation of how the Church communicates and the way of life that its message has generated. The point of the grand narrative is that it offers a corrective to the whole expression of the Church, not just the specifically doctrinal. The partial nature of the expression of the contemporary Church is therefore called into question and made subject to critique by the historically more complex and nuanced expression of the Church that is summarized in the grand narrative.

PART III

Abiding in a Liquid Ecclesiology

CHAPTER 9

The Call to Abide

Liquid Ecclesiology focuses theological attention on the multi-layered complexity of expression in the Church. The argument that has been developed throughout this book revolves around the challenges and possibilities for theological reflection on the Church when the "lived" becomes fully a part of the conversation. In this context, the case study serves to illustrate the inherent complexity of ecclesial expression. It demonstrates how through the dynamics of expression and the impact of cultural change, meaning, identity, spirituality and operant theologies are fluid in the contemporary evangelical Church. This fluidity is not peculiar to one particular church, however. I want to suggest that given a similar study of discourse in other churches, a very similar fluidity in expression and lived culture would be evident. This would manifest in different ways. In particular I would anticipate that the relationship between perceived "fixed points" of theology and practice would be very different in different ecclesial contexts.

Fluidity and complexity inevitably raise the issue of normativity in ecclesiology. What I mean by normativity is the necessity for the Church, and the theologian as part of the Church, to make decisions and come to some kind of judgement in the midst of the shifting ecclesial context. It should be stressed that judgement here is not meant to be a kind of disinterested arbitration about expression. Normativity speaks instead of the necessity for a faithful and prayerful attention to lived expression. The case study therefore serves to model how theological evaluation and normativity is enriched and nuanced through the kinds of insights that are generated through qualitative empirical work. Judgement in ecclesiology is fundamentally theological in the sense that it necessitates a discernment of the presence of Jesus Christ in and through cultural expression. This calling to "see Jesus" is far from straightforward.

Discernment in Theological and Empirical Discourse

There is a tension in any kind of empirically-orientated ecclesiology. This tension is brought to the fore in relation to questions of normativity where normativity is understood as discerning the presence of Christ. I have been reflexively aware while writing Parts I and II of a tension between confidence in speaking of the divine that is habitual in theological discourse, and a wariness

 | DOI 10.1163/9789004347359_011

about similar kinds of speech when dealing with empirical data. I have self consciously adopted a "theological voice" in Part I, but I have done so with the caveat that all theological speech is epistemically relative. This move serves to position both the theological voice and the analysis that can be developed through qualitative empirical work as equivalent. This equivalence operates at the epistemological level of expression. Of course the theological voice is seeking to express an ontological hierarchy. It cannot be taken as being that ontology itself, however. The real, that is, the presence of Christ in the Church and in the world, is always distinct from expression, even as that expression seeks to understand. In the case study I focussed on the espoused and the operant theological voices that are evident in empirical discussion about the contemporary evangelical Church, although Cameron et al. refer also to the formal theological voice. This aspect of the "four voices" typology is significant in that it suggests the fundamental connection between academic theology and the life of the Church.[1] Academic theology is therefore simply one of the voices in the complex fluidity of discourse in the Christian community.

Relativizing the theological voice in this way should not be taken as the negation of normativity. Expression is not an option. The Church must be made and remade, and judgement plays a fundamental role in this construction. Judgement then is part of the paradox of a Liquid Ecclesiology. It is a call to faithful ecclesial expression while accepting the contingency of that expression. This chapter explores this paradox in Liquid Ecclesiology that comes from normativity as the discernment of the presence of Christ. In what follows, I argue that seeing Jesus has two aspects. The first relates to the revelation of Christ in the scriptures. The second involves seeing this same Jesus in the present-day expression of the Church. This second aspect of seeing requires a disciplined attention to the lived complexity of believing, while the first is a call to contemplation and wonder, to behold the glory full of grace and truth. Both are a call to see, and hence to see and to develop a critique of the expression of the Church and the way of life that this expression gives rise to requires an approach that arises from worship and wonder. Liquid Ecclesiology situates normativity in worship and wonder. This is the call to abide in Christ. Abiding then becomes the continual point of return for theological reflection.

Visibility and Seeing

Contemplation and reflection rest on the conviction that Jesus Christ can be "seen." Seeing involves a re-orientation from the position of the distanced and

1 Cameron et al., *Thinking about God in Practice.*

objective observer to the participant who is continually drawn into relationship. This seeing, according to Paul Fiddes, involves specific skills and the mastery of a body of knowledge, but it is fundamentally a sharing in the dynamic life of God.[2] Seeing Jesus connects with the twin dynamics of contemplation and reflection. Jesus is seen first in the scriptures. This seeing provides the orientation and the perspective that enables the seeing of Jesus in the Church and also in the world. This is reflection. Reflection is both a process of disciplined attention and a relational journey into the life of God. Reflection rests on the transforming light of Christ shed forth in the world and in the Church. It is the light of the gospel of the glory of God (2 Cor 4:3). The Christ that we see in the Church and the world is the one who is reflected in the shining face of those who are animated by the Spirit. Seeing, then, is the discipline of learning to attend to those who also see and are reflecting the light of the gospel. Hence believers are transformed by the glory of God in the freedom of the Spirit. Reflection is a theological discipline of paying attention to discerning the light of Christ in the life of the Church and also in the wider culture. This reflection is not other than the life of the Church. It is also a reflection, a participation in the work of the Spirit. Seeing therefore refers both to contemplation and to reflection, and both have their place in the renewal of the Church and the gospel that it shares and lives by.

Behold the Lamb of God

Seeing finds its root in the command of the Baptist in the first chapter of John's Gospel. The Baptist's disciples are instructed to look for and to see Jesus the Christ. So John the Baptist reacts to his encounter with Christ with these words, "Behold the Lamb of God who takes away the sin of the world" (John 1:29). In chapter 20, John explains the purpose of the gospel in the following way, "Now Jesus did many other signs in the presence of his disciples, which are not written in this book. But these are written so that you may come to believe that Jesus is the Messiah, the Son of God, and that through believing you may have life in his name" (John 20:30-31). The Baptist's invitation to "behold," is not only there to guide his disciples. It is an invitation to all who read the gospel. Believers are invited, drawn into the gospel narrative in order that they might "see." What the reader sees is quite simply that in Jesus the Father is revealed. This is the whole point of the gospel, says John. These stories, and the words of Jesus, have been recorded in order that the reader may believe. To believe is to see the Father revealed in Jesus Christ. So the words and the stories are there

2 Fiddes, *Seeing the World*, 188.

to enable encounter with God through the work of the Holy Spirit. The Living Water wells up in and through the stories of Jesus.

In the incarnation, Jesus reveals God. This visibility comes to believers in the present through the gospels, but at root it is a Trinitarian act of revelation. The Son is the "image of the invisible God, the first born of creation" (Col 1:15). In him the invisibility of God is made visible. The Son reveals the invisibility of the Father, says Irenaeus, making the Father "manifest" through his own manifestation.[3] For no one knows the Son but the Father, or the Father but the Son and those to whom the Son shall reveal the Father. The incarnation is the divine purpose of revelation, making God known to all of humanity. "The Father therefore has revealed Himself to all, by making His Word visible to all; and conversely, the Word has declared to all the Father and the Son since he has become visible to all."[4] Through the revealing of the Word all may see because "the Father is the invisible of the Son but the Son the visible of the Father."[5] Visibility enables "seeing," but this does not make God the object of our knowing. Seeing leads to knowledge, but this knowledge leads to relationship and to worship rather than comprehension. Contemplation arises from the visibility of Jesus in the incarnation, but this visibility is carried into the life of the Church through the work of the Holy Spirit. The Church is the body of Christ, the reflection of glory, image being transformed into image. Discerning the body, i.e., reflection, rests on the revelation of Christ seen in the scriptures and in particular the gospels. So while reflection demands the attention and discipline that is required to draw close to the complexities of the lived experience of believing, it finds its life and energy in Jesus Christ the Light of the world, the image of God, reflected in the gospel as it is made alive and vivified by the Holy Spirit in the Christian community. Contemplation and reflection are a turning towards scripture and a turning towards the lived. Both have a complexity that echoes and engages with the other. It is only in this two-way turn to complexity that Liquid Ecclesiology can find a way to demonstrate how the foreshortened form of the evangelical gospel can be animated and made alive.

The Door and the House

There is a significant correspondence between the rich and varied complexity of the lived experience of believing and the deep and layered nature of the

3 Irenaeus *Ad Her* IV, 6.3.

4 Irenaeus *Ad Her* IV, 6.5.

5 Irenaeus *Ad Her* IV, 6.6.

gospel's account of the revelation of Jesus Christ. It is tempting to treat the evangelical gospel as reductive or simply misguided. This needs to be resisted, however. There is one very important reason why resistance is necessary, and it is found in attentiveness to the lived practice of the Church. The evangelical gospel may reduce the complexity of believing to a few quickly communicated and easily understood propositions, but this formula has opened the door into believing for millions. Lived believing is incredibly rich and varied in practice and expression. The gospel of the "Bridge to Life" diagram has proved to be the doorway into the life of faith for many thousands. At the same time while it may be the door, it is not the whole house. In practice, what has happened is that the "house," i.e., the faith that people choose to live with and live by, pays very little attention to the gospel message that initially sparked the faith. The evangelical gospel is a construction based on the much more complex and layered text of the scriptures, and in particular, the gospel accounts of the life and ministry of Christ. The truth of the short statements in the Four Spiritual Laws or the Bridge to Life diagram are not self-evident, nor indeed are they true simply because they lead people to an experience of God. The truth of the gospel lies in the person of Jesus Christ, who is the way the truth and the life. The purpose of the gospel is not to say all that could be said, or even to make a definitive theological statement. The evangelical gospel has been developed to communicate quickly and effectively. It is meant to lead believers into a more sustained relationship with Jesus Christ in their daily life, and through the scriptures. These twin dynamics of turning to the complexity of scripture and to the lived experience of faith both need to be brought into play when the dislocation between the gospel and the operant lived theology of the Church is addressed.

Contemplation and Reflection

Contemplation and reflection introduce the move towards the two complexities in Liquid Ecclesiology required to reintegrate the fullness of Christ into the inhabited spaces of lived faith. This is a call to continually revisit the Jesus of the gospels to worship, to receive living water, and to be renewed in the Spirit. This worship is to be found in a close attention to Jesus revealed in the scriptures. This is what it means to contemplate. Contemplation involves a reorientation towards Jesus as he is seen in the gospel narratives. The calling is not to seek to simplify or even to look for a specific message, however. Contemplation and reflection are acts of worship that draw on the worship of Christ made visible. This practice is akin to the spiritual theology of the

Eastern Church in relation to praying with icons. For orthodox theology, the icon is an image or a material representation that is possible because of the visibility of the Word made flesh in Jesus Christ. As John of Damascus says: "In former times, God without body or form could in no way be represented. But today, since God has appeared in the flesh and lived among men, I can represent what is visible in God."[6] The icon is material and yet the worship is not fixed on the form but passes beyond, through, and within the form to the image of God in Jesus Christ. Contemplation and reflection rest on a similar spiritual practice that locates seeing in the material but does not fix the presence of Christ in cultural forms. By turning towards the dual complexities of the lived and living Word, reflection and contemplation seek to be actions of transforming worship.

It is the Spirit that leads the believer into truth. The Holy Spirit, Jesus explains, will guide the disciples and show them the truth. Although in the gospel the disciples have been with Jesus and they have heard what he has said, they will continue to need the Spirit at work in them. "I still have many things to say to you but you cannot bear them now. When the Spirit of truth comes, he will guide you into all truth; for he will not speak on his own, but will speak whatever he hears and he will declare to you the things that are to come" (John 16:12-13). The Spirit will glorify Jesus, "because he will take what is mine and declare it to you" (John 16:14). The Spirit-led journey into truth is not a journey beyond or away from the Jesus of the Gospels, but a journey deeper into the glory of the Gospel shining in the face of Christ. It is this encounter with glory and truth that transforms. The evangelical gospel in its shortened form opens the way. It is the door and the worship songs and the personalized spirituality of the believers that generates a lived and vibrant faith. These elements are not in themselves wrong; they simply require the enrichment of a focused and disciplined continual return to the Jesus of the Gospels and a development of a self awareness and attention to present-day practice that will in turn enable a reconnection between espoused and the operant. This is contemplation and reflection.

Contemplation and reflection should not be confused with developing theologies or doctrinally-based principles for ministry. Truth eludes specific formulations, because it is not an idea but a person: Jesus Christ. Seeing Jesus in the gospels involves reading or hearing, and through this practice, the Spirit takes the believer to Jesus and invites him or her to worship. This is the contemplation of God revealed in Jesus. It is what it means to worship in Spirit

6 John of Damascus quoted in John Meyendorff, *Christ in Eastern Christian Thought* (Crestwood, NY: St Vladimir's Seminary Press, 1975), 179.

and in truth, to abide in the presence of Christ. In the gospel stories there is the "light of the gospel of the glory of Christ" (2 Cor 4:4) and it is the God who caused light to shine "who has shone in our hearts to give the light of the knowledge of the glory of God reflected in the face of Jesus Christ" (2 Cor 4:6). Hence to worship in truth is to gaze on Christ and to continually return to gaze on him such that the community is transformed from one degree of glory to another (2 Cor 3:18). By turning towards the dual complexities of the lived and living Word, reflection and contemplation seek to be an action of transforming worship. This kind of seeing is best described as the call for the Church to abide in Jesus Christ.

A Church that Abides

Seeing, i.e., the practice of Liquid Ecclesiology as contemplation and reflection, is a relational participation in the Trinitarian life of God. These practices of seeing are not techniques for ministry or methods for practical theology. They are the freedom of the Spirit and a sharing in the Jesus who is light and the life of the world. To see is to be indwelt and to indwell the life of God. This indwelling or abiding shapes what it means to believe. For St Athanasius, abiding is linked fundamentally to seeing Jesus Christ. This theology is a development of the Johannine theology of the vine, where to be joined to Christ as an organic unity is spoken of as abiding.

Abiding is the charge on the Church to continually return to contemplation and reflection. Abiding finds its classic ecclesial expression in John's Gospel. Jesus is the vine and his followers are the branches. Joined to Christ, branches are incorporated into him for he is the "whole" that is the vine. Being one with Christ, the disciples are tasked with abiding.

> Abide in me as I abide in you. Just as the branch cannot bear fruit by itself unless it abides in the vine, neither can you unless you abide in me. I am the vine, you are the branches. Those who abide in me and I in them bear much fruit, because apart from me you can do nothing. My Father is glorified by this, that you bear much fruit and become my disciples. As the Father has loved me, so I have loved you; abide in my love. If you keep my commandments, you will abide in my love, just as I have kept my Father's commandments and abide in his love. (John 15: 4-5 and 8-10.)

Ecclesial practice springs as a fruit from being made one with Christ, the vine. Apart from the vine there is no fruit. In fact, the unfruitful branches are cut off and thrown on the fire. The life of the believer and the life of the Christian community have no other source and orientation than what is found in union with Christ. C. K. Barrett talks about the union of believers with Christ "originating in his initiative and sealed by his death on their behalf, is completed by the believers' responsive love and obedience, and is the essence of Christianity."[7]

The image of the vine is the "supreme image" of the people of God. Israel is the vine that was brought out of Egypt and planted by God.[8] The "chosen" nation is often pictured as a degenerate and unfruitful plant.[9] In John's Gospel the image of the vine is taken up by Jesus and used as a reference to himself. He is the true vine, just as he is the true light, and the true bread.[10] Jesus is the chosen one and his are the true people of God made such by being joined to him. Union with Christ in the image of the vine is paralleled in Paul's characteristic phrase of being "in Christ."[11] James Dunn speaks of the "in Christ" language in Paul as indicating a "mystical sense of the divine presence of Christ within and without." This divine relationship brings about and nurtures the individual and community through the gospel.[12] Being in Christ, Dunn argues, is never to be seen as a mystical removal from the world or everyday life. Instead it becomes the "starting point and base camp for a quite differently motivated and directed life."[13] The image of the vine in John can also be seen in parallel to the image of the body of Christ in Paul.[14] Here the practice of spiritual gifts is set in the context of unity. Unity among believers is derived from the oneness of the Spirit and the oneness of Christ.[15] This unity transcends not only ethnic and social differences, but it also forms the basis for a community where there may be "varieties of service" and "varieties of activities" (1 Cor 12:5-6). Ministries of every kind spring from the work of the Holy Spirit. It is the baptism in the Spirit that joins the community together into the body of Christ.[16] Unity is derived

7 C. K. Barrett, *The Gospel According to St John: An Introduction with Commentary and Notes on the Greek Text*, 2nd Edition (London: SPCK, 1978), 470.

8 Ps 80:8; Richard Burridge, *John: The People's Commentary* (Abingdon: Bible Reading Fellowship, 1998), 180.

9 Isa 5:1-7; Jer 2:21; Ezek 15:2-8; 19:10-14. See R.H. Lightfoot, *St John's Gospel* (Oxford: Oxford University Press, 1956), 281.

10 John 1:9; 6:32.

11 For example, Rom 6:11; 1 Cor 1:2; Galatians 15; Phil 2:5.

12 James Dunn, *The Theology of Paul the Apostle* (Edinburgh: T and T Clark, 1998), 401.

13 Dunn, *The Theology of Paul*, 411.

14 1 Cor 12:1-31.

15 1 Cor 12: 4-6.

16 1 Corinthians 12:13 and 12:27-28.

from Christ who is one, but so also is diversity. The force of Paul's argument, says Gordon Fee is that, "even though the body is one, it does not consist of one member but of many." So the body image rests on unity by being joined to Christ but it also supports difference.[17]

Like the image of the body, abiding in John's Gospel is based on union with Christ. This union finds its orientation and description in the relationship that Jesus has with the Father. As Craig Koester says, "Jesus's bond with the Father shows what it means to bear fruit. He abides in his Father's love and shows this by keeping his Father's commandments" (John 15:10). His love is expressed in obedience.[18] This abiding of the Father and the Son is set in parallel to the abiding of the followers of Christ. To be fruitful it is necessary to abide in the love and in the words of Jesus and walk the path of obedience.[19] Abiding is characterised by mutuality. "Those who abide in me and I in them bear much fruit" (John 15:5). Abiding echoes the talk of the dwelling places that are to be prepared in the Father's house for believers. The Father and the Son dwell in each other and make their home in believers. "Do you not believe that I am in the Father and the Father is in me? The words that I say to you I do not speak on my own; but the Father who dwells in me does his works. Believe me that I am in the Father and the Father is in me; but if you do not, then believe me because of the works themselves."[20] The believer is to abide or to "indwell" Christ and Christ is to abide or indwell the believer. "The Christian is unthinkable," says Barrett, "except in union with Christ."[21] The call to abide also echoes Jesus' words about the Bread of Life. "Those who eat my flesh and drink my blood abide in me, and I in them" (John 6:57). In this context again, mutual abiding is explained analogically by reference to Jesus' relation to the Father. "Just as the living Father sent me, and I live because of the Father, so whoever eats me will live because of me" (John 6:57). To abide is to grow up "in all things into him" (Eph 4:15). To dwell in Christ is to continually be made clean by the words that Jesus has spoken. This is not a metaphorical use of words, but a reference to the actual words that Jesus has spoken.[22] For Rudolf Bultmann, abiding signals a steadfast loyalty to the cause of Christ, although this persistence comes from the experience of being "held" or allowing oneself

17 Fee, *The First Epistle to the Corinthians*, 601.

18 Craig R. Koester, *The Word of Life: A Theology of St John's Gospel* (Grand Rapids, MI: Eerdmans, 2008), 196.

19 Koester, *The Word of Life*, 196.

20 John 14:10-11, see also 14:2 and 23. 181. Richard Burridge, *John: The People's Commentary, 181.*

21 Lightfoot, *The Gospel of St John*, 474.

22 Lightfoot, *The Gospel of St John*, 283.

to be held.[23] To abide, "means holding on loyally to the decision once taken, and one can hold on to it only by continually going through it again." [24] Abiding involves a habitual return to the words of Christ of the Gospels. To abide requires a continual focused attention on Jesus and it is in the gospels that the words and the actions of Jesus are made available for contemplation. To worship in Spirit and in truth is to develop the discipline of returning to this Jesus to "Behold." This practice is quite distinct from the disembodied "you" of contemporary worship. It involves complexity and wonder, while the "you" of worship finds its content and life in the Jesus of the scriptures. We recognize the presence of Jesus Christ in the Church by the power of the Spirit through disciplined attention to what has been "made" known. Glory and truth come through incarnation.

The purpose and function of the evangelical expression of the gospel lies in bringing people to Christ. In the evangelical subculture, tracts such as the Four Spiritual Laws or the Bridge to Life diagram perform an essential function. They provide a way to conversion. They give a framework to a deep spiritual mystery of rebirth. At the very basic level, this gospel provides a set of doctrines that are to be accepted as part of the journey into faith. They make faith imaginable and attainable. As has been explored in previous chapters, this "gospel" then takes something of a back seat as the Christian life becomes a journey with the community and the Spirit. The call to "abide," it should be stressed, does not in anyway overturn this pattern of believing, but it does challenge it as a long-term sustainable spiritual pathway. Fundamental to this challenge is the belief that the "gospel" is Jesus Christ in all his mystery and visibility, revealed and yet also veiled. Evangelical spirituality has in most respects got the basic orientation exactly right. The revelation of Jesus Christ brings encounter with God and new birth, and this is sustained through worship. The problems arise when this gospel, because of its reduced form, becomes neglected rather than being the deep and enduring source of continually enriching and renewing the Church. In a sense the gospel has been emptied of its richness by making it communicable. The call to abide is a call to rediscover the deep and the complex, to seek the elusive Jesus of the Gospels. This seeking of Jesus is possible because Christ is made known through the work of the Spirit in the present, but the touchstone and reference point for this knowing is not in the first place subjectivity, but the scriptures, for it is in the gospels that Christ is made visible.

23 Rudolf Bultmann, *The Gospel of John* (Oxford: Blackwell English Translation, 1971), 535.

24 Bultmann, *The Gospel of John*, 536.

Abiding in Athanasius

Visibility is not in the first instance the basis for doctrinal formulation or for the construction of more effective forms of ministerial practice. The visibility of Jesus Christ is about the rich and sustained salvation of God in the believer through the work of the Holy Spirit. For Athanasius, the "visibility" of the Son becoming incarnate in bodily form becomes a source for a renewal of the image of God in humanity. By taking a body, the Word is able to teach through his actions. He grabs the attention of those who are "looking in the other direction."[25] In the incarnation, the Word acts on the same level as humanity. "He teaches those who would not learn by other means to know Himself, The Word of God and through Him the Father."[26] The Word, says Athanasius, is like a good teacher coming down to the same level as his pupils. "The Saviour of us all, the Word of God, in his great love took to Himself a body and moved as Man among men, meeting their senses so that those who were seeking God in sensible things might apprehend the Father through the works which He, the Word of God did in the body."[27] Thomas Weinandy argues that the body of Christ is central to Athanasius' thinking.[28] The bodily actions of Christ form a connection to humanity. The Word becomes accessible to the senses. It is through these deeds in the body that Jesus reveals the Father. "In re-orientating humanity toward remaining in God, the incarnation thus repairs the convergence between God's transcendence and nearness. God who is invisible and unknowable and pre-eminently accessible through the humanity of Christ."[29] This reorientation comes through the contemplation of Christ and this is what it means to abide.

It is abiding, says Athanasius, which sustains humanity. At creation, God's wish was for humanity to remain.[30] Remaining is made possible by the creation of men and women in the image of God. It is this image that both enables and is sustained by the continual contemplation of Christ who is the image of God. "For having nothing to hinder his knowledge of the Deity, he ever beholds, by his purity, the Image of the Father, God the Word, after whose

---

25 Athanasius, *On the Incarnation* (Crestwood, NY: St Vladimir's Seminary Press), 14.

26 Athanasius, *On the Incarnation*, 14.

27 Athanasius, *On the Incarnation*, 15.

28 Thomas Weinandy, *Athanasius: A Theological Introduction* (Aldershot, UK: Ashgate, 2007).

29 Khalid Anatolios, *Athanasius: The Coherence of his Thought* (London: Routledge, 1998), 37.

30 Athanasius, *Contra Gentes, Nicene and Post Nicene Fathers*, Volume IV (Edinburgh: T and T Clark), 3; Anatolios, *Athanasius*, 35.

image he himself is made."[31] The disobedience of the fall means that this contemplation is interrupted, and the image of God in humanity is lost.[32] It is this loss of the image of God in humanity that brings about the Incarnation. God becomes man to restore humanity's true nature. This gives rise to the famous verse from *De Incarnatione*: "For He was made man that we might be made God."[33] The image of God in humanity is derived from God's being and its restoration comes from the same source. Athanasius is not saying that believers become gods or even sons of god like the Word. Rather it is through the work of grace and appointment that we share in the nature and truth of the Word. "The logos took a body, so that in it we might be renewed and deified."[34] "He was made man for us, and our brother by similitude of body, he is therefore called and is 'first-born' of us, because, all men being lost, according to the transgression of Adam, His flesh before all others was saved and liberated as being the Word's body; and henceforth we becoming incorporate with It, are saved after Its pattern."[35] The Word entering into human flesh is like a great king who enters into a city. By living in that place the whole city is honoured. So it is with the King of All, says Athanasius. By his dwelling in flesh, all of humanity is released from death.[36] The Word takes a human body and he surrenders this body to death, "in place of all."[37] We share in his death and also in his resurrection and as a consequence mortality is brought to an end.

> For this reason, therefore, He assumed a body capable of death, in order that, through belonging to the Word Who is above all, might become in dying a sufficient exchange for all, and, itself remaining incorruptible through His indwelling, might thereafter put an end to corruption for all others as well, by the grace of the resurrection.[38]

Christ's resurrection is the first fruits of what will be at the eschaton the incorruptible humanity of every Christian.[39] Through sharing in the incorruptible humanity of Christ, human beings are restored into "full communion with

31 Athanasius, *Contra Gentes*, 2.

32 Francis Young, *From Nicea to Chalcedon: A Guide to the Literature and its Background* (London: SCM, 1983), 71.

33 Athanasius, *De Incarnatione*, 54.

34 Young, *From Nicea*, 73.

35 *Athanasius, Adversus Arius* ii, *Nicene and Post Nicene Fathers*, Volume IV, 61.

36 Athanasius, *De Incarnatione*, 9.

37 Athanasius, *De Incarnatione*, 8.

38 Athanasius, *De Incarnatione*, 9.

39 Weinandy, *Athanasius*, 34.

the incorruptible Father and Son and so fully share in their communion of love."[40] The incarnation makes possible the restoration of the image of God in humanity, but it also acts as the means to a renewal of contemplation. So the incarnation effects salvation in two ways. "First, he puts away death from humankind and renews it through the resurrection, and secondly, he makes visible what is invisible, that he is 'Word of the Father, and Ruler and King of the universe'."[41] The works of Christ made in bodily form enable humanity to "see" and thus to know the Father.[42] In the worship of Christ communion is restored. The call to abide is an invitation into relationship. This relationship is a participation in the Trinitarian life of God and as such it is transformative. Through the contemplation of the Word believers are changed from one degree of glory to another. Abiding situates indwelling and being indwelt in the continuous return to see Jesus.

Abiding and Normativity

The use I have made of the biblical charge to abide is in no way meant as a specifically focussed theological fix for the kind of problems that have been identified in the case study. Rather, the practice of abiding is a basic requirement for an ongoing healthy Church life in every kind of church. Liquid Ecclesiology is an argument for seeing, i.e., the call to discern Jesus Christ in the paradox of the ongoing life of the Church. This form of abiding takes the Church into the wonder and mystery of Jesus Christ revealed in the gospels. Contemplation is not meant primarily as a time where believers formulate new principles for ministry or seek new truth to preach or to share. This comes later. The task of contemplation is to worship Jesus Christ and to be transformed by his glory. This is not in the first instance the glory of the ascended Christ, but the glory of Jesus, who is incarnated, crucified, and who has risen again. It is this Jesus who the Spirit opens up to us as we worship in the scriptures. This is the Jesus that the Church is called to "behold." Those who worship in Spirit and in truth are those who continually return to this Jesus and rest in his presence and are drawn thereby into the life of the Trinity. It is in this context that the invocation to abide takes ecclesial form.

Believers, as part of the wider community, are instructed to continually return to Jesus Christ and his words. His words are to dwell in them and this is

---

40 Weinandy, *Athanasius*, 34.

41 Athanasius, *De Incarnatione*, 17.

42 Athanasius, *De Incarnatione*, 45.

the basis for fruitfulness. The call to abide carries with it the acceptance that some Christian communities may have significant problems. This lack of fruitfulness may result in branches being cut off and thrown into the fire. Becoming unfruitful arises from a disconnection from Jesus who is the source. To remain in Christ involves a measure of continual correction or pruning. Craig Koester speaks of pruning as the discipline that comes through an encounter with the words of Christ. Pruning (*kathairo*) carries the additional notion of cleansing. The words of Jesus therefore bring about a cleansing of the community.[43] The "words" that cleanse do not become a separate "gospel" from the person of Jesus Christ. This is what it means for Jesus to be the way. As has been noted already in John's Gospel, the truth is a person, not a set of ideas or doctrines. So when Jesus says "I am the Way the Truth and Life," there is a personification of wisdom. This is the *Logos* of the prologue. Truth is embodied in the person of Jesus. Jesus is the one who was with God and who came from God. He is the Word. Yet interestingly, Jesus the Truth is linked in this "I am" saying with the way and the life. Way and life both carry the sense of something that is in process. Life is something that is lived out and a way is something that can be journeyed along. The truth appears not so much to be something that is found out but someone who takes the believer on a journey and this journey and this life are also identified with Jesus. The "truth" therefore is not a kind of objective and distanced observation, but an invitation into complexity and a certain degree of puzzlement. This is what Mark Stibbe refers to as the elusiveness of Jesus in the Fourth Gospel. This elusiveness does not come from any kind of explicit disguise on the part of Jesus, but from the movement of Christ evading his captors and from the complexity of his language and communication.[44] The prologue, argues Stibbe, sets up the key dynamic of the gospel. Here the term *logos* is introduced with no real explanation. Who is the Word, what is the Word, where does the Word come from? These are questions that remain unclear.[45] When the "truth" is revealed in verse 5 that the word is the "light" of the world, elusiveness continues, because as the writer makes very plain, the "world" somehow has not understood or received that which is its light and life. As Stibbe points out, "understood" (*katalambano*) might better be translated as "grasped" or "comprehended."[46] Here is the deep challenge of the gospels to the simplified evangelical gospel. Complexity and elusiveness are almost the complete opposite of the approach to faith that produced the

43 Koester, *The Word of Life*, 40.

44 Mark Stibbe, *John's Gospel* (London: Routledge, 1994), 6.

45 Stibbe, *John's Gospel*, 13.

46 Stibbe, *John's Gospel*, 13.

Four Spiritual Laws and the Bridge to Life diagram, but this is what it means to remain in the words of Jesus Christ: to abide.

Believing in Jesus is not at all the same as grasping and comprehending. Believing is a relationship that transforms those who see and believe to become children of God. Being a child is suggestive of what it means to believe. Believing does not deliver comprehension or indeed absolute certainty. Instead, believing situates the believer as one who is indwelt and indwelling the person of Christ through the power of the Holy Spirit. Belief is a form of knowledge, but it is relational. There is a cognitive element to this knowing, says D. Moody Smith, for to know Jesus is to know from where he has come, i.e., his origin in God.[47] Those who know Jesus also know God, but to not know Jesus is equally to not know God, because Jesus is the one who reveals God. As a result, says Moody Smith, "knowledge of Jesus, and of God, is not an external, objective cognitive relationship, however, but a more intimate and personal one."[48] This insight into what it means to know Jesus Christ is a clue as to how the simplified gospel of the evangelical church might be enriched and made more complex through the contemplation of Christ and the practice of abiding. The assumption behind the evangelical gospel is that the message can be expressed in a very small number of simple propositions and that these can be "understood" and thereby lead people into the presence of Christ and re-birth. This basic format has been a mainstay of evangelicalism for decades, but it is becoming more problematic as the disconnection between the operant theology of the church and the espoused theology of lived believing becomes more marked. The cognitive is simply the means towards relationship. It is for this reason that the operant theology and the practice of the church has focussed on worship and living life with Jesus on a day-to-day basis. This move in the way that belief operates in communities is a deep sensibility and it connects directly to the theology of abiding.

Introducing Construction

Contemplation and reflection are a prelude to construction. Construction is the theological task of cultural creativity. Construction involves an awareness of the fluidity of culture and the possibilities and limitations of theological expression. Reflection is focussed on what has been made, i.e., constructed.

---

47 John 17:7-8:25. D. Moody Smith, *The Theology of the Gospel of John* (Cambridge: Cambridge University Press, 1995), 97.

48 Smith, *Theology of the Gospel of John*, 97-98.

Reflection seeks to discern the presence of Christ through the work of the Spirit in what has been constructed. Reflection is necessary because construction in a fluid cultural environment is complex. In saying this it needs to be stressed that churches of all kinds are more than able to generate forms of ecclesial life that bring life and become places for divine encounter. Construction is not really the big challenge. The main issue is the ability to make Church in a way that is continually self-critical, i.e., based around abiding as both contemplation and reflection. This kind of self-criticism needs to go beyond trying to figure out what is most effective, or what can work best, or what can grow the Church most efficiently. Self-criticism needs to have at its core a theological encounter of abiding. Self-critique in this sense is not really self-criticism at all, but the intentional practice of being open to the reforming work of the Holy Spirit. This openness demands the willing surrender, not just of the "self" or the "heart," or of the individual life of the believer, but a reflexively self-aware surrender of the Church and its expression. I recognize such a suggestion might be vague and depends on the ability of individuals and communities to effect changes in ecclesial culture, but nevertheless, if "abiding" and worship start to be seen as encouraging this openness to the Spirit, correcting and bringing about changes that are not simply individual and personal, but also ecclesial and communal, this will go a considerable way towards generating some of the changes I have suggested. Such a practice is not alien to the Church. Self-criticism is actually part of the ongoing fluid movement of communities. What is innovative here is the suggestion that this regular reform and renewal should form a part of the ongoing practice of worship and that the gospel narratives should move to centre stage in a Liquid Ecclesiology.

The Need for Self-Awareness

Alongside self-criticism, abiding in ecclesiology suggests a basic self-awareness in the Church. This is fundamental to reflection and it consists in generating a mindset that is open to the continual renewal of practices and expression. Contemplation and reflection involve a commitment to look at the practice and expression of the Church with new eyes. It requires the ability to look at what is happening in the day-to-day life of the Church and be constructively critical. This is demanding, because Church culture is generally somewhat resistant to this kind of examination. Leaders and believers together are often impatient for the next programme that will be effective and will solve their problems. Reflection and contemplation are far from being a quick solution. Seeing and abiding requires an attentiveness to the present moment and the forms of expression that have gained a purchase in the life of the Church. Church culture is also resistant because it likes to think that it is right. Needing to be right almost inevitably means that it becomes quite a challenge to entertain the possibility that some things might not be what they should be. Resistance is also there in a general blindness that inhabits our Church life. Church culture is very often quite immune to self-analysis, simply because it casts itself as being that which is normal and self-evident. This generates a viewpoint that things are the way they are because that is the "way" they are. Contemplation and reflection challenge these perspectives and argue that the Church needs to continually review its life and communication. The call to correct the practice of the Church is not in the first place to do with the success of programmes or the effectiveness of the message. The call is to return again to Jesus Christ and to dwell in him and be indwelt by him. This is the call to abide.

Fundamental to reflection is the willingness to simultaneously find the expression of the Church to be a place of blessing and yet also a flawed and muddied complexity. This is a difficult psychological position to occupy; it is to believe and meet God, while also having a weather eye out for the problems and contradictions that accompany divine encounter. This approach is not entirely alien for those who are actively involved in generating the Christian culture of the Church, however. Preachers, for instance, are very aware of the limitations of their messages, even as they believe that they can become places where God might change those who are in the congregation. The same holds true for worship leaders and song writers who may be rather embarrassed by their abilities to play, or to compose, and yet their imperfect offering can become a place where those who believe can find renewal, and the Spirit can be present. These kinds of reactions show that reflection is not alien to the everyday practice of the Church, and it certainly should not be seen as a threat or as unsympathetic criticism. The point is that ministers and leaders are continually reflecting on their practice. What I am suggesting is that this everyday openness to the limitations of expression should become intentionally located in the practice of abiding. Expression, and the sensibility that what has been made has limitations, should be seen in and through the light of Jesus Christ revealed in the gospels and reflected in the animation of the Holy Spirit in the community. Here again there are indications that at the level of practice, many Christian leaders have a spiritual self-understanding that embraces this kind of abiding. What is not evident, however, is the extent to which reflection and self-awareness is habituated in the general and public expression and practice of the Church.

CHAPTER 10

Seeing and Learning: Theological Education in the Church

Liquid Ecclesiology has been an exercise in developing a theological perspective that addresses the central paradox of the Church. This paradox centres on the relationship between cultural expression and the presence of Jesus Christ. I have argued that a Liquid Ecclesiology must take account of forms of knowledge drawn from the empirical as well as the biblical and theological traditions. The intention here is to show how disciplined attention to the lived can and should be central to the ongoing life of the Church. The lived in this sense does not simply mean the cultural, the social, or the historical, because what is alive is the Church, and the life of the Church comes from the work of the Spirit, making Christ present in new ways for each generation. The Spirit thereby keeps the Church young, but this youth aptly comes through expression in the cultural forms that are part of the flow of the everyday. This everyday fluid culture is fundamentally and enduringly generated and regenerated by the creative energy of people.

The life and energy of the Church is not self-regulating, nor, indeed, without significant problems. By following the prompting of the Spirit, the Church grows and is made alive, but in the process it is often the case that some significant problems begin to emerge. The case study illustrates this dynamic, but the same issues and contradictions are present across ecclesial traditions. Liquid Ecclesiology argues that a critical evaluation of problems such as those identified in the case study needs to start by paying close attention to discerning the body of Christ in the practices of the lived community. This means developing ways of reading the cultural in terms of both representation and also in relation to the way that individuals and communities take up representation and internalize it as their sense of self in relation to the world. Attention is a move within the work of the Spirit, because to see is to seek the wisdom of God. Seeing aright arises from the worship of Jesus Christ through contemplation and abiding in the presence of Christ by means of a continual return to Jesus in the scriptures. This continual return to Christ also has to lead to reflection and then to construction. Hence the task of expression, even though it is provisional, is a necessity, because the Church must always make and re-make itself. This proposal in a sense begs the question of "how?"

 | DOI 10.1163/9789004347359_012

A Plan for Theological Education

In this final chapter I set out in outline form a plan for theological education that makes Liquid Ecclesiology an approach that can assist in renewing the Church. The purpose here is to offer a more practical agenda that can help churches and those formally engaged in theological education to incorporate some of the insights that come from combining empirical methods and theology. There are five elements that make up this proposal for theological education: Contemplation, Reflexivity, Attention, Expanding the Fragments and Construction. It is not intended that these elements should form a pattern or a programme for study and learning. They are not, for instance, a version of the Pastoral Cycle.[1] Rather, I want to suggest that Contemplation, Reflection, Attention, Expanding the Fragments, and Construction are not individual stages or moments that make up theological reflection, but are elements that should be present simultaneously in the process of seeing and learning. At various points one element may be more significant than another, but each is related and needs to be present and part of what it means to both see and learn.

Contemplation

Seeing and learning find their true location in Jesus Christ, the way the truth and life. Seeing is seeing Jesus Christ and learning is an invitation into relationship with the Trinitarian God. It is important to realize that this is not

1 An example of the Pastoral Cycle is offered by Paul Ballard and John Pritchard. Here theological education is shaped as a series of stages to move through. The starting point in the process of reflection is the everyday context of *experience* where the prompt for reflection is the experience of an interruption or a tension. This interruption sets off the need for *exploration*. This is a stage where the situation is subjected to analysis in order understand what is taking place. Exploration then leads to *reflection*. Reflection is a process where a variety of different forms of knowledge and of knowing are brought to bear on the situation. These will include the theological resources of the Christian Faith. The final stage is *action*. Growing out of the two stages that precede it a plan for a new approach to a pastoral situation is developed. Action then completes the cycle because it takes the reflection into the field of experience and practice. Paul Ballard and John Pritchard, *Practical Theology in Action: Christian Thinking in the Service of Church and Society* (London: SPCK, 1996), 77-78. For an alternative version of the Pastoral Cycle, see Richard R. Osmer, *Practical Theology and Introduction* (Grand Rapids, MI: Eerdmans, 2008) and for the origins and development of the Pastoral Cycle see Judith Thompson with Stephen Pattison and Ross Thompson, *Theological Reflection* (London: SCM, 2008).

simply a kind of theological rubric that has to be enacted before the Church figures out the best thing that needs to be done or the most "effective" way of communicating the faith, or the most imaginative approach to generating an attractive and successful Church. Theological education needs to start by helping the Church, and particularly its leaders, quit the obsession with the bottom line. The key to seeing and learning is love: love of God, love of the Church and love for the world. This love is the same love that is shared in worship. Worship is integrally related to seeing and learning, since all of these are a call into relationship with Jesus Christ. There is an everyday familiarity with this proposition, since the contemporary Church has embraced worship as a place of self-giving and sacrificial praise. The Church that is only interested in worship for what it gives is mistaken. The everyday wisdom of the Church knows that it is a problem to focus on worship simply as a place that delivers what believers want, even though at times it may fail to live up to this ideal. Nevertheless, the same dynamic is at play in seeing and learning. Theological education is thus a journey in God and towards God. It is characterized by wonder and worship. Anything less is not to see and not to learn, because these have their life in the life of Jesus Christ. The Church is made alive and young again through the Holy Spirit. Being made alive and young is what it means to bear fruit in union with Christ.

In practical terms, this means that the sensibilities and habits that are generated in worship need to be continued into classrooms and seminars. This connection needs to be made explicit. Here I am not necessarily suggesting that an intentional link to worship comes from starting every session with twenty minutes of songs or by sharing in the liturgy, but rather developing practices that call to mind the experience and sensibility of worship. The educational environment should foster the sense that wisdom, or ways of thinking about ourselves and about the world, find their true orientation in the worship of Jesus Christ. Worship in this sense needs to be slightly relearned and repositioned away from the mindset that says, "We are now moving into a time of worship," i.e., a mindset that divides time and practices into sacred and non-sacred moments, and into a way of thinking that draws from the intimate and the deep encounter that is wisdom and is hence a way of being and seeing that facilitates learning. Believers need to start to connect up aspects of themselves in the action of learning that in the practice of the Church might have become inadvertently fragmented. Critical thinking and worship therefore need to be seen as part of the same script in that they come from love, the love of God, the love of the Church, and love of the world. This connection should be found in helping learners to summon up how they are in worship and to bring this worshipping self into the more reflective, analytical, and critical arena of the classroom.

Contemplation is the practice of abiding in Christ. Abiding involves a continual return to worshipping Jesus Christ as he is revealed in the gospels. This approach to the bible draws directly on the theological interpretation of scripture.[2] In this interpretative pattern, the gospel is read as a text that takes the reader into the transforming presence of God. Such a move does not necessarily preclude a critical treatment of the biblical text, but it repositions academic biblical studies as a resource for the theological renewal of the Church through the work of the Holy Spirit. Here again, in practical terms, theological education should find its creative interaction with the scriptures, not primarily through academic biblical studies in the first instance, but through worship. Starting with worship and the use of scripture means finding space to meditate upon the scriptures in any educational program. Biblical studies as an academic discipline can form a part of this spiritual interaction with the scriptures, but the sensibilities and practices of worship should position rational and critical engagement with the text. How this is done as part of personal study and classroom practice can be quite varied and creative, but the main purpose should be to facilitate abiding in Jesus Christ as revealed in the gospel.

Reflection

Worship of Jesus Christ through the scriptures needs to be more than a journey into another world. The bible is of course "other" in terms of culture and time, and it is "other" in terms of its position as a source of revelation, but this should not mean that those who come to worship leave behind their world and what they see in that world. Worship of Jesus Christ in this sense is meant to bring the present into perspective. This is what it means to be reflective in the context of contemplation. In terms of theological education, this means that there need to be practices that help those learning to consciously bring their everyday into the presence of Christ as he is contemplated in the scriptures. This could mean little more than developing forms of bible study that suggest that the experience of the Church in the present should be reflected on in connection with the scriptures. Here the temptation is to try to find conceptual ways of linking the bible to context. This is helpful, but it may not be a way of learning that connects most sympathetically with the operant theology of worship. Practices of prayer and staying with the two realities of the everyday and the gospel stories, without developing mediating theological constructs may be more helpful in the first instance. Believers pray about their everyday lives and

2 Fowls, *Theological Interpretation.*

experiences all the time. Expanding the operant theology might mean that this kind of prayer can be done in and around the worship of Christ in the scriptures. The patterns of theological reflection that have been developed in practical theology have tended to focus on problems. These problems are then used to trigger reflection using the pastoral cycle. This can be very helpful, but what I am talking about here is simply a move towards a regular spiritual practice that involves bringing the everyday and the lived experience of faith into the presence of God through prayerful contemplation of Jesus in the gospel stories. Again the key here is to gently develop learning by encouraging regular life-giving practices of prayer and worship to be expanded through a gradual re-orientation towards the lived and towards Jesus in the scriptures.

Attention

So far, under contemplation and reflection, I have talked about theological education becoming embedded in the ongoing spiritual practices of worship, prayer, and bible reading. This habituated pattern needs to be the basis for learning, but there is also a need for theological education to help students and the wider Church to develop disciplined forms of attention that can enrich and support the life of the Church. These practices need to be such that they help the Church to embrace ways of thinking that are both scholarly and critical. In the case study I modelled what is meant by this kind of attention. Fundamental to the approach has been the conviction that seeing is a practice that is relational and participatory. One of the most significant blockages to learning in the Church is the sense that academic work is something that is entirely distinct from the lived. It requires a new way of thinking. For some this is exciting, but for many it is problematic, because they find that they think one way in their Church and another way in the classroom. Overcoming this divide requires a shift in the theory of knowledge that lies behind theological education. Knowing has for too long been seen as structured around subject and object relations. The knower is distant and required to be objective and hence critical. A participatory form of learning acknowledges the situatedness of the learner and the sources that might be drawn into the learning process, e.g., academic and scholarly writing, and all of these are in turn located in the Trinitarian relational life of God. This shift is not simply a reordering of how the learner and those teaching think about thinking. It is more self-involving than this, because it requires that the self be brought into knowing and learning. This is what has been introduced so far as contemplation and reflection. Learning is therefore participatory.

There are two orientating sensibilities that should operate in developing practices of academic attention in learners. Humility requires that the self-confident church is able to both continue to move forward in creative ways and at the same time be sufficiently self-aware to recognize that what it produces and promotes may need to be examined critically from time to time. Here again the everyday practice of the Church is actually self-critical. Churches and Christian organizations are continually looking for ways to develop and renew their ministries. Theological education should therefore orientate itself so that it works with the flow of this basic orientation and then locate academic and critical sources within the ongoing discussion as helpful conversation partners. This form of operation requires the second orientating sensibility: empathy. Theological educators need to generate an atmosphere around learning that is fundamentally empathetic to practice. This requires not simply an interest in practice, but a deep attention to what it is about the expression of the Church that gives believers life and keeps them on the Christian journey. What is being suggested here is an empathetic attention that should be passed on to students. To see is to be involved and to learn is to work in the direction of the flow of the Spirit. This does not mean that critical things cannot be said. The purpose of seeing is to discern the body and discernment requires judgment, i.e., deciding between things and coming to a view on the way forward.

The four theological voices theory indicates that understanding practice demands attention across a range of expressions.[3] Theological educators should develop the methods that are required to pay attention to the lived practice of the Church in all of these voices. Practitioners themselves are experts in ways that theological educators may not be, but this expertise needs to be expanded and developed by equipping practitioners with analytical approaches that help them to examine the lived and the operant in more focused ways. This means, in the first instance, helping them access the increasing numbers of empirical studies that have been written over the last ten years. These studies are often not specifically theological in nature. Many are located in the sociology of religion, anthropology or in religious studies. Accessing these sources for theological reflection means building an awareness of the theoretical and methodological frameworks that give rise to particular studies, and generating a critical and reflexive interaction with these sources. In other words, practitioners should be encouraged to learn what they can from a variety of different disciplines that study the Church, but to also be aware that the interests of those writing such studies may have led them to different perspectives

3 Helen Cameron et al., *Thinking about God in Practice.*

and indeed conclusions from those of practitioners.[4] This kind of attention does not mean rejecting social scientific perspectives wholesale, but neither does it mean that the insights that are found in other disciplines are to be absorbed uncritically. Alongside pre-existing studies, those involved in theological education also need to include specific training in practice-based empirical research methods, including the various issues around observation and interviewing, data collection and data analysis. Empirical research is deeply important, but it is not the only kind of attention that needs to be fostered and developed. The Christian tradition has deep and significant resources in Biblical Studies, Theology, and Church History as well as Christian ethics, that can and should be utilized as part of what it means to develop a disciplined attention. The Pastoral Cycle is helpful in this regard because it encourages practitioners to engage with the various forms of knowledge as stages in a process of reflection. This staged approach means that as part of learning, practitioners develop the habit of turning in a focused way to theological and social scientific resources. The problem with the staged approach is that it can tend to give the impression that thinking takes place in separate disciplinary boxes. The reality is that academic disciplines are not quite so disconnected, and a participatory understanding of teaching and learning collapses these distinctions in even more radical ways. The truth is that thinking progresses through articulation in much the same way that creativity takes place in the everyday life of the Church. Connections need to be encouraged as do critical perspectives that cross boundaries. This is what it means to pay attention.

Alongside the use of studies from a range of different disciplines, as part of their theological education, practitioners should also be encouraged to develop the skills that are necessary to conduct their own empirical studies. There is no space here to detail how this kind of work might be done, but it should be the responsibility of those involved in theological education to offer small-scale research training.[5] This training should cover some of the basic methodologies and also the ethical issues around conducting research in the context of ministry. The value of small-scale research is that it encourages ministerial practitioners to pay attention, and above all to listen to those with whom they work. This kind of listening is an everyday activity at its most basic level, but what small-scale research can do is develop a continual curiosity in clergy or

4 For more on this see Pete Ward *Perspectives on Ecclesiology and Ethnography.*

5 For more on qualitative empirical methods see John Swinton and Harriet Mowat, *Practical Theology and Qualitative Research;* Pete Ward, *Perspectives on Ecclesiology and Ethnography, Explorations in Ecclesiology and Ethnography* and for small scale research in a ministerial context see Mary Clark Moschella, *Ethnography as a Pastoral Practice.*

Church workers about the effects of what they are doing and how expression does actually make a connection with people's lives. Research should not be focused entirely on the ways that communities build lives and how they operate in the world, but also on the kinds of expression and habituated operant theologies that are circulating in cultural forms most often used in Church. There should thus be a place for attention to prayer, worship songs and talks, for instance. It should be the aim of theological education that empirical research of this kind becomes a basic tool for all who are heading into ministry and leadership.

Construction

The purpose and product of theological education needs careful consideration. In an academic context the conventions of assessment mean that students are expected to produce written work. This written work is required to conform to certain conventions. Academic writing has the strength of encouraging the assimilation of knowledge and a critical engagement with ideas. Through writing, students are able to demonstrate that they have developed these skills and those teaching them are then able to assess how well students have achieved these aims. This process in and of itself, while it has merit, is not really what theological education is about. The product that we are aiming for should not be more writing or better writing, but a renewed Church. Renewing the Church calls for expression, and this expression takes place not in the two dimensional world of theological writing, but in the multi-dimensional world of cultural construction. There is a word of caution here: I am currently writing an academic text, after all. Writing can form part of the process of contemplation, reflection, and attention and it is indeed construction, but it is not the end point or the product. Nevertheless, writing can help in the process of theological education if it leads to the generation of a renewed Church.

Practitioners can benefit from learning the skills of academic writing, but theological education is incomplete if it does not automatically enable practitioners to also make Church. Methods of practical theology, such as the Pastoral Cycle, include some element of revised practice, but what they do not tend to do is frame this in terms of cultural production. In other words, practitioners are often left writing papers about practice rather than constructing in the modes and expressive conventions of the Church. Thus students typically consider the communication of the Church and generate "theological reflection," but what they might not do so readily is formulate new ways of praying or writing songs or planting a church. There are practical reasons for this, e.g., the limitations of classroom-based learning, but there are also certain academic assumptions that hold sway. Chief among these is the belief that "ideas" will generate new forms of practice. This basic approach to knowledge needs to be challenged in theological education. Ideas may lead to renewed practice, but construction in the cultural forms of the Church will always be preferable, because that is the basic milieu of the practitioner. This is where the life of the Church takes place.

Construction in cultural forms means that theological education needs to pay as much attention to how Church is made as to writing essays and dissertations. Making, as has been discussed in the previous chapter, involves a complex cultural dynamic between processes of production, representation and the various ways that individuals and communities take up what is represented and make it part of the lived and habituated. Theological educators should take these dynamics much more seriously. Again this does not mean theology becomes reduced to the cultural and to the social scientific. It means that theology takes seriously the way that God is present in the world. While the development of new ways of thinking and different theoretical frameworks remain highly significant, theological education should also encourage more "three dimensional" forms of construction.

Expanding the Fragments and Editing Expression

In *Liquid Ecclesiology* I have argued that the Church is a fluid cultural expression indwelt by the presence of Christ through the power of the Holy Spirit. This perspective assumes that where there is life there are problems as well, because cultural expression is complex, multi-layered and contradictory. The overriding core value for theological education should be a deep regard for the Church as a living, moving, cultural form. This regard is essential to theological education because it builds on a respect for what has been made meaningful by communities and by the investment of individuals, but it also recognizes how meaningful places are made what they are by the work of God who is Trinity in relationship. All that has been said so far about what it means to "see" and how this is linked to an epistemology of wisdom and participation should permeate theological education such that those who are learning generate the attitudes and spiritual sensibilities of wisdom in relation to their own formation within a tradition in the Church and also in the traditions of others. Theological education is not distinct from, but is a part of the life that vivifies the Church. By consciously incorporating worship and prayer and spiritual practices into educational programs, this connection becomes more explicit.

The proposal is that the experience of worship expresses an explicit value of building on the life that already exists in the Church as the origin for learning and renewal. Here the proposal is that theological education should seek its starting point in the habituated ways in which believers find God in their everyday operant theologies. In other words, learning takes people from what they know and from that which helps them expand, into new areas and ways of seeing. This approach to theological education affirms what is already there and then builds on it. Faith is expanded and developed in the power of the Spirit and the primary means for this is worship. The next constructive move I call "expanding the fragments." What I mean by this is that the point of departure and creative development for theological education should be the various ways that biblical and theological themes are already at large in the ongoing discourse of the Church. Concerning the worship songs, for instance, I have discussed the way that biblical narratives and theological themes are embedded in a fragmentary way in lyrics and other forms of expression. Theological education should help students develop these references and give them a context in the wider flow of biblical narrative and theology. Taking the fragments that are already seen as meaningful and part of the operant theology of the Church and then developing them offers a more likely form of education that may enable practitioners to re-integrate what they are learning into the everyday expression and practice of the Church.

Conclusion

Valuing the lived expression of the Church and expanding the fragments should be the core values of theological education, but are not the full extent of what should take place. The purpose of contemplation and reflexivity is that through worship of Jesus Christ and through learning to pay attention to expression and the everyday life of the Church, practitioners should become confident and able to be self-critical. Criticism in this context might be too strong a word. Perhaps a better word might be the ability to "edit." Editing is an interesting term because it takes account of the ongoing flow of expression that is part of the life of the Church. Ministers are editing all the time as they make choices between different kinds of cultural/theological expression. Sermons, for instance, are often edited to take out sections that are less well-expressed and to include better illustrations or insights. This kind of everyday editing is a part of the fluid life of the Church. On a larger scale it is clear from the activities of entrepreneurial evangelicalism that the development of new initiatives and projects often arise from a perceived lack or gap in what the Church is currently doing. Thus conferences might be set up to encourage women into leadership roles or programs might be launched to help churches engage in social and justice issues in their local communities. Here the process of construction has been generated from a critique of the current practice of the Church. The same might be observed about the shifts in the narratives of encounter in song lyrics. These changes have come about in part because new ways of speaking about God seem to fit the current time much better, or have more resonance. These changes have not usually arisen because of any explicit critique of the previous theology of encounter, but rather have come through a general orientation towards change and the collective sense or wisdom as the Church takes up these forms of expression and new narratives of encounter as its own. Theological education needs to be positioned within these vivifying practices of renewal, while also helping students become self-aware about the changes that they are themselves participating in as they make choices and as they edit. This awareness can be taught in classrooms and modelled by leaders, but it finds its origin in the practice of abiding.

Bibliography

Adams, Nick and Charles Elliott. "Ethnography is Dogmatics: Making Description Central to Systematic Theology." *The Scottish Journal of Theology* 53/3 (2000).

Adey, Lionel. *Hymns and the Christian Myth*. Vancouver: University of British Columbia Press, 1986.

Ammerman, Nancy T. *Congregation and Community*. New Brunswick, NJ: Rutgers University Press, 1997.

Anatolios, Khalid. *Athanasius: The Coherence of his Thought*. London: Routledge, 1998.

Athanasius. *On the Incarnation*. Crestwood, NY: St Vladimir's Seminary Press.

Athanasius. *De Incarnatione. Nicene and Post Nicene Fathers*, Volume IV. Edinburgh: T and T Clark.

Athanasius. *Contra Gentes. Nicene and Post Nicene Fathers*, Volume IV. Edinburgh: T and T Clark.

Ballard, Paul and John Pritchard. *Practical Theology in Action: Christian Thinking in the Service of Church and Society*. London: SPCK, 1996.

Barrett, C. K. *The Gospel According to St John: An Introduction with Commentary and Notes on the Greek Text*. London: SPCK Second Edition, 1978.

Barth, Karl. *Church Dogmatics* I.1, translated by Geoffrey W. Bromiley. Edinburgh: T and T Clark, 1975.

Barth, Karl. *Church Dogmatics* I.2, translated by G.T. Thomson and Harold Knight. Edinburgh: T and T Clark, 1956.

Barth, Karl. *Church Dogmatics* II.2, translated by Geoffrey W. Bromiley et al. Edinburgh T and T Clark.

Barth, Karl. *Church Dogmatics* IV.2, translated by Geoffrey W. Bromiley. Edinburgh: T and T Clark, 1958.

Barth, Karl. *Church Dogmatics* IV.3.2, translated by Geoffrey W. Bromiley. Edinburgh: T and T Clark, 1962.

Barth, Karl. *Anselm: Fides Quaerens Intellectum: Anselm's Proof of the Existence of God in the Context of His Theological Scheme*. London: SCM Press, 1960.

Bauman, Zygmunt. *Liquid Modernity*. Cambridge: Polity Press, 2000.

Bebbington, David. *Evangelicalism in Modern Britain: A History From the 1730's to the 1980's*. London: Unwin Hyman, 1989.

Bender, Kimlyn. *Karl Barth's Christological Ecclesiology*. Eugene, OR: Cascade Books, 2013.

Bevans, Stephen B. *Models of Contextual Theology*. Maryknoll, NY: Orbis 2nd Edition, 2002.

Bevans, Stephen B., and Roger G. Schroeder. *Constants in Context: A Theology of Mission for Today*. Maryknoll, NY: Orbis, 2004.

Bhatti, Deborah, Helen Cameron, Catherine Duce, James Sweeney and Clare Watkins. *Living Church in the Global City: Theology in Practice*. ARCS Project, 2008.

Bonhoeffer, Dietrich. *Christology*. London: Collins, 1966.

Borlese, Craig and Mike Pilavachi. *Live the Life: The Soul Survivor Guide to Doing it*. London: Hodder and Stoughton, 1998.

Bosch, David J. *Transforming Mission: Paradigm Shifts in the Theology of Mission*. Maryknoll, NY: Orbis, 1991.

Bright, Bill. *Would you Like to Know God Personally?* Campus Crusade, 1965.

Bultmann, Rudolf. *The Gospel of John*. Oxford: Blackwell English Translation, 1971.

Burridge, Richard. *John: The People's Commentary*. Abingdon: Bible Reading Fellowship, 1998.

Cabasilas, Nicholas. *The Life in Christ*, translated by Carmino J. Decatanzaro. Crestwood, NY: Saint Vladimir's Seminary Press, 1974.

Cameron, Helen, Deborah Bhatti, Catherine Duce, James Sweeney, and Clare Watkins. *Talking about God in Practice: Theological Action Research and Practical Theology*. London: SCM Press, 2010.

Campbell, Heidi, Gordon Lynch, and Pete Ward. "'Can you Hear the Army?' Exploring Evangelical Discourse in Scottish Youth Prayer Meetings." *Journal of Contemporary Religion* 24/2 (May 2009).

Cannell, Fennella, ed. *The Anthropology of Christianity*. Durham, NC: Duke University Press, 2007.

Carpenter, Joel A. *Revive Us Again: The Reawakening of American Fundamentalism*. Oxford: Oxford University Press, 1997.

Clark Moschella, Mary. *Ethnography as a Pastoral Practice: An Introduction*. Cleveland, OH: Pilgrim Press, 2008.

Cray, Graham. *Youth Congregations and the Emerging Church*. Cambridge: Grove, 2002.

Creasy Dean, Kenda. *Practicing Passion: Youth and the Quest for a Passionate Church*. Grand Rapids, MI: Eerdmans, 2004.

Creasy Dean, Kenda. *Almost Christian: What the Faith of Our Teenagers is Telling the American Church*. Oxford: Oxford University Press, 2010.

Davids, Peter H. *The First Epistle of Peter: New International Commentary on the New Testament*. Grand Rapids, MI: Eerdmans, 1990.

Doornebal, Robert. *Crossroads: An Exploration of the Emerging-Missional Conversation with a Special Focus on Missional Leadership and its Challenges for Theological Education*. Delft: Eburon, 2012.

Dunn, James. *The Theology of Paul the Apostle*. Edinburgh: T and T Clark, 1998.

Eddison, John, ed. *Bash: A Study in Spiritual Power*. London: Marshal Morgan and Scott, 1982.

Edwards, Jonathan [1746] "A Treatise Concerning Religious Affections," in *The Works of Jonathan Edwards*, John E. Smith, ed. Vol 2 (Newhaven: Yale University Press, 2009).

Fancourt, Graham. *Brand New Church? The Church and the Postmodern Condition*. London: SPCK, 2013.

Fee, Gordon. *The First Epistle to the Corinthians: New International Commentary on the New Testament*. Grand Rapids, MI: Eerdmans, 1987.

Ferguson, Everett. *The Church of Christ: A Biblical Ecclesiology for Today*. Grand Rapids, MI: Eerdmans, 1996.

Fiddes, Paul. *Seeing the World and Knowing God: Hebrew Wisdom and Christian Doctrine in a Late-Modern Context*. Oxford: Oxford University Press, 2013.

Finney, Charles. *Lectures on Revival*. Grand Rapids, MI: Bethany House Publishers, 1935 (1988).

Fowl, Stephen. *Theological Interpretation of Scripture*. Eugene, OR: Wipf and Stock, 2009.

Gay, Doug. *Remixing the Church: Towards an Emerging Ecclesiology*. London: SCM, 2011.

Gittoes, Julie, Brutus Green, James Heard, and Ian Mobsby, eds. *Generous Ecclesiology: Church, World and the Kingdom of God*. London: SCM, 2012.

Graham, Billy. *Peace With God*. Surrey, UK: The Kingswork Limited, 1954.

Guder, Darrell, L., ed. *Missional Church*. Grand Rapids: Eerdmans, 1998.

Guest, Mathew. *Evangelical Identity and Contemporary Culture: A Congregational Study in Innovation*. Milton Keynes, UK: Paternoster, 2007.

Gumbel, Nicky. *Questions of Life*. Eastbourne, UK: Kingsway Publications, 1993.

Gunton, Colin and Daniel Hardy, eds. *On Being the Church: Essays on the Christian Community*. Edinburgh: T and T Clark, 1989.

Hall, Stuart, ed. *Representation: Cultural Representations and Signifying Practices*. London: Routledge, 1997.

Hall, Stuart. "Introduction." *Production of Culture/Cultures of Production*, edited by Stuart Hall and Paul du Gay. London: Routledge, 1996.

Hardy, Daniel. *Finding the Church*. London: SCM Press, 2001.

Hatch, Nathan. *The Democratization of American Christianity*. New Haven, CT: Yale University Press, 1989.

Healy, Nicholas, M. *Church, World and the Christian Life: Practical-Prophetic Ecclesiology*. Cambridge: Cambridge University Press, 2000.

Heelas, Paul. *The New Age Movement*. Oxford: Blackwell, 1996.

Heelas, Paul and Linda Woodhead. *The Spiritual Revolution: Why Religion is Giving Way to Spirituality*. Oxford: Blackwell, 2005.

Hegstad, Harald. *The Real Church: An Ecclesiology of the Visible*. Eugene, OR: Pickwick, 2013.

Holmes, Stephen R. "Three Versus One? Some Problems of Social Trinitarianism." *Journal of Reformed Theology* 3 (2009).

Ignatius. "Epistle to the Ephesians." *The Apostolic Fathers with Justin Martyr and Irenaeus*, translated by Philip Schaff. *Ante Nicene Fathers*, Volume 1. Grand Rapids, MI: Eerdmans, 2001.

Irenaeus. "Against Heresy." *The Apostolic Fathers with Justin Martyr and Irenaeus*, translated by Philip Schaff. *Ante Nicene Fathers*, Volume 1. Grand Rapids, MI: Eerdmans, 2001.

Johnson, Douglas. *Contending for the Faith: A History of the Evangelical Movement in the Universities and Colleges*. Leicester, UK: Inter-varsity Press, 1979.

Kilby, Karen. "Perichoresis and Projection: Problems with Social Doctrines of the Trinity." *New Blackfriars* (October 2000).

Kilby, Karen. "Is an Apophatic Trinitarianism Possible?" *International Journal of Systematic Theology* 12/1 (January 2010).

Koester, Craig R. *The Word of Life: A Theology of St John's Gospel*. Grand Rapids, MI: Eerdmans, 2008.

LaCugna, Catherine Mowry. *God For Us: The Trinity and Christian Life*. San Francisco: Harper Collins, 1991.

Lightfoot, R. H. *St John's Gospel*. Oxford: Oxford University Press, 1956.

Luhrmann, Tanya M. *When God Talks Back: Understanding the American Evangelical Relationship with God*. New York: Vintage Books, 2012.

Luzbetak, Louis J. *The Church and Cultures: New Perspectives in Missiological Anthropology*. Maryknoll, NY: Orbis, 1963.

Mannion, Gerard and Lewis Mudge, eds. *The Routledge Companion to the Christian Church*. London: Routledge, 2008.

Marti, Gerado and Gladys Ganiel. *The Deconstructed Church: Understanding Emerging Christianity*. Oxford: Oxford University Press, 2014.

McClendon, James. *Doctrine: Systematic Theology, Volume 2*. Nashville, TN: Abingdon Press, 1994.

McClendon, James. *Ethics: Systematic Theology, Volume 1*. Nashville, TN: Abingdon Press, 2002.

McClendon, James and James Smith. *Convictions: Diffusing Religious Relativism*. Norcross, GA: Trinity Press International, 1994.

McClintock Fulkerson, Mary. *Places of Redemption: Theology for a Worldly Church*. Oxford: Oxford University Press, 2007.

McDannell, Colleen. *Material Christianity: Religion and Popular Culture in America*. New Haven, CT: Yale University Press, 1995.

McGann, Mary. *A Precious Fountain: Music in the Worship of an African American Catholic Community*. Collegeville, MN: Liturgical Press, 2004.

McGrath, Alister. *A Scientific Theology: Volume 2, Reality*. London: T and T Clark, 2001.

Mellott, David. *I Was and I Am Dust: Penitent Practices as a Way of Knowing*. Collegeville, MN: Liturgical Press, 2009.

Meyendorff, John. *Christ in Eastern Christian Thought.* Crestwood, NY: St Vladimir's Seminary Press, 1975.

Miller, Donald E. *Reinventing American Protestantism: Christianity in the New Millennium.* Berkeley, CA: University of California Press, 1999.

Mitton, C. Leslie. *The Epistle to the Ephesians: Its Authorship, Origin and Purpose* Grand Rapids, MI: Eerdmans, 1951.

Moody Smith, D. *The Theology of the Gospel of John.* Cambridge: Cambridge University Press, 1995.

Moore, Laurence. *Selling God: American Religion in the Marketplace of Culture.* Oxford: Oxford University Press, 1994.

Moynagh, Michael. *Church in Every Context: An Introduction to Theology and Practice.* London: SCM, 2012.

Ormerod, Neil. *Re-Visioning the Church: An Experiment in Systematic Historical Ecclesiology.* Minneapolis, MN: Fortress Press, 2014.

Orsi, Robert A. *The Madonna of 115th Street: Faith and Community in Italian Harlem 1880-1950.* New Haven, CT: Yale University Press, 1985.

Osmer, Richard R. *Practical Theology and Introduction.* Grand Rapids, MI: Eerdmans, 2008.

Percy, Martyn. *Shaping the Church: The Promise of Implicit Theology.* Farnham, UK: Ashgate, 2010.

Peterson, Cheryl, M. *Who is the Church? An Ecclesiology for the Twenty First Century.* Minneapolis, MN: Fortress Press, 2013.

Pickard, Stephen. *Seeking the Church: An Introduction to Ecclesiology.* London: SCM, 2012.

Pollock, John. *Billy Graham.* London: Hodder and Stoughton, 1966.

Roeland, Johan. *Selfation: Dutch Evangelical Youth Between Subjectivization and Subjection.* Amsterdam: Pallas Publications.

Sanneh, Lamin. *Translating the Message: The Missionary Impact on Culture.* Maryknoll, NY: Orbis 1991.

Sanny, Lorna C. *The Pioneer a Condensed Life History of Dawson E. Trotman.* http://www.discipleshiplibrary.com/pdfs/dawson_trotman_more.pdf.

Schweitzer, Albert. *The Quest of the Historical Jesus.* London: A and C Black, 1911.

Ramsey, Michael. *The Gospel and the Catholic Church.* London: Cowley, 1936.

Scharen, Christian. *Public Worship and Public Work: Character and Commitment in Local Congregational Life.* Collegeville, MN: Liturgical Press, 2004.

Scharen, Christian. "Judicious Narratives: Ethnography as Ecclesiology." *The Scottish Journal of Theology* 58/2 (2005).

Scharen, Christian and Aana Marie Vigen, eds. *Ethnography as Christian Theology and Ethics.* London: Continuum, 2011.

Scharen, Christian, ed. *Explorations in Ecclesiology and Ethnography*. Grand Rapids, MI: Eerdmans, 2012.

Scharen, Christian. *Fieldwork in Theology: Exploring the Social Context of God's Work in the World*. Grand Rapids, MI: Baker, 2015.

Schultze, Quentin J., Roy M. Anker, James D. Bratt, William D. Romanowski, John W. Worst, and Lambert Zuidervaart. *Dancing in the Dark: Youth, Popular Culture and the Electronic Media*. Grand Rapids, MI: Eerdmans, 1991.

Smith, Christian with Melinda Lunquist Denton. *Soul Searching: The Religious and Spiritual Lives of American Teenagers*. Oxford: Oxford University Press, 2005.

Stibbe, Mark. *John's Gospel*. London: Routledge, 1994.

Stott, John. *Basic Christianity*. Leicester, UK: Inter-varisty Press, 1958.

Swinton, John and Harriet Mowat. *Practical Theology and Qualitative Research*. London: SCM Press, 2006.

Thompson, Judith with Stephen Pattison, and Ross Thompson. *Theological Reflection*. London: SCM, 2008.

Torrance, Thomas, F. *Theological Science*. Oxford: Oxford University Press, 1969.

Torrey, R. A. *Personal Work*. London: Pickering and Inglis, 1974.

Turner, John G. *Bill Bright and Campus Crusade for Christ: The Renewal of Evangelicalism in Postwar America*. Chapel Hill, NC: University of North Carolina Press, 2008.

Twitchell, James B. *Branded Nation: The Marketing of Megachurch, College Inc and Museum World*. New York: Simon and Schuster, 2004.

Van Gelder, Craig and Dwight J. Zscheile. *The Missional Church in Perspective: Mapping Trends and Shaping the Conversation*. Grand Rapids, MI: Baker, 2011.

Van Deusen Hunsinger, Deborah. *Theology and Pastoral Counselling: A New Interdisciplinary Approach*. Grand Rapids, MI: Eerdmans, 2010.

Volf, Miroslav. *After Our Likeness: Church as the Image of the Trinity*. Grand Rapids, MI: Eerdmans, 1998.

Von Campenhausen, Hans. *Fathers of the Greek Church*, translated by Stanley Godman. London: A and C. Black, 1955.

Walker, Andrew. *Telling the Story: Gospel, Mission and Culture*. London: SPCK, 1996.

Walker, John. *Testing Fresh Expressions: Identity and Transformation*. Farnham, UK: Ashgate, 2014.

Andrew Walls. *The Missionary Movement in Christian History: Studies in the Transmission of Faith*. Edinburgh: T and T Clark, 1996.

Ward, Pete. *Growing Up Evangelical: Youthwork and the Making of a Subculture*. London: SPCK, 1996.

Ward, Pete. *Liquid Church*. Peabody, MA: Hendrickson, 2002.

Ward, Pete. "Union with Christ: The Subplot of Evangelical Soteriology." *Journal of Youth and Theology* 2/1 (2003).

Ward, Pete. *Selling Worship*. Milton Keynes, UK: Paternoster, 2005.

Ward, Pete and Heidi Campbell. "Ordinary Theology as Narratives: An Empirical Study of Young People's Charismatic Worship in Scotland." *International Journal of Practical Theology* 15/2 (2011).

Ward, Pete, ed. *Perspectives in Ecclesiology and Ethnography*. Grand Rapids, MI: Eerdmans, 2012.

Ward, Pete. "Blueprint Ecclesiology and the Lived: Normativity as a Perilous Faithfulness." *Ecclesial Practices* 2/1 (2015).

Ward, Pete and Paul Fiddes. "Affirming Faith at a Service of Baptism in St Aldate's Church, Oxford." In *Explorations in Ecclesiology and Ethnography*, edited by Christian Scharen. Grand Rapids, MI: Eerdmans, 2012.

Warner, Robert. *Reinventing English Evangelicalism 1966-2001*. Milton Keynes, UK: Paternoster, 2007.

Warner, Robert. "Autonomous Conformism—the Paradox of Entrepreneurial Protestantism Spring Harvest: A Case Study." *Religion and the Individual: Belief, Practice and Identity*, edited by Abby Day. Aldershot, UK: Ashgate, 2008.

Warren, Rick. *The Purpose Driven Church: Growth Without Compromising your Message and Mission*. Grand Rapids, MI: Zondervan, 1995.

Watkins, Clare, with Helen Cameron, Deborah Bhatti, Catherine Duce, and James Sweeney. "Practical Ecclesiology: What Counts as Theology in Studying the Church?" *Perspectives on Ecclesiology and Ethnography*, edited by Pete Ward. Grand Rapids, MI: Eerdmans, 2012.

Watson, Francis. "Hermeneutics and the Doctrine of Scripture: Why They Need Each Other." *International Journal of Systematic Theology* 12/2 (April 2010).

Webster, John. "Editorial." *International Journal of Systematic Theology* 12/2 (April 2010).

Webster, John. "'In the Society of God': Some Principles of Ecclesiology". *Athanasius: A Theological Introduction*, edited by Thomas G. Weinandy. Aldershot, UK: Ashgate, 2007.

Williams, Raymond. *The Long Revolution*. Harmondsworth, UK: Penguin, 1961.

Williams, Raymond. *Culture and Society 1780-1950*. Harmondsworth, UK: Penguin, 1961.

Wright, Andrew. *Christianity and Critical Realism: Ambiguity, Truth and Theological Literacy*. London, UK: Routledge, 2012.

Woodhead, Linda. "Introduction." *Religion and Change in Modern Britain*, edited by Linda Woodhead and Rebecca Catto. London: Routledge, 2012.

Young, Francis. *From Nicea to Chalcedon: A Guide to the Literature and its Background*. London: SCM, 1983.

Zizioulas, John. *Being as Communion: Studies in Personhood and the Church* Crestwood, NY: St Vladimir's Seminary Press, 1985.

Index

Index of Biblical Sources